William Johnston was born in Belfast, Northern Ireland, in 1925, and was educated in Liverpool and at the National University of Ireland.

He joined the Jesuit order and then went to Japan in 1951, where he has lived ever since, receiving a doctorate in Mystical Theology from Sophia University, Tokyo, in 1968. He has made a special study of Buddhism and has taken an active part in the dialogue between Zen Buddhism and Christianity.

William Johnston is now Director of the Institute of Oriental Religions of Sophia University, and has lectured widely on East-West mysticism in Europe, the United States of America, Australia and Oceania. He has also been Visiting Professor at universities in San Francisco and Cleveland, Ohio.

Known as a translator from Japanese into English, William Johnston has written widely on East-West mysticism and contributed many articles to learned journals. He is the author of *The Mysticism of "The Cloud of Unknowing"*, *The Still Point: Reflections on Zen and Christian Mysticism*, *Christian Zen*, *Silent Music* and *Letters to Contemplatives*.

BY THE SAME AUTHOR

The Mysticism of "The Cloud of Unknowing"
The Still Point: Reflections on Zen and Christian Mysticism

AVAILABLE AS FOUNT PAPERBACKS

Being in Love
Silent Music: The Science of Meditation
The Wounded Stag
Letters to Contemplatives

TRANSLATIONS

Silence, a novel by Shusaka Endo, translated from The Japanese
The Cloud of Unknowing and The Book of Privy Counselling,
newly edited from the Middle English

LORD, TEACH US TO PRAY

WILLIAM JOHNSTON

Christian Zen

and

The Inner Eye of Love

Fount

An Imprint of HarperCollins*Publishers*

Fount Paperbacks is an imprint of
HarperCollins*Religious*
part of HarperCollins*Publishers*
77–85 Fulham Palace Road,
Hammersmith, London W6 8JB

First published in Great Britain in 1990 by
Fount Paperbacks
Reprinted 1991

Christian Zen was previously published by Harper & Row, Publishers,
San Francisco and *The Inner Eye* of Love by William Collins Sons &
Co. Ltd in Great Britain and by Harper & Row in the USA

Printed in Great Britain by
HarperCollins Manufacturing Glasgow

"He was praying in a certain place, and when he ceased, one of his disciples said to him 'Lord, teach us to pray, as John taught his disciples.' "

LUKE 11:1

Contents

Preface

Once upon a time Jesus was praying in a certain place and when he had ceased his disciples said: "Lord, teach us to pray, as John taught his disciples." No doubt they were impressed, attracted, fascinated by the transfigured countenance of Jesus as he faced his Father; and they asked the question the whole world is now asking: "Lord, teach us to pray."

For the modern world, from Tokyo to London and from Los Angeles to New Delhi, is asking about prayer and meditation. "Lord, teach us to pray." Now we begin to see that colour television, elaborate washing-machines and success in the stock exchange do not satisfy the aspirations of the human heart. Something is missing. And so we seek that dimension of human living that was written on the radiant face of Jesus. "Lord, teach us to pray."

At one time we thought that theology would satisfy our longing. Does not theology tell us about God and his wondrous working? Does it not probe the baffling mystery of his infinite being? It certainly does. And yet speculative theology can somehow disappear in the clouds, leaving us with no experience of the living God it describes. It can leave us cold and dissatisfied, resonating with that holy man who said he would feign have compunction than know its definition. And so we turn our eyes from theologians to teachers of prayer. Please teach us as Jesus taught his disciples and as John taught his disciples.

*

Yes, the longing for prayer grows stronger every day. Something is afoot in the modern world. Something is stirring in the hearts of contemporary people. From Tienanmen Square to the Berlin Wall, from the spires of the Kremlin to the halls of the Vatican, something is at work in the innermost being of men and women and children. What are people looking for? What do they want? One might say they are demanding that human dignity be respected. One might say that they refuse to allow their basic humanity to be trampled on. And this is true. But there is more to it.

Look more clearly and you will see that humanity is like the woman who, having ten silver coins, lost one coin and lighted a lamp and swept the house high and low until she found it. Humanity is now searching for the lost coin of prayer. Where will we find it?

We Christians will find it in the Gospel and the psalms and in our great religious traditions. But we can also look further afield. All the great religions are schools of prayer teaching their children to give praise and thanksgiving or to enter into sacred silence. There is no religion that does not teach worship or prayer or meditation or wondering silent before the unutterable mystery of existence. And can we not learn from one another?

Here let me pause to make an important comment. It is widely thought in Western religious circles that Asian religions specialize in techniques – that they teach only posture and breathing and bodily training as ways to union with the Absolute. What a superficial view this is! For authentic Asian religion puts all the stress on faith. Think of Buddhism and how often fervent Buddhists speak of great faith, of total commitment, of willingness to die in the search for enlightenment. Their faith is an inspiration to all of us. But let me return to my theme.

*

One of the great turning points in history was 17th October, 1986 when leaders of world religions prayed together at Assisi. It was prayer for peace, and it was an experience of peace. At 9 a.m. John Paul entered alone into the Basilica of St Mary of the Angels to pray for a moment at the place where the ecstatic Francis breathed his last while lying on the bare ground. Then there was the deeply moving entrance of the Dalai Lama and thirty religious leaders, followed by a similar number of Christian leaders, while the choir sang Psalm 148: "Let everything that lives praise the Lord."

As I reflect on that tremendous scene, I am brought back in spirit to New Testament times. In the ancient temple at Jerusalem was a wall that separated Jew from Gentile. And Paul wrote powerfully that Jesus broke down that wall, making one person in place of the two and bringing hostility to an end. "For he is our peace, who has made us both one and has broken down the dividing wall of hostility. . . ." (Ephesians 2:14). The collapse of that wall was a stupendous event. But now with the Second Vatican Council and the great, symbolic meeting at Assisi, yet another wall has been broken down. Yes, the ugly wall that separated Christian from Buddhist, Muslim from Hindu and Jew from Gentile has come crashing down, with consequences that are incomparably more earth-shaking than those which follow the demolition of the cruel wall that divided Berlin. For now we are aware that one is our origin and one the transcendent goal towards which we walk. "For he is our peace."

I said that we are like that woman who lost her silver coin. Are we not all – Buddhist and Christian and all – searching together? I said the silver coin was prayer. But now I would like to change the metaphor and say that the silver coin is also peace. We realize that world peace will never come – never, never – unless we learn to pray together. "Lord, teach us to pray, as John taught his disciples."

*

And men and women of prayer have risen charismatically before our eyes in recent times. I think of Mother Teresa and Padre Pio; I think of the Dalai Lama and Ramana Maharshi. I think of the monks in Japan and Thailand, of the Sadhus in India and the fervent Muslims in North Africa. I think of the Staretz in Russia and the millions of Catholics who kneel daily before the tabernacle. There are today thousands, nay, millions of men and women of prayer whose names are written only in the Book of Life. Here rests our hope. For, as the poet tells us, more things are wrought by prayer than this world dreams of.

We pray together. But that does not mean we abandon our

cherished religious identity to become an amorphous mass. It means that we pray for one another, talk to one another, listen to one another, accept one another, respect one another, learn from one another, love one another and lay down our lives for one another. This is the work of dialogue to which we must devote our energies more and more if we are to be faithful to the Gospel of Jesus Christ.

Prayerful dialogue is at present going on between Buddhist and Christian monks. Pope John Paul, speaking to assembled monks, emphasized that dialogue is more than a sharing of ideas. It is a religious experience leading to profound union of hearts in interior silence. Here are his words:

> Your dialogue at the monastic level is truly a religious experience, a meeting in the depths of the heart, animated by the spirit of poverty, mutual trust and profound respect for your own traditions. It is an experience which cannot always be translated adequately into words, and which can best be expressed in prayer-filled silence.

What is this prayer-filled silence about which the Pope speaks? I believe it is the realm of pure faith. I doubt if we will have a profound meeting at the realm of thoughts and ideas or at the realm of pictures and images or at the realm of visions and locutions. Our meeting with Buddhists will be at the level of pure faith; that is to say, at the mystical level of deep silence.

The books in this volume relate the course of my own dialogue with Buddhism over a period of twenty years. I have learned much about prayer and, as I came to love and respect Buddhist religion and culture, I grew in my commitment to Jesus Christ and the Gospel. "Lord teach us to pray, as John taught his disciples." I hope the time will come when that woman who has been searching for her silver coin will call together her friends and neighbours saying, "Rejoice with me, for I have found the coin which I had lost."

SOPHIA UNIVERSITY
TOKYO
June, 1990

CHRISTIAN
ZEN

FOR
George
Isidore
John
Rich
and even
for
Pier Paolo

CONTENTS

Some Japanese Words
Used in the Text

bonyari	idle
dokusan	private interview
gedo Zen	unorthodox Zen
hakama	divided skirt, traditionally worn by Japanese men
koan	paradoxical problem
kyosaku	stick
makyo	illusion
mu	nothing
muga	non-self
nembutsu	repeating the name of the Buddha
oshosan	priest in charge of a temple
roshi	Zen Master
sake	Japanese rice wine
satori	enlightenment
seiza	traditional Japanese sitting posture
sesshin	retreat (usually seven days)
shikan taza	just sitting
tatami	matting used in Japanese room
teisho	sermon
zazen	sitting in zen meditation

PREFACE TO
THE SECOND EDITION

Almost ten years have elapsed since this book was first written, and I know that I could not write the same book today. When questioned about one of his early works, Thomas Merton remarked: "The man who wrote that book is dead." Indeed, Merton the writer died and rose many times, as does every author who lives and grows and develops. That is why I can borrow his words and say that the man who wrote *Christian Zen* is dead.

Yet even if the man who wrote this book is dead, it is also true that he is alive. And as I glance through these pages I realize, sometimes with a jolt, that most of my ideas remain basically unchanged. Some were discarded, only to be taken up again. Others hopefully have deepened and developed. But all in all I can still stand by what I wrote in the autumn of 1970.

At that time the great meditation movement which subsequently spread to the whole Western world was in its early phase. Transcendental meditation and yoga and Zen were already in vogue. Christians were asking if it was possible for them to avail of the riches of oriental spirituality while remaining committed to Christ and to the Gospel. And to this I wanted to answer that Christians might not only avail of the riches of oriental meditation but that they should become leaders in a movement of which Christ would be the centre – a meditation movement which would humbly learn from Zen and the East while being totally penetrated by the Gospel.

I still think this. And in this second edition of *Christian Zen* I have written a fairly long postscript which contains practical instruction on the art of Christian meditation in an oriental setting. Furthermore towards the end of this postscript I describe how my own relationship with Zen developed after publication of this book.

Only one thing would I change if I were to rewrite this book; and this concerns not Zen but Ireland. Here and there I made slightly flippant remarks about the sectarian trouble in the part of the world where I was born. Now I ask my reader to recall that when this book was written the violence had not escalated to the cruel and tragic proportions which we later saw – and which caused untold suffering to many. When I wrote it was possible to laugh at the whole thing. It is no longer a joke.

No more need be said. Here only let me express my belief that authentic Christian meditation is a key factor in healing the wounds of a divided society. For meditation is inextricably bound up with reconciliation and forgiveness and the prayer of Jesus that we may all be one.

SOPHIA UNIVERSITY
Tokyo, 1979

1

Beginning

Some years ago, Arnold Toynbee declared that when the historian of a thousand years from now comes to write the history of our time, he will be preoccupied not with the Vietnam War, not with the struggle between capitalism and communism, not with racial strife, but with what happened when for the first time Christianity and Buddhism began to penetrate one another deeply. This remark is profoundly interesting and, I believe, profoundly true. Christianity and Buddhism are penetrating one another, talking to one another, learning from one another. Even the stubborn old Catholic Church, in a flush of postconciliar humility, feels that she has something to gain by sitting at the feet of the Zen *roshi* and imbibing the age-old wisdom of the East. Surely this is progress.

I have called this book *Christian Zen*, but the contents are less ambitious than the pretentious title might suggest. Rather than treating of the confluence of two vast traditions of East and West, I simply try to say something about how Zen and Christianity have met in me, setting down some practical conclusions that this meeting has evoked. In the twenty years that I have spent in Japan – so meaningful and rich that this land is almost my land – I have had some contact with Zen, whether by sitting in Zen meditation or through dialogue with my Buddhist friends. All this has been tremendously enriching; it has deepened and broadened my Christian faith more than I can say. Indeed, I sometimes reflect (not without dismay) that had I remained in my native Ireland instead of coming to the East, I might now be an intolerant and narrow-minded Papist hurling bricks and bottles at my Protestant adversaries in the cobbled streets of Belfast. Contact with Zen, on the other hand, has opened up new vistas, teaching me that there are possibilities in Christianity I never dreamed of. It is about this I want to write. So this is a personal book about what I have gained and about the problems that face the person who wants to practise Zen without rejecting his Christian faith – or more correctly, to practise Zen as a way of deepening and broadening his Christian faith. For inevitably the Christian who does Zen hits up against problems. He or she is faced with a method of meditation that at first sight looks atheistic or pantheistic or whatever you want to call it.

People have frequently asked me why I got interested in Zen at all, and as so often happens, this question is far from easy to answer. Who knows why he gets interested in anything? Yet I suppose some reasons can be given, even though I cannot vouch for the fact that they are the real ones.

For one thing, the contemplative ideal in Buddhism has always fascinated me. I never tire of gazing at the statues of the Buddhas and Bodhisattvas rapt in deep silence, in nothingness, in unknowing. They remind me of the exquisite words in which John of the Cross describes contemplative experience:

> Silent music, sounding solitude,
> The supper that recreates and enkindles love.

And then there is the gentle smile of compassion that so often plays around the lips of the Bodhisattva. All this is beautiful. And it reflects the great Buddhist intuition that the highest wisdom is found not in Cartesian clear and distinct ideas but in the tranquil silence that transcends all thought, all images, all ideas, all reasoning, in the total extinction of craving and desire. This is what shines through the exquisite silence of the Buddha, a silence that echoes through every corner of Asia.

As I have said, all this attracted me. Consequently, when one of my students offered to bring me to Engakuji, the big Zen temple at Kamakura, I jumped at the opportunity of going there to sit in meditation. At that time it seemed somewhat strange to Christians – and also to non-Christians – that a Catholic priest should meditate in a Zen temple. It seemed like mixing things up; Japanese Christians themselves were vaguely pleased but vaguely puzzled. On the other hand, these were the years leading up to Vatican II, years in which it was becoming increasingly clear that Christians must recognize and promote the true values in religions other than their own. Besides, it was also becoming obvious, alas, that Christianity had failed in Asia mainly because of its intransigent refusal to learn from the local culture and religion. There could be no hope for an Asian Christianity which ignored things like Zen or looked on them with hostility. Other priests had been meditating in Zen temples. Catholicism was on the move.

So I went to Engakuji for several hours on Sunday afternoons, and the young *oshosan* who took care of one of the little temples in the vast complex kindly taught me how to sit.

I was greatly taken by him. A stocky, broad-shouldered ascetic from Okinawa, he was barefoot and dressed in the traditional Japanese *hakama*. Up and down the meditation hall he crept silently, ready to strike or to scold with the utmost severity. But when the meditation was over and we drank green tea together, he radiated all the gentleness and compassion of the great Bodhisattvas.

One day he called me aside. "Thank you so much for coming," he said. "Now I would like to see a Christian monastery."

I was somewhat taken aback. I felt that there was not in Tokyo a Christian monastery to which I could introduce him with reasonable hope that he would be edified. Plenty of Christian contemplatives there were (more indeed among the Japanese than elsewhere), but our monasteries were so Western, so much like offices – and he would probably have to wear shoes. The incident made me realize how great is the need for contemplative renewal within Christianity and how much can be learnt from Buddhism.

But to return to the meditation. Soon I found myself together with a small group of people sitting in the half-lotus position and gazing at the wall in silence. This kind of meditation was not, however, entirely new to me. John of the Cross had been my guru for many years, and at this time I was reading *The*

Cloud of Unknowing (about which I subsequently wrote a somewhat academic book), which teaches a species of silent, imageless meditation not unlike Zen. At the beginning of one of his
minor treatises, for example, the anonymous author of *The
Cloud* confronts his disciples with the stern words: "When thou
comest by thyself . . . forsake as well good thoughts as evil
thoughts." The author's idea is that all discursive thinking
should be abandoned in order that an interior dynamism (which
he beautifully calls "the blind stirring of love") may arise in the
depth of one's being. His doctrine resembles that of John of the
Cross in advocating abandonment of thinking in order to make
way for what the Spanish mystic calls "the living flame of love".

I might add here that imageless prayer is not uncommon
among Christians devoted to meditation, but there is not much
talk about it. One time, while conducting a retreat for sisters in
the south of Japan, I suggested that we spend some hours in
silent, Zenlike meditation, gazing at the wall. After this experi-
ment, quite a few of the sisters remarked, "But I always meditate
that way anyhow".

And the same was true for me when I first went to Kamakura.
As far as interior disposition was concerned I changed nothing;
but I found that I was enormously helped and, so to speak,
deepened simply by the half-lotus posture which I then took on
for the first time. After an unbearably painful beginning (for
some strange reason I always got a headache), I began to realize
that this is indeed the ideal posture for contemplative prayer –
for putting into practice the advice of the good author of *The
Cloud* to "forsake as well good thoughts as evil thoughts".
The fact is that this lotus position somehow impedes discursive
reasoning and thinking; it somehow checks the stream of consciousness that flows across the surface of the mind; it detaches
one from the very process of thinking. Probably it is the worst
position for philosophizing but the best for going down, down
to the centre of one's being in imageless and silent contemplation. This position had the further simple advantage of keeping me quiet, since a certain nervous restlessness had made me
want to pace up and down my room in time of so-called medi-

tation. Now I found myself rooted to the earth in silent unification.

The Kamakura experience somehow helped my daily meditation, which I continued to make in the half-lotus position (I could never manage the full lotus – alas for Western legs) in some kind of Zen style. I say this because some people would probably deny that what I did was Zen, and whether or not it could be called Zen I did not know. As I have already said, it was a continuation, but at the same time a remarkable deepening, of what I had been doing before I ever heard of Zen.

After some time I attended by first Zen *sesshin* (that is to say, a retreat) at a small temple on the Japan Sea. This was an unforgettable experience, though the whole thing was very severe and gruelling. Perhaps I was not yet ready for it. We arose at 3 a.m., sat in *zazen* for ten periods of forty minutes each, and retired at 9 p.m. Even our meals were taken in the lotus posture in the meditation hall. During the time allotted to the reciting of the sutras, a Jesuit colleague and I were kindly permitted to celebrate Mass, which we did in the small *tatami* room that had been given to us. Each morning the *roshi* gave an instruction, called *teisho*, in which he expounded some of the principles of Buddhist philosophy in addition to giving hints for the practice of Zen. In one of these instructions he remarked that Zen was found everywhere and in all true religions – in Hinduism, in Islam, in Christianity, and so on. Such Zen he called "*gedo* Zen." "*Ge*" means outside, and "*do*" means the way; so "*gedo* Zen" is unorthodox or heretical Zen. The real Zen, he went on the say, was not Hinayana nor even Mahayan – it was just Zen divorced from all categories and affiliations. I was interested to hear that he did concede that there was Zen in every religion, and this made me think that what I was doing might be called Zen after all.

In the course of another *teisho* he spoke about *dokusan* or spiritual direction. This, he explained, was usually a brief affair and dealt only with the actual practice of Zen. "I don't want to hear about your financial problems," he said, "nor about your family problems. And if you talk about these things I'll stop you. All I want to know is what you are doing during your *zazen.*" To me this simple remark was quite striking, and I felt it could give Christian directors food for thought. As a seminarian studying for the priesthood, I had frequently gone to spiritual directors and found this attitude the contrary of that of the *roshi*. They asked about practical problems of adjustment to life, and by and large they were good counsellors; but they shied away from the central problem of "What are you doing at the time of meditation?" Perhaps this stemmed from a natural reluctance to talk about something sacred. Yet is it true that we can all learn much from the Zen *roshi*, who know about the working of the human mind in an intimate way. That is why they can lead persons to *satori*.

Anyhow, I squatted in the queue, and when my time came I struck the gong and went in for *dokusan*. The *roshi* was seated on a slightly raised platform, and down below, some distance away, was the cushion on which I was to squat. I wondered why he was so far away; later I put this question to a Japanese who knew the temple pretty well. Almost furtively he said, "I'll tell you the reason. The *roshi* drinks sake, and he doesn't want you to smell his breath." Seeing my surprise he went on hastily, "I don't mean that he drinks too much. He doesn't. But he drinks some, and he doesn't like people to know."

I reflected that, after all, Zen *roshi* were human beings, good men like the Irish Catholic pastors. As for my conversation with the *roshi* it was, as far as I recall, more or less as follows.

"How are you getting on?"

"My legs are aching so much that I can scarcely bear it any longer."

"Stretch them out! Stretch them out! I'll tell the young man in the meditation hall not to bother you. If the thing is too painful, you'll simply have to give it up. And I don't want you to give it up, I want you to continue. So don't overdo it. But tell me, what about your Zen? What are you doing?"

"I'm doing what you, I suppose, would call '*gedo* Zen'."

"Very good! Very good! Many Christians do that. But what precisely do you mean by '*gedo* Zen'?"

"I mean that I am sitting silently in the presence of God without words or thoughts or images or ideas."

"Your God is everywhere?"

"Yes."

"And you are wrapped around in God?"

"Yes."

"And you experience this?"

"Yes."

"Very good! Very good! Continue this way. Just keep on. And eventually you will find that God will disappear and only Johnston San will remain."

This remark shocked me. it sounded like a denial of all that I considered sacred, of all that lay at the very centre of my so-called Zen. One should not, I suppose, contradict the *roshi*, but nevertheless I did so. Recalling the teaching of *The Cloud* that there are mystical moments when self totally disappears and only God remains, I said with a smile, "God will not disappear. But Johnston might well disappear and only God be left."

"Yes, yes", he answered smilingly. "It's the same thing. That is what I mean."

Yet, as I have said, his seemingly radical denial of God was a shock to me. But afterward, reflecting on the whole matter and discussing it with my friends, I came to the conclusion that his words did not necessarily deny the existence of God at all. Underlying them is a denial of dualism and an approach to God which is different from that of the traditional West. Now I maintain that this way of speaking throws light on the very notion of God, helping Western Christians to purify and clarify their ideas. But this realization only came later, and the remark of the *roshi* shook me.

*

All this happened some years ago. Today Zen has entered Christianity with more confidence. Outside Tokyo there is now a simply built Christian Zen meditation hall in which are conducted monthly *sesshim*. In the centre of Tokyo (yes – noisy, dirty, smoggy, grimy Tokyo) is a quiet place where Christians and others come to sit in silence. In sitting together with these young Japanese people, it has never been my intention to guide and instruct them in Zen; all I have wanted is to be with them and to learn. I have told Japanese Christians — and I believe it is true — that they have an important role to play in the development of Christianity. Their vocation is to renew meditation within the Church and interpret it to the West. At the same time they must humbly and gratefully acknowledge their debt to Buddhism, as I myself must express my gratitude for the unfailing kindness and courtesy with which my friends and I have always been treated by Zen *roshi*.

Renewal of meditation in Christianity! There has, after all, been renewal in almost every other field. The organ has been replaced by the guitar; ties have replaced Roman collars; nuns' skirts have moved from maxi to mini and back to midi; scriptural and theological progress has been breath-taking. But surely all this progress will be so much junk (if I may be pardoned the word) if religion is not renewed at its very heart, that is to say, at the mystical level. That such renewal is badly overdue is proved by the fact that many people, discontented with old forms of prayer, discontented with the old devotions that once served so well, are looking for something that will satisfy the aspirations of the modern heart.

And is it not just possible that the vocation of the East lies here?

2

Dialogue

One of the beautiful things of our age – which, alas, has all kinds of ugly things also – is that we have learnt to talk to one another. Slowly we are mastering the art of dialogue. And the religions of the world, after centuries of rivalry and quarrelling, are learning to wipe the blood off their hands, beat their swords into ploughshares, and exchange the kiss of peace. Truly an interesting and exciting age.

Since I myself hail from a somewhat intolerant corner of the earth, I have always felt that dialogue with other religions is something of a sacred duty. Somehow I ought to make amends. That is why I have been so glad to attend meetings between Christians and Zen Buddhists that have taken place in various parts of Japan. Most of these meetings have been more or less unofficial (that is to say, the people present were not officially appointed by central religious authorities) and have been conducted in a spirit of the utmost cordiality and friendship. We meet on terms of equality – no attempt, of course, is made at proselytizing – in the belief that none of us possess the totality of the truth. To us Catholic Christians the Vatican Council brought the refreshing news that we are still seekers, members of a pilgrim Church, and so we can join hands with other searchers, whether they be Buddhist, Hindu, Muslim, or anything else, in our common quest for truth. Needless to say, we have Christ, who I believe spoke of God as no man ever spoke; but I do not think we can claim to understand the revelation of Christ in all its fullness. Perhaps we are still at the beginning. Moreover I also believe that in sundry times and in diverse ways God spoke to our fathers through the prophets, and these include prophets whose voices echo beautifully in the *Gita*, the *Lotus Sutra*, and the *Jao Jeh Ching*.

I am aware that it sounds awfully patronizing to give Christianity the plum of Divine Sonship and throw a few crumbs of prophethood to Buddhists and Hindus, but I have found that Buddhists, at least those I have met and know, do not take this amiss. They want to know what we think without camouflage or dilution, and in the same way we want to know what they think. None of the Christians are particularly disturbed to hear that they possess the Buddha nature. The fact is, however, that we are only now advancing from the backwoods of intolerance and have not yet found a formula that will keep everyone happy. Perhaps we never will.

The dialogue with Zen owes much to the initiative and enterprise of the Quakers, to whom we are all eternally grateful. No doubt the great similarity between Quaker meditation and Zen (though there are great differences too) was instrumental in prompting their ecumenical interest. The first meeting was held in Oiso, near Tokyo, and the participants talked frankly about their personal religious experience, searching for a link that might bind them together. Conducted in a spirit of great charity, it revealed that the interior life of Buddhists and Christians has much in common; they can be united at the deepest part of their being, at the level of psychic life which Eliot calls the still point of the turning world. But the participants were unable to enunciate any theological or philosophical statement all could agree upon.

When the time came round for the next meeting, this time to be held in Kyoto, it seemed to me that we should leave the subjective realm of religious experience and get down to something objective. Perhaps the whole discussion could centre around the problem of ultimate reality – we Christians could explain what we meant by "God", pointing out that we did not believe in an anthropomorphic being "out there" but in the supreme source of existence in whom we live, move, and are. The Buddhists, on the other hand, could explain what they mean by nothingness, emptiness, the void, and so on. In this way a lot of misunderstanding might vanish like smoke; we might discover that we had something in common after all, and what a break-through this would be in religious thinking! Now I realize that I was naïve. Or a victim of my Hellenistic education.

Anyhow, with this in mind I spoke to a Buddhist friend who was to be a participant. He listened kindly, and his answer, typically Buddhist and deeply interesting, was more or less as follows. "Do you really thing that you can talk about nothingness, emptiness, or the void? Do you really think you can talk about God? Of course you can't. You are part of the void; you are part of the nothingness; you are part of God. All is one."

And here I found clearly and directly expressed something that runs all through Zen, whether it be in the thinking of the simplest Master or the most sophisticated scholar: that is to say, there is no duality, no "I and Thou" (alas for Martin Buber), no "God and myself". All is one. This is the so-called monism that underlies all Mahayana Buddhism. Let me illustrate it further with a story about the great Dr Suzuki.

One time the old philosopher gave a talk on Zen to Western people in Tokyo. He spoke of the silence, the emptiness, the nothingness, and all the rest, together with the deep wisdom that comes from *satori*. When he had finished, one of his audience rose to his feet and, not without a touch of irritation, exclaimed, "But Dr Suzuki, what about society? What about other people? What about the other?"

Whereupon Suzuki paused for a moment, looked up with a smile, and remarked, "But there is no other!"

There is no other, and there is no self. This is the answer he had to give, and this basically was the answer of my Buddhist friend. What they meant by it (for it is by no means as simple or as terrible as it sounds) I would like to discuss later; for the present, let us return to the dialogue.

We met in Kyoto, where we spent a wonderful week, fifteen of us. The atmosphere was permeated with good will and deep religious faith. Not only did we talk together, we also sat together in a wordless dialogue of silent communication. The meeting was highlighted by a talk from an eminent *roshi* who described with great enthusiasm the experience of enlightenment that had made him wild with ecstatic joy. His head seemed to be shattered and for several days he did not know where he was or what he was doing. *Satori* could never be described or explained, he said, but there was undoubtedly enlightenment in the words of Jesus:

> Before Abraham was, I am.

This, he said, was perfect enlightenment – no object, no duality, just "I am".

Here I might digress to say that I have been impressed and moved by the respect and reverence with which Buddhists have always spoken of Christ in my presence. However dim a view they may take of us, and I suppose they have reason on occasion, they have not concealed their admiration for the founder of Christianity. In this case his words gave me food for thought. I had heard it said before that "I am" is an expression of perfect *satori*. It should be noted, however, that when the words "I am" rise up in the depth of the enlightened being, this "I" is not the empirical ego; it is not the little self that is compounded of desires and does not really exist in Zen. This "I" is the very ground of being, the heart of the universe, the true self which rises in the depths and overwhelms everything. It is the voice of the "big self" which drowns all consciousness of the "little self" because it is all that is. I saw then clearly that when Jesus said "I am", the "I" that spoke was not the "I" of a man, but that of the eternal Word that was in the beginning and through whom all things were made. Jesus, I believe, was so filled with God that he no longer had a human personality – within him was only the personality of the eternal Son. That is why the "I" that cried out within him was the same as that which spoke to Moses saying, "I am who I am".

Be that as it may, our talk had gone on over cups of coffee and green tea, while at other times it has been more formal, with tape recorders and press correspondents. Perhaps the reader will ask where it is all going and what we are getting out of it. Yet this is, perhaps, a question no one can answer. In some ways dialogue is a dangerous and tricky business. At one meeting a Buddhist professor humorously made the remark that we all feel the cultural and religious danger. After all, if you leave yourself open, if you recognize the other's position, if you treat with others on terms of equality – then God alone knows what might happen. But the risk is worth taking, and progress will be made. As for myself, my principal preoccupation at present is with learning from Buddhism. I can't help feeling that Western Christianity (like Western everything else) is badly in need of a blood transfusion. Somehow or other we have become effete – is this the old theory about the decline of the West? – and we need new perspectives. Just as a whole new era opened up for Christianity when Thomas introduced Aristotle in the thirteenth century, so a new era, an even bigger one, could be opened up by the assimilation of some Buddhist ideas and attitudes. And the time is particularly ripe for this now that we see Christianity as an open-ended religion, a religion on the march, a religion that has taken things from Hellenism and communism and will only reach something like completion when it sees the truth through the eyes of all cultures. Indeed, it is precisely because of its claim to universality that Christianity needs the insights of other religions. And here I might add that many Buddhists I have met are also on the march, happy and willing to learn from Christianity.

But now about the blood transfusion. What can Christians learn from Zen? Or in a book like this it might be better to ask what I have learned, or am in the process of learning, from Zen. And first of all it seems to me that Zen can teach us a methodology in prayer. Let me explain what I mean.

Every religion that is worth its salt has taught people how to pray. Some religions are poor in theology and organization; but if they have prayer or meditation we can respect them and recognize that they are trying to do their job. In Buddhism and Hinduism there have always been people – gurus and *roshi* – who have so mastered the art of meditation that they can lead their disciples through the tortuous paths of the mind to a high level of concentration. Now Christianity, too, has a similar tradition (how could it otherwise have survived?), as also has Judaism. Recall how the disciples said to Jesus, "Teach us to pray, as John taught his disciples to pray". They expected Jesus to be a Master of prayer, as were John and the other rabbis who moved around the countryside. The fathers of the Church, too, taught prayer; and later on we find men like Ignatius of Loyola wandering around Paris simply instructing people in the ways of meditation. Ignatius had a method – it is outlined in his *Spiritual Exercises* – and he aimed at bringing people to something like *satori*. His method continues and flourishes even today.

Yet the method of Ignatius was grossly misunderstood, and became tied up with rationalism, with reasoning and thinking and a so-called "discursive prayer" that appeals little to modern man, who wants mysticism. Modern people, like Hamlet, have had too many words, words, words. Perhaps it is that they are wrung out and exhausted by television, radio, advertising, and all the stuff that McLuhan calls the extension of man's nervous system throughout our planet. What they want is deep interior silence. And this can be found through Zen, as it could be found through Ignatius' method if it were properly understood. Zen has simple techniques, however, for introducing people to inner peace and even to the so-called Christian "infused contemplation". The Japanese, as is well known in the world of economics, are an eminently practical people, and they have perfected the Zen method that came to birth in China: the sitting, the breathing, the control of the mind.

But the key thing in Zen is not just sitting in the lotus posture. The key (or so it seems to me) is detachment, the art of which is highly developed in Zen. It should be remembered that all forms of Buddhism are built on detachment and that the roots of Zen are here.

What then is the Holy Truth of the Origination of Ill? It is that craving which leads to rebirth, accompanied by delight and greed, seeking its delight now here, now there, i.e., craving for sensuous experience, craving to perpetuate oneself, craving for extinction.

What then is the Holy Truth of the Stopping of Ill? It is the complete stopping of that craving, the withdrawal from it, the renouncing of it, throwing it back, liberation from it, nonattachment to it.

True to these principles, Zen inculcates a renunciation or asceticism that is truly extraordinary. One must be detached from everything, even from oneself. Nor does Zen detachment simply mean doing without alcohol and tobacco (this is the usual Christian understanding of the word); it goes much deeper to include detachment from the very process of thinking, from the images and ideas and conceptualization that are so dear to Western men and women. And through this detachment one is introduced to a deep and beautiful realm of psychic life. One goes down, down to the depths of one's being – or, if you want a Zen physiological explanation, to the pit of one's stomach. As the process continues, one becomes detached even in those subliminal regions in which are found infantile fixations, unconscious drives, and all the rest. When detachment sets in here, Zen had something in common with psychoanalysis and can even be therapeutic for those who are able and willing to take the medicine. But I have written about this in my little book *The Still Point* and need not repeat it here. All I want to say is that so far as detachment is concerned it resembles greatly the Christian contemplative path of John of the Cross. So striking indeed is the similarity that some scholars hold that John of the Cross received Buddhist influence through Neoplatonism. But this is by no means certain.

Anyhow, detachment is only one side of the coin. One becomes detached in order that something else may shine forth. In the Buddhist this is his Buddha nature. For, contrary to what is often said, true Zen is based on a very great faith – faith in the presence of the Buddha nature in the deepest recesses of the personality; faith that, as the Four Noble Truths point out, there is a way out of the morass of suffering and that man be transformed through enlightenment. I believe this point is worth stressing for one frequently hears that there are in Zen no faith, no presuppositions, "no dependence on words and letters". In one sense this is all true. It is true that no conceptualized system can be present in the mind in time of *zazen*, it is also true that one cannot point to any one sutra and say, "Here is the essence of Zen". But in spite of this the fact remains that the whole thing is penetrated with the spirit of Buddhism, the spirit of the patriarchs, the spirit of the sutras. If one speaks to Zen people one finds this immediately, if one listens to the talks in the temples it is quite clear. There is a great faith here.

In Christian Zen this faith may take the form of a conviction that God is present in the depth of my being or, put in other words, that I am made in the image of God. Or it may express itself in the Pauline words, "I live, now not I; but Christ lives in me". The deepest and truest thing within me is not myself but God. As Christian Zen develops, self disappears (here is the Christian *muga* or nonself situation), and God lives and acts within me; my activity is no longer my own but the activity of God who is all in all. In the last analysis there is nothing except God. Paul says that there is nothing except Christ. "There is no such thing as Jew and Greek, slave and freeman, male and female; for you are all one in Christ." This is how Christian Zen will develop. The point I have tried to make here, for I consider it important, is that some kind of faith is necessary in a practice like Zen, and that one is not floating in the air as much as some people have said. This is true of all forms of deep meditation, and it is probably for this reason that a man like Aldous Huxley, who had great interest in meditation but no particular belief in anything, just didn't get anywhere. You can't go on detaching yourself indefinitely in the hope that something may or may not turn up inside. One may of course begin meditation without much faith, and many of the people who come to our place in Tokyo do just that, but the time comes when faith is necessary, and without it no one goes through to the end.

In short, it seems to me that Christians can profit greatly from Zen methodology to deepen their Christian faith, and here in Japan an increasing number of Christians, both Japanese and Western, are discovering this. A growing number of Catholic Japanese nuns, for example, are quietly practising Zen, and I believe it has a future within the Church. Surely it would be a good idea to take up this methodology and start once again teaching people how to pray. For the sad fact is that, while Catholic monks and nuns are teaching all kinds of things from botany to business English, not many are teaching people how to pray.

There is, of course, more to the methodology than the couple of points I have mentioned; but I think it better to leave the discussion of the *roshi* and the *koan* to a later chapter. What I want to say here is that impoverished Western men and women are in need of something like this, because the contemplative life is fantastically underdeveloped in the developed and affluent nations. Western civilization has become horribly one-sided and unbalanced, so much so that serious people cannot see the distinction between a computer and a man. When this happens, and when the contemplative dimension existing in every one becomes starved, then people go berserk and do crazy things. And this is what is happening. Moreover it is ghastly to think that it is happening even among some monks and nuns. Here are people whose lives are geared to *satori*, yet they feel that all is meaningless unless they are moving around the place making noise in the name of Christian charity.

If young people look into Hinduism and Buddhism for the contemplative education they instinctively long for, may this not be because modern Christianity has projected the image of a churchgoing religion rather than a mystical one? May it not have too much bingo and too little mysticism? Too much theological chatter and not enough subliminal silence? Words, words, words! Perhaps this is why we need the blood transfusion from the East.

There are other important lessons to be learned from Zen, which I shall take up in the next chapter.

3

Monism and Dualism

From what has been said it will be clear that if Christianity and Buddhism cross spiritual swords, the issue at stake is monism versus dualism. This was the point of the old *roshi* who told me that God would disappear and only Johnston would remain. This again was the point of my friend who said that one cannot even talk about God and Nothingness. The *roshi* was referring to this when he spoke of Christ's enlightenment, expressed in the words "I am". And Dr Suzuki was getting at this when he said, "But there is no other". So it all comes down to a basic problem: Are there many things or is there only one thing?

The monism versus dualism conflict has, of course, been a live issue in the West for many centuries, and Christians have been warned about the dangers of pantheism and nihilism and all the horrible things for which people like Eckhart were clobbered in the fourteenth century. But now that the pure and fresh breeze of dialogue and tolerance blows through the world, we can begin to ask other questions. We can ask: What is good in this "monism"? What can we learn from it? What does it really mean? Is it really the enemy of Christianity? What message does it have for the West?

Let me immediately give my own answer to this question. I believe that the Christian West needs a touch of this so-called monism. Modern people are looking for it, and most of it can be understood in a Christian sense. This, I believe, was one of the insights of the great Thomas Merton. I had the privilege of meeting the famous Trappist in Gethsemani (though our meeting was sadly brief, as he was called away by the bell), and afterwards we exchanged letters. A few days before we were to meet again in Japan I was shocked to hear of his sudden death – electrocuted by a fan in Bangkok. I had kept him informed about our poor Zen efforts, and he followed the whole thing with the keenest interest. Because of legal complications I have had to paraphrase the letter instead of quoting it directly. Here it is:

DEAR FATHER JOHNSTON,

Many thanks for your kind letter. I was interested to hear about the *sesshin*. I myself think that the lotus posture is quite unimportant. But perhaps Father Lassalle and yourself want to look like the real thing in the eyes of the Japanese and for this reason it may have some relevance. The problem of *satori* is more delicate.

Though I am far away and have no direct knowledge of what is going on in Japan, I will attempt to give an opinion that might have some value.

Possibly the Zen people have their own idea of what we mean when we say that we believe in God. Perhaps they think that it necessarily implies dualism and the establishment of an I-Thou relationship – something concerned with subject and object. And of course this would make *satori* impossible. I wonder if they know about Eckhart who says that it is possible to be so poor that one does not even have a God. And Eckhart is not here propounding Christian atheism and the death of God. He is simply speaking about an experience that is found clearly in all forms of apophatic mysticism. Also the Zen people may think about Christian mysticism in terms of the bride and the bridegroom. And this takes us pretty far from *satori* too.

But let's look at the thing from another standpoint. Perhaps someone like Father Lassalle who wants as a Christian to get *satori* ends up in a situation which makes *satori* psychologically impossible. Because to get the true *satori* one must have no plans whatever about a Christian getting *satori* – one must be completely detached from such plans. Perhaps the Zen people have a kind of intuition that Christians practising Zen are in such a psychological position.

I myself believe that a Christian can get *satori* just as easily as a Buddhist. It is simply a case of going beyond all forms, images, concepts, categories and the rest. But it may be that the type of Christianity we now have makes this difficult. Probably the best thing to do is to use Zen for purposes of inner purification and liberation from systems and conceptual thinking without bothering about whether or not we get *satori*. At the same time, if Father Lasselle feels that it is his vocation to get there, I am all for him. Please tell me more about all this. Have the German books of Dumoulin and Lassalle been translated into English? I'm trying to review them, but my German is not so good.

With every best wish,
Yours in Christ
THOMAS MERTON

Truth to tell, I don't go along with everything that Merton says in the above letter. Probably the cross-legged position is more important than he thinks – though he is right in saying it is not essential. Again, I don't think that any of us Westerners are particularly anxious to be the real thing in the eyes of the Japanese. And I think we have always known well enough that the person striving for *satori* with attachment never gets there. So far for my gripes. They are no more than small reservations about the thought of the great man. What he states well and with rough clarity is that Zen goes beyond all categories and all duality and that Christianity can do the same. In certain areas of apophatic experience (the Rhineland mystics make it clear) the subject-object relationship disappears. And this is no mere Christian atheism or denial of God but simply another way of experiencing God. All this is worth saying, and I am so grateful to the busy Merton for taking the trouble to sit down at his typewriter and bash out this letter to me. Let me try to elaborate on his ideas while adding my own.

For the past few centuries popular Christianity has spoken of God in a dualistic and even anthropomorphic way. I say popular Christianity because mystics like Eckhart, the anonymous author of *The Cloud*, John of the Cross, and the rest were never guilty of this oversimplification. But the popular brand of Christianity preached from the pulpit undoubtedly did tend to speak about the God "out there" that has been pilloried by Robinson in *Honest to God*. Perhaps this was partly due to an interpretation of the Bible that was too fundamentalist, a literal interpretation of the God who walked in the garden with Adam, who was angry with his people, and who is called "Father". Be that as it may, popular Christianity had the strong, if unconscious, tendency to put God *in a place*, and this tendency still persists. How many Christians, even those advanced in interior things, want to put God either above the clouds or (if that is unacceptable to modern man) in the depths of the heart or in the core of the being. But in all cases God is *somewhere*.

Now it is quite certain that an orthodox Zen monk will deny the existence of such a God; he will say that there is nothing resembling this God in his meditation nor is there any dialogue with a transcendent being. He will even go so far as to say that considerations about such a being destroy Zen. This is completely natural, for he is totally committed to a nondualism. He is the unrelenting opponent of all subject-object relationships; he is against all activity of the discriminating intellect. How could he possibly accept the idea that God is *there* and I am *here*?

And there is, of course, much truth in what he says, as Merton points out. Christians must recall the old, old philosophical truth, stressed and restressed by the mystics and elaborated by good Aquinas himself, that God is not in a place. He is not *there* in the sense that I am *here*. It is true; of course, that we may think of him in a place for convenience' sake, just as we may paint pictures of God the Father. But we must always remember the inadequacy of such an approach, recalling the fact that God is nowhere. He simply is. To put God in a place is to limit and restrict one who by definition is unlimited. If you say God is *there*, you imply that he is not *here*. Which is an absurdity. And perhaps many people saw the absurdity of this and rejected God altogether. Hence the death-of-God wave that burst over the Western world.

Turning to the Christian mystics, however, we find a different story. Here are men and women whose meditation (or contemplation) is more akin to that of the Zen Masters in that it embraces an area of experience which is beyond subject and object. I was particularly impressed by this while writing my book on *The Cloud*. The English author, in one of his minor treaties called *The Book of Privy Counselling* (which I recommend to anyone interested in Zen), is no less unrelenting than the Masters in his efforts to withdraw his disciple from subject-object relations. God is your being, he says (not "god is in you or in your being", etc.) – though your being is not the being of God. Simply be! Lose the sense of your own being for a sense of the being of God! This English author stands clearly in the great tradition of "theology of negation" that stems from Dionysius, passes to the Rhenish mystics, and reaches a climax with John of the Cross. Merton, too, belongs to the same tradition and that is why he has such sympathy for Zen.

It might be argued that this doing away with subject-object relations is not in the Bible, which is dualistic to the hilt. This is sometimes maintained even by great theologians like Karl Barth, who are unvarnished enemies of the dionysian tradition. They look on the whole apophatic stream culminating in John of the Cross as a monistic contamination of the beautiful spirituality that flows from the Bible. But in this I do not go along with them at all. Because apart from the fact that the Bible is not the whole of Christianity and necessarily restricts itself to Jewish cultural patterns – apart from this, if one reads the Bible carefully one can find there the seeds of the theology of negation. They are there in embryo. Not that this mystical stuff is expressed in terms of nothingness and emptiness and the void, because the Jews just didn't talk that way. But they had their own way of saying that God is unknowable and that he is not in a place and so on. This they said by forbidding the making of images, with the assertion that God is not like any of these things – for no man has ever seen God. Moreover the story is told – and it is a story that really appeals to me – that when the victorious Pompey strode into the Holy of Holies curious to see what was there, he found nothing (how close at last to Buddhism!). For this was the Jewish way of proclaiming the supreme unknowability of God. In addition, the seeds of apophatic mysticism are scattered throughout *Job* and *Deutero-Isaias* (or so it seems to me).

I say all this because it is of great importance for the dialogue with Zen and for those Christians who would like to practise Zen while cleaving to God. It means that it is not necessarily atheism to say that God will disappear and only Johnston will remain. It means that Christians can practise Zenlike meditation being intensely aware of God without making him an object of thought. God is not, strictly speaking, an object. He is the ground of being. If this is not grasped, Zen will be called atheistic and its introduction to Christianity will be roundly opposed or regarded with suspicion.

Nor is this to deny the dualistic aspect of reality, which for the Christian always remains. And here we come to the famous problem of "the one and the many", which has occupied the finest minds in the West from Parmenides and Aristotle to Aquinas. There is one thing; yet there are many things. Such a delicate and difficult problem as this I would not venture to tackle here, even if I had the ability to do so. Suffice it to say that the Aristotelian tradition (which, I believe, has still something to say) holds to both limbs – the one and the many. Though I am not a philosopher I have always thought this eminently sensible, since it tallies with experience. Everyday life tells us that there are many things; experience like Zen tells us that there is one thing. Why not stick to both? Must we deny one area of experience?

The point I want to make here, however, is that Christian prayer must find room for both facets of reality. Like Zen it can be silent, imageless, without subject-object relationship, and beyond dialogue. In this kind of meditation all is one. God is all in all, "I" am lost. Such in the prayer of the mystics. But there can also be dialogue between creature and Creator, made by the creature who raises up his hands like Moses to intercede for his people and for the world. Generally the prayer of Christians advanced in meditation is a mixture of both – it has its moments of imageless silence and its moments of dialogue with the Father. Consequently, coming to practice, I would suggest that Christians who do Zen use both methods of meditation. Let them follow their deepest spiritual instincts, since it is here that the Spirit is working. There will be times when they wish to be totally silent in the absence of subject-object relationship and in interior unification. And then they should follow this inclination. Many Christians educated in the I-Thou dualism have a scruple about doing this (this I have discovered from my Christian friends who do Zen), as if the abandonment of dualism meant the abandonment of God. But they should put aside such scruples. Let them enter into the area of apophatic experience that is, in fact, filled with the beauty and immensity and goodness of God. Even though it is God in darkness. On the other hand, if words of dialogue rise up in the heart – if, for example, they want to repeat the famous "Jesus prayer" or cry out to God; if they want to praise and thank God or make a prayer of petition – let them do so. Let us be for freedom. Let us follow the Spirit.

In this whole matter, however, it should be recalled that dialogue in Christian prayer reaches its perfection when it is no longer "my dialogue with God" but "Christ's dialogue with the Father in me". That is to say, the real Christian prayer is not *my* prayer but Christ's prayer. It is the voice of Christ within my soul crying out, "Abba, Father!" How wonderful this is in Paul! In such prayer we have the nonself (the *muga* or the sanskrit *anatta*), since it is no longer I that live, but Christ that lives in me.

At this point I would like to quote a passage from Gregory of Nyssa, who has been called "the father of Christian mysticism" (though I believe that he isn't – for Christ is the father of Christian mysticism), in which he speaks of the passage through Zen-like silence to the culminating cry of "Abba, Father!"

Then I would leave behind the earth altogether and traverse all the middle air; I would reach the beautiful ether, come to the stars and behold all their orderly array. But not even there would I stop short, but, passing beyond them, would become a stranger to all the moves and changes, and apprehend the stable Nature, the immovable Power which exists in its own right, guiding and keeping in being all things, for all depend on the ineffable will of the Divine Wisdom. So first my mind must become detached from everything subject to flux and change and tranquilly rest in motionless repose, so as to be rendered akin to Him who is perfectly unchangeable; and then it may address Him by the most familiar name and say: "Father."*

Here the word "Father" is no simple utterance; it is something that issues from the depth of one's being when, detached from all things, one rests tranquilly in motionless spiritual repose. Such an experience may seem a thousand miles from Zen, but there are still similarities – not only in the silencing of the faculties, the deep repose, the detachment and the integration, but also in the nonself condition in which the word "Father" rises up in the heart. For, reading Gregory and the mystics in depth, one sees that this cry does not issue from the empirical ego (which has been lost). It is the cry of Christ to his Father, the Son offering himself to the Father in Trinitarian love, the Son who is within as in the Pauline "I live, now not I; but Christ lives in me". So Christian prayer ends in a Trinitarian context. It ends with the frightening paradox that there is dialogue within a being that is totally one.

But would it be an oversimplification to say that the East has stressed unity and that the West has stressed diversity? And that they need one another? Or better, to say that the mystic East teaches us in a striking way that all is one, while the scientific West has brilliantly grasped the diversity and the many? And that they need one another. Perhaps we should shy away from such wild generalizations. Yet I like to think this way in our dialogue with Zen.

St Gregory of Nyssa: The Lord's Prayer, Hilda C. Graef, trans. and annot. (London: Burns and Oates, 1954) p. 37.

4

Christian Zen (1)

During the summer of 1970 I lectured on mysticism in San Francisco. People had told me that California is the centre of yoga and witchcraft, Zen and sorcery, drugs and nudity, and everything under the sun. They said that there were all kinds of *swamis* and *roshis, gurus* and transcendental meditators floating around the place, and that the atmosphere was haunted by the ghost of Aldous Huxley swallowing mescaline and claiming to have had the Beatific Vision. In short, California was the home of mysticism true and false. Whether or not this is true I do not know. All I know is that I fell in love with the wide open spaces of California and with the breath-taking beauty of Big Sur. I left some of my heart in San Francisco.

I tried to invest my classes with a veneer of academic learning (after all, *noblesse oblige*); but feeling that with such a subject theory must be supplemented by practice, I invited the students, and anyone else who wanted to come, to sit in *zazen* for forty minutes each evening. Obviously it was not my intention to turn them into mystics but merely to give them some tiny experience and savouring of the *silentium mysticum* (this, I believe, is possible) and to introduce them to a meditation that would be without thought, without images, without desire, in interior unification and peace. This I tried to do by developing a few simple techniques, and with a short explanation which I shall outline in a moment. I wanted to have the minimum of theory so that they could just sit.

To my surprise fifty or sixty showed up, and many kept coming. So we sat in the university chapel, facing the wall and thinking about nothing. In some ways it was much less impress-

ive than the solemn meditation halls in Engakuji or Eiheiji, since
we didn't have the set-up to do the thing in style. Some used
pillows and blankets in place of the beautiful little Zen cushion
that is called a *zafu*, and we didn't have the neat, straight-lined
and disciplined atmosphere of the Zen temple; but then, needless
to say, Western legs don't take easily to the lotus posture and
the Western back tends to sag. Yet in spite of all this there was
a hushed silence (latecomers sensed it instantly), a sense of
union and an atmosphere of supernatural presence. Since some
students complained that "just sitting" was somehow driving
them into isolation, we began and ended with a good old hymn,
"We are one in the Spirit, we are one in the Lord. . . ." Even to
write about it gives me a pang of nostalgia for those happy days.
It was, after all, a primitive endeavour, but it has convinced me
that Zen in some shape or form has a future within Christianity.
Western Christianity, I repeat, needs this kind of thing – the
people are longing for it.

There was a little opposition, though less than I expected. I
confess that I can understand the feelings of my critics. Conciliar
ideas take some time to filter into the psychology of certain
good people, and I saw at once that the recent influx of Oriental
religions has perplexed not a few solid Christians in the California area. They don't know whether to thrust the whole damn
business into the category of a Fellini-Satyricon end of the
Roman Empire (an apocalyptic omen of the end of the West),
or to welcome it with postconciliar comprehension, co-operation, and charity. I was not surprised, then, to find a few who
looked on me as a Buddhist missionary out to topple the idols
of Christianity. To a conservative Irish Catholic like myself, this
was a little painful. Yet Irishmen gave me small support. I have
always felt that my staunch fellow countrymen are among those
less open to the gentle breeze of spirituality that blows from the
Orient. They are more at home with "Hail, Glorious Saint
Patrick" than with the lotus posture, and they look with alarm
at the saffron robes, the beards, and the bare feet that speak of
the esoteric East. Conversely, I found that if one wants to sell
something like Zen, a guttural Teutonic accent pays better divi-
dends than a brogue. This latter, in the United States, is more

often associated with Irish coffee than with Oriental studies; and many people did not suppress their surprise and amusement at hearing an Irishman talking about Zen. Alas, in such circumstances what can one do but transcend the confines of time and space, entering into the serene air of pure nothingness?

Anyhow, since misunderstanding could arise, I thought it better to call the thing "Christian Zen" and make the business clear. Yet this was a bit embarrassing in view of the fact that I had just published a book in which I attacked all the talk about "Christian Zen" as being confusing. Now I was obliged to eat my words. Certainly the term will always be controversial, and some people won't like it. Nevertheless, after thinking the thing over again, I now am of the opinion that the term "Christian Zen" can be meaningful, provided one makes the necessary distinctions. Probably the strongest argument in its favour is the fact, already mentioned, that some of the Masters concede that Zen exists in Christianity. Perhaps they do not rate our brand as highly as their own – though even that is not certain – but they do recognize it. And if they recognize it, why not use the term? Anyhow, let me now recount briefly how I introduced the subject of Zen and how some people reacted.

First of all, I felt it necessary to distinguish between Zen and Zen Buddhism. This latter is a Buddhist sect which, it is said, originated in Canton in the sixth century AD when the Indian monk Bodhidharma, after sitting in meditation for nine years, finally obtained enlightenment. So long and with such determination did he sit facing the wall that his arms and legs fell off. And the little armless, legless statues of Dharma Sama can still be found all over Japan. Bodhidharma is a legendary figure, and scholars say that Zen originated from the confluence of Mahayana Buddhism and Taoism. Certainly marks of the India origin still remain in the vocabulary. The sanskrit *maya* becomes *Makyo, dhyana* became *ch'an* in China and *Zen* in Japan; *samadhi* becomes *sanmai*, and so on. It is to the undying credit of Zen Buddhism, especially to the two great sects of Soto and Rinzai, to have preserved and developed Zen with such purity and severity. So much for Zen Buddhism.

The word Zen, on the other hand, means meditation, and

that is why it need not be restricted to Buddhism. Not any old meditation at all, of course – not the discursive meditation wherein one reasons and thinks and makes resolutions. Rather is it a state of consciousness in which one sees into the essence of things; it extends throughout the day, so that one can say that Zen is walking, Zen is working, Zen is eating, Zen is life. It is meditation without an object. It is what elsewhere I have called "vertical meditation", because it is sometimes described as a "going down", a breaking through layers of consciousness to the depths of one's spirit or the core of one's being. One pays no attention to the thoughts and images that pass across the surface of the mind. One simply ignores them in favour of a deeper activity. In Christian terms it may be better to call it contemplation rather than meditation, since it is so akin to the mental exercise described by the great Christian contemplatives. This, like Zen, is sometimes spoken of as darkness, emptiness, silence, nothingness. It has been called "the dark night", not because it is particularly painful but because of the absence of clear-cut thoughts and images in the mind. Again, it is called the cloud of unknowing, because one is, as it were, in a cloud without clear images and ideas. Sometimes it is spoken of as "thinking of nothing"; but I like this terminology less because it can give rise to the misconception that Zen or contemplation is a form of idling. A better term is "super-thinking".

This meditation is existential in that it is not preoccupied with past or future, right or left, up or down. One is simply in the present (in the lotus posture one may have the feeling of being locked there), in the eternal now, face to face with reality like two mirrors. And all this may some day culminate in the transforming experience known as *satori*. The bodily position is not without importance, because Zen is meant to drive conviction right down into the guts. Here it is in contrast with Western prayer, which for the past couple of centuries has tended to be very cerebral and has not rooted itself deeply in the personality, with the result that many Christians, even nuns and priests, can jettison long-held convictions in moments of emotional crisis. Probably they would not be able to do this if their convictions were lodged at the gut level through Zen.

This, more or less, was the way I explained the thing. Now it has often been said that you cannot understand Zen unless you do it and that there is no substitute for experience. This is probably true. And yet I found that the people I met got the idea rather quickly, even before they actually sat. They got it much more quickly than the people of a generation back. For the latter all this talk about interior darkness and emptiness was so much rigmarole; and even spiritual writers were reluctant to write about it except for the initiated. They seemed to feel that they were dealing with an area of psychic life which could be sacred or diabolical and which, at all events, should be handled with delicacy. On the other hand, modern people are much more familiar with it all. Why?

One reason, I believe, is the widespread knowledge of psychoanalysis. Since the Freudian revolution people are acutely aware of their interior drives, subconscious anxieties, childhood fixations, archetypes, and all the rest. They are familiar with the description of the mind as an iceberg with only a fraction of its massive bulk protruding from the water. It is not hard for them to imagine depth upon depth in the mind, depths normally dormant until their powers of energy are released by something like Zen. When they are told about a meditation that penetrates through layers of consciousness to the very bottom, they somehow get an idea of what it's all about.

There is, I believe, a second reason why modern people get the hang of Zen rather easily, though I hesitate to mention it lest I be misunderstood. Anyhow, it is this: the widespread use of drugs. Now I am by no means advocating drugs. I have never experimented with them myself, and am quite prepared to believe the horrendous things that are said about them. All I say here is that they seem to have introduced some people to a level of psychic life that has something in common with Zen and mysticism. I don't mean that the experience they induce is the same as Zen – it isn't, for it has altogether different effects – but similar psychological faculties may have been brought into play. The result is that some people who have used drugs understand a little about Zen, since they have been awakened to the realization that there is a depth in the mind worth exploring. I have heard of people who began with drugs and ended up with Zen. Surely this is a consummation devoutly to be wished.

There were serious Christians who had difficulties about Zen. I don't mean prejudiced people, but others who were open but perplexed. Their problems, I believe, can be reduced to three.

First, there was the whole problem of the place of God in Zen. I have already spoken of that and need not go into it again.

Secondly, there was the problem of the place of Christ in Zen. Some people felt that Christian Zen must be centred on Christ. And where was Christ in this void of imageless darkness? This is an important problem. I myself believe that Christian Zen can be Christ-centred, but I shall leave that to a later chapter.

The third problem can be dealt with here. Some asked: But how does Zen differ from "quietism"?

Quietism is one of these words that are bandied about by well-meaning people who don't quite know what they mean. If I understand it correctly, which is not certain, it is a form of idling that crept into contemplative prayer in the seventeenth century, taking the form of suppression of thought and activity. Undoubtedly it was a grotesque distortion of the real thing. And that similar distortions exist today when people are so anxious for kicks is beyond question. I suppose it is a matter that should be taken seriously, since it is certainly possible to sit in comfortable silence, enjoying a species of physical euphoria that has no religious significance whatever and makes nobody wiser than before.

But it should be remembered that Zen literature, no less than its Christian counterpart, is filled with anathemas against such things. "*Bonyari Zen*", which means "idling Zen", is roundly condemned by true Masters, who rightly insist that, far from idling, the true Zen demands a fantastic effort of mind and will and body. Thought is not just suppressed. As has been pointed out, the upper levels of consciousness are ignored in order that one may concentrate at a deeper level. Put in other words: one is not preoccupied with thought but with the ground of being from which thought takes its origin. Here lies the true self. Nor is there any question of just letting the mind run amuck. Deep down there is a concentration that is silent but intense; people practising Zen are urged to use all their powers and energies to break through. And the key is the detachment that we have considered. In short, quietism could be a danger in Zen as in Christian contemplation; but, properly understood, Zen is not quietistic. Anyone who has been beaten by the stick or *kyosaku* knows this.

Again, if quietism means the negation of activity in such a way that one does no work, it is clear that no such charge can be levelled at Zen, which emphasizes work immensely. Indeed, to do one's work with total concentration and energy is one form of Zen practice and is a substitute for sitting in the meditation hall. This is frequently said by the Master.

Going further, it might be possible to define quietism in a broader sense. Then for Christians it would mean rest in anything that is not God. For Zen Buddhists it would mean rest in anything. And for practical purposes both are saying the same thing. The fact is that if you want to persevere to the end you must rest in nothing. Nothing, nothing, nothing, says John of the Cross, and on the mountain nothing. This means renunciation, not of alcohol and tobacco, but of all thoughts and desires (even thoughts and ideas of God), of all visions, sensible experiences, and the rest. The *Ascent of Mount Carmel* is a detailed catalogue of all things from which you must be detached, particularly those sweet spiritual experiences to which the mind cleaves. "Unless a man renounces everything he possesses he cannot be my disciple." And everything means everything. How often people get attached to the joyful euphoria of their own *samadhi*, and they cling to it, they rest in it. And this, I believe, is a form of quietism that hinders progress. John of the Cross speaks of such attachments as the tiny thread around the foot of the bird, hindering it from soaring into the clear blue sky in serene freedom. A Buddhist author puts it in another way. A man is standing in the underground train leaning on his umbrella when the train lurches. He must let go of the umbrella and grasp the rail — otherwise he is lost. So let go of your umbrella. Let it go. Don't cling to it or you'll fall flat on your face.

I write this to underline the radical nature of true mysticism, whether Buddhist or Christian. It is rest in nothing; it is no search for a beautiful experience or a thrilling kick. But let's remember, too, that renunciation is but one side of the picture. There is the treasure hidden in the field and the pearl of great price. To find these the suffering is worthwhile.

5

Christian Zen (2)

I have tried to say that, on the admission of some Masters, Zen is found in religions other than Buddhism. If this is true, Zen ought already to exist in Christianity; and in that case the task of the Christian will be to find it, develop it, and make it relevant to our day with the help of the East. But where is Zen within the Christian tradition?

I confess that I would hate to go on record as stating that Zen is found in Christianity in exactly the same form as in Buddhism. This would be one of those simplified statements that drives everybody out of their mind, Christians and Buddhists alike, and I am not particularly anxious to lose all my friends. What I can safely say, however, is that there is a Christian *samadhi* that has always occupied an honoured place in the spirituality of the West. This, I believe, is the thing that is nearest to Zen. It is this that I have called Christian Zen.

I have already spoken briefly about this *samadhi* which flourished in the great schools of spirituality that drove their roots into the rich cultural soil of medieval Europe. There were schools of Cistercians, Dominicans, Carmelites, Franciscans, and the rest. Then there were the Victorines – and schools of mysticism in the Rhineland and in Flanders and even in stolid old England. To say nothing of the great Orthodox schools that gave us the *Philokalia* and taught the prayer of the heart. All these schools had their way of leading to contemplative silence and peace, beyond words, beyond images, beyond ideas, and beyond desire. The contemplative experience went by various names. The author of *The Cloud* describes it beautifully as "the blind stirring of love". It is blind because it contains no thoughts and images, being just like nothing; it is no more than a delicate and simple interior movement of love in silence. Again, the same author speaks of it as "the naked intent of the will". Mention of the will indicates the element of love, while nakedness or nudity is traditionally used in Christian prayer to indicate complete detachment from all things, even from thoughts and images and desires. "Be sure that it be naked", the English author tells his disciple, and he repeatedly warns him to be "unclothed" in his approach to God. Other authors speak of it as the *silentium mysticum*, indicating that beyond all thought and speech there lies a realm of exquisite silence. Again, it is called "spiritual sleep" because it has a depth and a quietness and a strength like that other beauty sleep which is chief nourisher in life's great feast. John of the Cross (my great guru) calls it "the living flame of love", referring to the dynamic nature of this *samadhi*, which developing into a roaring flame, comes to possess one's whole being and drives one on in total self-forgetfulness. The same author refers to it as the dark night because of the spiritual nudity or absence of thought that characterizes the state of deep *samadhi*. The terminology stems from a much earlier writer, Dionysius.

> In the earnest practice of mystical contemplation, do thou leave behind the senses and the working of the intellect, and all things that the senses and the intellect can perceive, and all things which are not and all things that are, and strain upwards in unknowing, as far as may be, to union with Him who is above all things and above all knowledge. For by constant and absolute withdrawal from thyself and all things in purity, abandoning all and set free from all, thou shalt be carried up to the ray of Divine darkness that surpasseth all being.*

This ray of divine darkness pierces brightly through the whole apophatic school of mysticism of which John of the Cross is the chief spokesman. His sister Teresa is less dark. For her, *samadhi* is found at the centre of the interior castle in the depth of one's

*My own translation.

being. She refers to interior and spiritual senses of listening, touching, and relishing, thus adding richness to the emptiness of interior silence.

Each school had its own typical approach, but one thing common to all was an emphasis on love or divine charity. Here, of course, the basic intuition comes from the Scriptures, particularly from the text which states that he who loves knows God and he who does not love does not know God. Enlightenment was the fruit of love, which was like a candle that gives light and enables one to see. "Proffer thy candle to the flame", writes the author of *The Cloud*, asking us to enlighten our hearts from the immense flame that is the love of God. Somehow love drives people down to the psychic level where *samadhi* is found (and I believe this is true also of human love) and wisdom is relished. For contemplation itself was not precisely love, but wisdom – the beautiful *sapientia* that medieval Christianity esteemed so much. "If anyone loves me he will be loved of my Father and we will send the Spirit. . . ." The spirit of wisdom was given to those who love.

In the technique of introducing people to *samadhi*, the Western tradition differed considerably from Zen. There was no lotus position and little about bodily posture. There does seem to have been considerable interest in breathing, particularly in the Eastern Church and in the tradition that flourished around Mount Athos, but much of this was lost or forgotten, and the farther West one moves the more cerebral the whole thing becomes. People were introduced to meditation by reading the Scriptures and reflection on their contents. Gradually this discursive meditation would develop into something more simplified (like the repetition of an aspiration or word), and eventually into the wordless and supraconceptual silence which is contemplation – or, if you prefer the word, Christian *samadhi*. This was a stage at which everyone seriously devoted to mental prayer should arrive. It was the ordinary development of meditation.

This is the way I was taught to meditate when I entered the novitiate (or joined the party) somewhere out in the bog. I was told to take the Bible, or some book about the Bible, and to chew and ruminate and digest and pray. For a start, this was pretty good, and I would recommend anyone to begin in this way. My only complaint is that in religious orders at that time, and now also, nothing further was taught. The old medieval tradition of leading people through various stages to *samadhi* was more or less lost. It just was not customary to introduce people to supraconceptual forms of prayer; and as for "mysticism", this was not a good word. Needless to say, if people stumbled on *samadhi* or got there under their own steam, as many did, there was nothing to stop them, but skilled direction and efficient methodology was greatly lacking.

Aldous Huxley and others have blamed the Jesuits for the decline in mysticism in nineteenth-century Europe, accusing the sons of Ignatius of teaching a species of prayer that was more like mathematics than contemplation. But perhaps this is not entirely fair. Other factors were at work. For one thing, a healthy reticence about mysticism was considered prudent in view of the wave of false mysticism that had wrought havoc in religious life at an earlier period. Then there was the spirit of the times (what my German friends, if I hear them correctly, call the *Zeitgeist*), which always hits monasteries hard – as the permissive society hits them hard today. In the last century it was a spirit of scientism, of rationalism, of dogmatism that esteemed concepts, images, mathematics, ideas, and was quite bewildered by the silent darkness of mystical wisdom. All this militated against the mystical tradition. Add to it the general decline of Western stamina in the last decade and you understand why so many religious orders have lost their mysticism, and with it their vision.

It is just at this juncture that Zen and other forms of Oriental mysticism appear on the horizon. I believe they have something to say to us. I believe they can help the tottering religious orders to rethink some problems and to make some changes. And they can also help the Christian layman to enter into *samadhi*. Faced with this phenomenon from the East, however, and anxious to learn from the Oriental treasure house, the Westerner can adopt either of two attitudes.

First, he can jettison his own tradition to become all Oriental.

Neglecting the great giants of his past, he can sit at the feet of the *roshi* and endeavour to obtain a *satori* that has been handed down through many generations from the time of Bodhidharma and even from the time of the Buddha. In this way he stands in the full stream of Eastern Buddhism, and if he is a Christian he can take his *satori* into a Christian framework. Some Western people have taken this line.

I myself, however, could never do things in this way. Perhaps Jung and Eliot have made me feel too deeply the power of tradition and the strength of those archetypes that are lodged down deep within me. Jung was enthusiastic about Zen and yoga; but he insisted that in their Eastern form they do not suit Western men and women, who have a different tradition and different archetypes. In a famous sentence he said that the West would have its own yoga, built upon the foundations of Christianity. Here, I believe, he had a charismatic flash of prophecy, uttering words that will soon be fulfilled. Together with Jung, Eliot keeps telling us that the past is present – that it is living in us, part of us, pushing us on. If this is so, is it possible to cast away one's past and substitute another? Is it possible to throw out Western archetypes and replace them with those of the East? For me it is not. And in spite of having lived in the East for twenty years, in spite of loving Japan very deeply, I still feel incorrigibly Western and even, alas, incorrigibly Irish. Obviously this is not to say that my own tradition is superior – I don't believe it is – but simply that it is a fact.

For this reason it has always seemed to me that the psychologically realistic way of doing things is to stand in the stream of one's own tradition and humbly take what is good and valuable from another. In particular it is the work of the great religious orders – Dominicans, Franciscans, Jesuits, and so on – to rediscover the mystical tradition they have lost and enrich it with the spiritual insights that the East has to offer. This may mean forgoing the apostolic joy of teaching mathematics, walking in demonstrations, and running bazaars. But the sacrifice would surely be worth while.

About this blood transfusion – learning what we can and integrating it with out past – I have already said something in an earlier chapter. Now let me add a few more words. How can Zen update and make relevant the tradition of Christian contemplation that goes back for more than a millennium and is now in dire need of renewal? First of all, I think that things like Zen can help us update and demythologize much of the theology that underlies Christian mysticism. Let me explain what I mean.

The Judaeo-Christian tradition, as is well known, is extremely theocentric. Everything hinges on God. This stems in large measure from the Bible, where all is attributed to the guiding hand of Yahweh. If the rain falls, this is the work of Yahweh. If someone goes astray, Yahweh hardens his heart. If he dies, Yahweh strikes him down. And so on. This is all the more stressed in the communication of God to human beings; the great experiences of Abraham, Moses, and Paul had nothing whatever to do with their own efforts, their own asceticism, their own prayer. All was the gift of Yahweh. This was carried over into the Christian mystical tradition, where everything was the work of God and the activity of people received little attention. What I have called Christian *samadhi* went by the name of infused contemplation because it was a pure gift poured into the soul by God alone.

Now this is a legitimate way of speaking. Ultimately it is very true, and the Hebrew was right in attributing everything to God. But it has the disadvantage of making people lazy in developing the human faculties that make for mysticism. It has the further disadvantage of being rather unacceptable to modern mankind, who is extremely anthropocentric and has difficulty with a terminology that incessantly (and to them needlessly) keeps harping on God. He has demythologized the action of God in the natural sphere by finding all kinds of secondary causes, and he finds difficulty with a Christian mystical theory which clings constantly to the direct action of God and is stubbornly theocentric.

As opposed to this, Zen is extremely man-centred and existential. You are simply told to sit and get on with the job. The instructions are concerned with your spine and your eyes and your abdomen; in a very practical way you are led to *samadhi* without too much theory. What you are asked to believe is that you possess the Buddha nature and that enlightenment is possible.

Here is something for Christianity. Terminology about acquired and infused contemplation, about ordinary and extra-ordinary prayer, about *gratia gratis data* and *gratia gratum faciens* – all these complications can quietly and conveniently be dropped. They aren't really necessary, because the experience itself is frightfully simple and uncomplicated. In my opinion we could even dispense with the word contemplation and put in its place "Christian *samadhi*". This would have the good effect of bringing us into line with other spiritual traditions which use this word. Besides, contemplation is a Latin word, translation of the Greek *theoria*. Must Christians for ever stick to the Hellenistic vocabulary?

By using a language that people understand and employing a technique they can practise, it should be possible to introduce a great number of people to Christian *samadhi*. This would be an enormous boon to Christianity – particularly to Catholic Christianity, which finds its people losing interest in the rosary, the way of the Cross, novenas, and all the devotions that have propped up the popular faith in the past. These can be seen as leading to a simple contemplation accessible to anyone with good will. The old Christian contemplation was for an elite – it was for Franciscans, Jesuits, Dominicans, and the good people I have spoken about. But the poor layman, a second-class citizen, was left with his beads. It need no longer be so. Just as the liturgy has broadened out to embrace everyone, so contemplation can broaden out too. The wretched wall that divided popular Christianity from monastic Christianity can be broken down so that all may have vision, all may reach *samadhi*.

Nor is this to say that the role of the poor Franciscans, the wise Dominicans, the wily Jesuits, and the rest has come to a happy end. No, these should be contemplatives by profession, leaders of the rest. In this way they can do a great service to the community and to the world. But if they persist in doing things that the world can do better, they will simply cease to exist. They will have no reason for existence and little relevance for society. Others will take their place.

6

Christk

Christ

Speaking about Zen to Christians I have found myself faced with the wide-eyed question, "But what about Christ? How does Christ fit into this void, this emptiness, this darkness that transcends thought?"

This is an obvious and inescapable question. Anybody with even a kindergarten grasp of Christianity knows that Christ is the centre of the whole business, and that to exclude Christ would be the prime sellout. Naturally, then, people are wary of a Christian prayer that seems to put aside the Scriptures (no dependence on words and letters) and excludes thoughts and images of Christ in order to enter into the darkness of nothing. And needless to say, all this is a pretty formidable challenge to anybody foolish enough to start gabbing about Christian Zen.

I myself believe that if Christian Zen is to be Christian and not simply Zen, it must be somehow Christocentric and some-how built on the Scriptures. But I ask myself if through Zen we may not find a new approach to Christ, an approach that is less dualistic and more Oriental. This statement may sound strange, but I believe that it is pretty reasonable.

Let me go back to something I tried to say earlier. Dialogue does not simply mean that Buddhists and Christians sit around sipping green tea and exchanging pleasantries in a palsy-walsy atmosphere of ecumenical good will. It means that they settle down and learn something from one another. They get new ideas, new attitudes, new insights. And it is this I am talking about now: from Buddhism we can get new insights into our approach to Christ.

We ought to be open to this kind of thing, because it is what our forebears did. Christianity, after all, began as a Jewish thing, but Augustine, Gregory, and the rest did not swallow the whole bit, hook, line and sinker as it came from Judaism. These men lived in a Greek culture; they carried Greek insights into the Jewish revelation, and so Christianity grew and was enriched. Now if Augustine and Gregory did not take the whole thing from the Jews, I can't see why the Orientals should take it hook, line and sinker from us. They will have their own insights, their own attitudes – and they will add a lot to Christianity, just as Greek culture added a lot.

That is what I mean by saying that if we go to Christ through Zen we find him in a different way from the person who goes to him through Aristotle. I love that passage in Second Corinthians where Paul speaks of the glory of God in the face of Moses and the glory of God in the face of Jesus. What radiant brightness and divine power is there! And do we little Westerners think we have seen all that glory? Do we claim to have exhausted all that beauty? Do we imagine we have explored all that wisdom? Far from it. In the face of Christ are myriads of contours yet to be explored; his voice speaks in rich and vibrant tones that Western ears have never heard; his eyes are pools of wisdom the Western gaze has never fathomed. And now it is the hour of the East to explore all this beauty and find what the West has missed. What an exciting adventure! But let me, a mere foreign barbarian who has spent twenty years in the mystic East, attempt to stammer some words about this new approach to the glory of God in the face of Jesus.

Once in a Buddhist temple I heard a good old *roshi* deliver a talk on detachment from words and ideas. Words, he said, using a traditional Buddhist simile, are like a finger pointing to the moon. Cling to the finger and you'll never see the moon. This I felt to be eminently reasonable and true. Words, any words, even the words of Scripture, are fingers that point to something else. As long as we cling to words we will never have real vision.

And, of course, Western man loves his little words and clings to them like a child clutching his favourite toy. He clings to his concepts, images, figures, adding machines, and computers, forgetting that all these things are fingers pointing to the moon.

Today his main problem is that he has got enmeshed and fouled up in mass communications and the secular city, forgetting again that these are no more than pointing fingers. Transferring this attitude to the Scriptures, he clings to the words and the phrases, and he is in danger of adoring images and concepts of God instead of God himself. A strange form of idolatry.

What I am getting at here is that words and concepts and images of Christ are not Christ. Let us at least reflect on the possibility that Christ can be known without ideas – that he can be known in the darkness, in the void, in the emptiness that transcends thought. The Scriptures are the finger (and we need the Scriptures just as we need the finger), but Christ is the moon. Let us not get so involved with fingers that we miss the moon.

Or take something else from Zen. Anybody who has dabbled a little in Suzuki and the others has heard the famous dictum: "If you meet the Buddha, slay him!" This is often taken as a blasphemous rejection of all that is religious or sacred – sometimes as proof that Zen holds nothing sacrosanct, even the Buddha.

But I do not read it this way. I prefer the interpretation that says, "If you see the Buddha, what you see is not the Buddha. So slay him!" The underlying idea is not unlike the finger and the moon. Anything – absolutely anything – that you see or hear or touch is not the genuine article. Kill it! It is no more than the finger pointing to the moon. It may be very precious; but if your right hand scandalizes you, cut it off.

Now I believe that there is something for Christians here. Properly and piously understood, one can say, "If you meet Christ, slay him!" And the meaning is: "What you see is not Christ."

The slaying metaphor, of course, is pretty grim and overstates the problem. Because, as I have said, concepts and images and pictures are as necessary as the finger, and it's not a good idea to do away with them altogether. On the other hand, the slay-the-Buddha motif is meant as practical direction for time of meditation. Get rid of the Buddha as an object of thought, it means, if you want to realize your Buddha nature. And in the same way one can say, get rid of images of Christ if you want the high contemplative union with the inner Christ who lives in the core of your being.

In short, what it comes to it this. It is not necessary to have clear-cut images and concepts of Christ. If you have no such concepts you may be in the stage where you have forgotten about the finger, fascinated by the pale and tranquil beauty of the autumn moon. And if so, how happy you are! You have left the dirty cave of Plato and are out in the beautiful sunlit air. Don't let these grubby little merchants drag you back to the murky underworld of conceptualization. Stay out. Enjoy your *samadhi*. Christ is with you.

Now I can immediately envisage some of my readers considering this a lot of nonsense. They will say that we can, in fact, have an image of Christ; we can have a picture of the eternal Galilean who dominates Matthew, Mark, Luke and John. After all, have we not his portrait? So how can you throw images and concepts out of the window as if they were so much garbage? And to this I would answer again that concepts are not trash but the finger pointing to the moon.

Christ is the moon because the men who wrote the Gospel are leading their reader to a vision not only of the historical Jesus (of whom we assuredly can have concepts) but of the risen Christ, the cosmic Christ, the Christ who was at the beginning. And it is he who escapes all images, all thoughts, all ideas, and all pictures. The risen Christ is so far beyond concepts that we find Paul struggling with all kinds of words to express the inexpressible. Here is Paul on Jesus:

> His is the primacy over all created things
>   For in him were created
>   All things in heaven and on earth;
> Everything visible and everything invisible
> Thrones, dominations, sovereignties, powers,
>   All things were created through him and for him.
> Before everything was created he existed
>   And he holds all things in unity.

Don't let anyone tell me that Paul is here speaking about some simple reality that can be expressed in concepts and images!

Nor is he speaking of Jesus just as he was in his earthly, preresurrection form. For Paul, Christ is a "secret" or a "mystery" or whatever you want to call it, and he keeps pointing one finger after another at the moon that no human eye can descry. The poor scholars get all tied up in Paul's fingers; the mystics turn toward the moon.

The living and risen Christ of Paul who is with men all days is the unknowable Christ, co-extensive with the universe and buried in the hollow recesses of the human heart. The deepest thing in Paul is not Paul but Christ. It is not Paul who lives, but Christ who lives in him. It is not Paul who cries out "Abba, Father", it is the spirit of Christ within who utters this cry. For Paul, to live is Christ and to die is Christ – and it is all the same. If this is true for Paul, it is true for anyone who believes. The deepest thing within him is not himself but Christ.

I believe that Paul is trying to say something like this to the Ephesians when he makes the prayer, "that Christ may dwell by faith in your hearts". The word "heart" here is a direct translation of the Greek; but Paul, a Jew born and bred, probably had in mind the Hebrew word, which means the core of being, the deepest self. So for Paul, Christ is beyond concepts, beyond images, beyond thought, beyond place. If we want to situate him anywhere, we should situate him where thought takes its origin, because he is our original face before we were born. That is why Paul can say that we were chosen in Christ before the foundation of the world.

One step further. If Christ is deep, deep down at the centre of reality and in the depths of the heart – if he is somehow like the true self, then there will be times when we do not know him reflectively. This is because there is no I-Thou relationship any longer. It is of the very nature of the deepest realms of our psyche to move, urge on, inspire, and direct without being known in a subject-object way – the charity of Christ drives us on, says Paul. Nor is it only Paul. Luke tells us how Jesus warned his disciples not to think too much when they were dragged before princes and kings.

"Keep this carefully in mind: you are not to prepare your defence because I myself will give you an eloquence and a wisdom that none of your opponents will be able to resist or contradict" (Luke 21). Face to face with the judge or the hangman, one shouldn't start asking, "What would Jesus do now?" No, get rid of all this dualistic stuff. Because the answer is going to come from your very guts where the deepest thing lies. Here Jesus and Zen are together. No reasoning. No reflection. The answer is going to come from a part of our being that you scarcely know exists.

I have talked about Paul and said a word about Luke; but John is just the same. The great John, the beloved disciple – what a fantastic sense he had of the glory of Jesus! "We have seen his glory. . . ." And for him Jesus was the "true" everything, the Greek *alethinos*. Jesus is the true vine, the true bridegroom, the true way, the true life, the truth itself. He is the genuine vine, and other vines that we see are second-class imitations of the real product. Here is another poetic way of speaking about the cosmic dimensions of a risen Christ who is at the centre of all that is. "And I, if I be lifted up from the earth, will draw all things to myself."

Of course when I talk about the cosmic Christ I want to maintain some balance, which is not easy in a world that is topsy-turvy and upside down. I mean that some theologians in their zest for the living Christ tend to cut the link between the cosmic Christ and the historical Christ. No doubt they feel that this is a felicitous, ecumenical virtue, since if the cosmic Christ is divorced from the historical Christ, the cosmic Christ can be equated with the all-pervading Buddha nature, and everyone feels happy in sweet, ecumenical unanimity. But alas, things are not so easy, and neither true Buddhists nor true Christians feel happy when things are ironed out in this way. If one has a minimum of fidelity to Paul and John and Luke and the rest, one sees that the cosmic Christ is precisely the Jesus who shed his blood. If anything is clear in the preaching of the New Testament, it is the fact that the once crucified Jesus is now alive – even the wildest exegetes cannot find in the Bible a discontinuity between Jesus of Nazareth and the Christ who has the primacy over all things. I want to stress this in parenthesis lest I be identified with a lot of gnostic rubbish that creates air pollution in the theological skies of our day.

Returning, however, to the cosmic dimensions of Christ who is at the deepest heart of man, this is something that can have enormous repercussions on the life of meditation for the Christian. It means that meditation need not be confined to the I-Thou brand that has been the warp and woof of popular Christian prayer. Not that the I-Thou approach is excluded. It must always be there. But it is not the whole story. Let me try, then, to sketch briefly a Christocentric path of Zen meditation.

The starting point will be the Scriptures, which should be read or heard or experienced in liturgy. This is the indispensable groundwork without which no Christian meditation can exist. And if we have Christian Zen meditation halls (as I hope we soon will) I believe that the air should be pervaded with Scripture and liturgy and the atmosphere of faith, without which the void might well become a literal void and not the rich fullness of mystical emptiness. Furthermore, in the early stages, meditation (particularly in the case of Western people) may be dualistic, or rationalistic, or whatever you want to call this reflection and dialogue with God that is traditionally central to Christian prayer. Paul began in a dualistic way. He began with a conversation with Christ on the road to Damascus, and the I-Thou approach seems to continue in *Philippians*, where he is running after Christ like an athlete in the Isthmian games. If a Christian, too, wants to start in the footsteps of Paul, running after Christ – well, this is all right. But if he wants to go on to anything like Zen, the thinking process must simplify, the words must decrease, the dualism must give way to the void of emptiness which is the *silentium mysticum*. Now he is doing something like Zen – *gedo* Zen, perhaps, but still Zen. He is getting away from the finger and beginning to look toward the moon. He cannot see the moon (for it is beyond the cloud of unknowing) but he is drawn to it even so, and he does not want to be bothered with pious reflections about the finger. He does not want to be ensnared even by its delicate silken beauty and its white-skinned softness. Its very beauty may be a temptation now, distracting him from the quiet splendour of the moon. It is the finger of enlightened men – Matthew, Mark, Luke and John – who saw something and want their readers to see it too. "These things I have written in order that you may believe." So let him forget the finger and, without any solicitude whatever, look quietly towards the silent beauty of that hidden moon. He may find, in Paul's masterly phrase, that his life is hidden with Christ in God. His self is hidden, Christ is hidden, and only God remains. (Shades again of my old *roshi*.) But if this is you, remember that you will be there, very much alive; Christ is there, very much alive; but you are not conscious of yourself or of Christ – because your life is hidden with Christ in God. Eventually enlightenment will come. Not any enlightenment, but the one toward which the finger points. Abba, Father!

7

Koan

People sometimes say that Zen is crazy and that anyone interested in the business should have his, or her, head examined. It's not my intention here to refute or substantiate this accusation, since, apart from everything else, protestations of personal sanity don't convince anyone anyhow. What I want to do is to discuss the *koan*, which is one of the seemingly crazy elements in Zen.

Koan literally means "a public document", but as used in Zen it has absolutely nothing to do with public documents (here we go on the first happy spree of irrationalities) and simply means a paradoxical problem. It is a problem that is kept before the mind's eye or, more correctly, held in the pit of the belly, not only in time of *zazen* but at all times, day in and day out, until one eventually breaks through to enlightenment. The *koan* is not solved by reason – it defies all logic – but by a process of identification. One lives the thing, forgets self, and in the end forgets the *koan* also. Zen is full of amusing anecdotes about people struggling and wrestling with *koan*. And then there is the story of the monk who, having solved his *koan*, slapped his poor old *roshi* on the face as if to say, "There now! I'm as good as you."

Here are some examples of *koan*.

What was the shape of your original face before you were born?

or

We know the sound of two hands clapping,

But what is the sound of one hand clapping?

or

Mu (Nothing)

Meditation on these paradoxes often begets great anguish until one breaks through to the joyful solution – which has nothing to do with logic and is utterly bewildering to the uninitiated. Here are some Zen questions and answers.

A monk asked Tung-shan, "Who is the Buddha?"

"Three *chin* of flax", came the answer.

or

A monk asked Chao-chou, "What is the meaning of the first patriarch's visit to China?"

"The cypress tree in the front courtyard", came the answer.

*

The *koan* has attracted the attention of not a few Westerners today. Perhaps this is because the cult of wisdom within the irrational has been in vogue for some decades and is still on the upswing. I can't help feeling that a little of this is due to my fellow countryman James Joyce, whose later writing is full of strange things that sound like *koan*. Perhaps it is no accident that Joyce is popular in Japan, and that not a few Japanese professors, visiting Ireland, have gone to Clongowes to gaze pensively at the spot where the great man suffered at the hands of his vicious persecutors. I myself don't fall down in admiration before Joyce, and consider him something of a nut or something of a leg-puller. For this reason I have been embarrassed to hear Japanese people say to me, "Irish? Oh, James Joyce!" Yet Joyce, even if a nut, is an interesting nut; and I suppose that in my heart of hearts, if the truth were known, I am proud of his stupid *koan* (though I shouldn't call them *koan* because they aren't) in *Ulysses* and *Finnegan's Wake*. I suppose he liked a leg-pull and laughed at the solemnity of his scholarly interpreters. This, however, is a temptation of all *koan*-makers and I suspect (though here I may be wrong) that even good old Dr Suzuki enjoyed a leg-pull from time to time.

Be that as it may, the *koan* is a baffling business. At one time I thought it was a gimmick to frustrate the mind at its upper level of discursive reasoning, thus forcing it to break through to a deeper level of psychic activity. I still think that this is one of its functions, and I believe I got a tiny glimmer of insight into it when I visited Expo '70 in Osaka. I was on my way to the south of Japan and took the opportunity to jump off the fast train and spend a few hours looking around that vast complex of glittering exhibitions from the countries of the world. What impressed me was the psychedelic dimension of the whole thing. The shrieking music, the flashing colours, the revolving screens, the wild designs, and all the rest. I wondered what wise old Aristotle would make of it all if he had the chance to toddle through this Babylon in his ragged old toga or whatever he wore. Would he have decided to add another chapter to the *Metaphysics*? Or would he in consternation have screamed for help to those pretty Japanese hostesses floating delicately around the place and flooding the air with smiling Oriental charm? What I mean is that there was little there to appeal to the discursive intellect with which Aristotle penetrated the earth and the stars. I saw at once that there was no use asking, "What does it all mean?" That was simply the wrong approach. I must go in, not to understand but to get the experience – to get the kick. This I did and found Expo '70 enthralling. I didn't scream to the pretty hostesses, but I added a chapter to my metaphysics.

Now I don't mean precisely that Expo '70 was one big *koan*, but to my mind it was something like that. And now I see that the *koan* contains an element of psychedelic wisdom that the discursive intellect (which I always foist off on poor Aristotle) cannot grasp. To get the hang of the *koan* you have to walk into it as I walked into Expo '70. You have to identify with it, live it. Since it is filled with paradox, it is filled with the anguish of life and the contradiction of existence. It is only by living through this terrible suffering of anguished contradiction that you can overcome the dispersion of dualism and reach the joy of enlightenment. If you look carefully at the *koan* you can see that they usually lead to unification or what we call (erroneously, I think) monism. For example, "the sound of one hand clapping" is obviously leading away from dispersion to unity. The *koan* may also, on the other hand, lead you down to the centre of your being, to the core of your existence. "The shape of your original face" is clearly leading to the depth of the mind, to the place from which all thought takes its origin. One is being led to the source from which thought bubbles up. This is the original face. This is "the big self".

But, I repeat, one cannot get there by discursive reasoning and thinking or by playing around with syllogisms. This wisdom can only be grasped by deeper faculties that are normally dormant, particularly dormant in a generation that has blunted its sensibilities with radio, television, orange juice, and steaks. The *koan* gets these things out of one's system, triggering the mystical faculties into action and opening up a new level of topsy-turvy psychedlic wisdom that we all possess without knowing it. To get those mystical faculties cracking we have to clear the mind of the trash that we collect in modern living and then focus it on something else. The *koan* has this effect; it purifies and leads to wisdom. Probably it has more in common with art than with philosophy or science. True art, as Eliot or someone said, can communicate before it is understood – a statement which is certainly true of *The Waste Land*. Here is a poem that has communicated to all kinds of people, but if anyone knows what it's all about I would like to meet him and sit at his feet. I have read the poem several times with my students. We enjoyed it immensely (and perhaps even got a shred of communal enlightenment), but we didn't understand so very much. I began to see what the critics mean when they say that art does not mean; it is. The same might be said of the *koan*. It does not mean; it is. It lives the contradiction and the anguish and the absurdity of existence.

Now I have often asked myself if all this has any relevance for modern Christianity. At one time I thought it had none, and this was the opinion of my colleagues also. We just didn't get the hang of it all. Perhaps this was partly due to an education that saw primarily the order and harmony of a universe proclaiming the existence of a divine artist, and only secondarily the disorder, the anguish, the contradiction, and the pain – all that we call the problem of suffering. Be that as it may, not being able to handle the *koan*, we decided to give it a wide berth. We avoided *Rinzai Zen*, which puts great emphasis on the *koan* exercise, and directed our attention to *Soto Zen*, which inclines more to *shikan taza*, meaning "just sitting". Now, however, I have changed my mind (I do that fairly often) and have come to the conclusion that the *koan* approach contains something of tremendous value. I see it as a help to the understanding of our Christian Scriptures and as a guide to a meditation based upon biblical paradox. But is there anything vaguely corresponding to the *koan* in the Christian Scriptures?

It seems to me that Paul was one of the great *koan*-makers of all time, and it takes a pretty enlightened person to get what he's at. Take, for instance, the beginning of First Corinthians. Here Paul makes it clear that Christ crucified is utterly crazy to Jew and Gentile alike; but once you get enlightened, he is the truest wisdom. And this is the *koan*: something that looks crazy but isn't. I believe that the Christian who stares at the crucifix for hours and hours (and how many have done just that!) is face to face with a heart-rending *koan*. What confronts him is not the absurdity of a crucified God, but the absurdity of his own suffering and the suffering of mankind. The whole thing is absurd, and it is epitomized in this twisted, crucified figure. So one does not try to understand by reasoning and thinking. One simply identifies with it, living the anguish, living the suffering; and eventually, after hours of wrestling with the crucifix, one may break through to the enlightenment of seeing sense in what looks like nonsense. Then comes resurrection. One has found unity in the terrible dispersion of a suffering Christ.

Taken in this way, the famous "Jesus prayer" of the Hesychasts, in which the word Jesus is recited rhythmically with the breathing, can be *koan*. For in Jesus are summed up all the contradictions and sufferings and anxieties of mankind as such. He is a great archetypal figure, set for the rise and fall of many;

he is the sign that is to be contradicted. By living death with him, one breaks through to resurrection and a Jesus enlightenment.

Nor is all this so far from Buddhism as might appear at first sight. A student of Theravada Buddhism once told me that she had asked her old Master the question, "What type of person is the perfectly enlightened man? What would he be like?"

And to her shocked surprise, the Master retorted, "He would be despised, laughed at, and scorned by everyone". The crucified, the servant of Yahweh, the murdered Socrates, the despised *roshi*. Don't they all form part of the big contradictory picture of malicious stupidity and martyred goodness which is the *koan* history of poor mankind?

The gospels, too, abound in *koan*. All this talk about plucking out your eye and cutting off your hand and what not. And then:

Let the dead bury their dead and come, follow me!

> or

He that loves his life will lose it.

> or

I am the vine and you are the branches.

> or

This is my body.

Will anyone doubt that this goes beyond reason? Will anyone say that it is less baffling than Zen? I believe it could be argued that any religion demanding faith has its *koan*. Perhaps it could be argued that Christianity is one tremendous *koan* that makes the mind boggle and gasp in astonishment; and faith is the breakthrough into that deep realm of the soul which accepts paradox and mystery with humility. Quite certainly there were points in which Jesus makes it clear that he is talking in *koan* that defy explanation. Take celibacy. He that has ears to hear, let him hear. As if to say, if you don't understand, I can't help you – not, at any rate, at the level of discursive thinking.

All this makes me think that the *koan* opens up for Christians a new, yet old, approach to their Scriptures. I was set thinking along these lines by the remark of a Buddhist monk to a Christian friend of mine to the effect that Christians would get enlightenment if only they knew how to read their own Scriptures. I thought it rather big of him to say this, to admit so clearly that the Christian Scriptures contain enlightenment for the reader capable of getting it.

So let us use the Scriptures as *koan*. We need this to counterbalance the academic approach to the Bible that has characterized the last century. I mean that wise scholars have deciphered old languages, dug up pots in the desert, discovered musty manuscripts in dark caves, and unearthed ancient cities; and this has sometimes led them to the bright conclusion that they have plumbed the depth of biblical wisdom. But however valuable their pots and manuscripts (and they are valuable, very valuable), they don't help you solve the *koan* that flash-out and hit you from the pages of the Scriptures. The old, old doctrine on which à Kempis and company went to town was that unless the Spirit speaks from within, you cannot really understand. This is what I mean when I say (in language that is a little demythologized) that the discursive faculties don't get a message that is grasped only by the deeper mystical faculties operating where the Spirit speaks to the human person.

So I suggest that you read the Scriptures as *koan*. Walk into them as you might walk into the psychedelic glory of Expo "70. Put aside for a while your critical faculties of reasoning and arguing. Stop asking whether Jesus did or did not walk on the waters, whether there was or was not a star to guide the Wise Men. Stop asking what it all means; because what it means is less important than what it does to you. Forget all the complications and let the words enter the visceral area of your body, where they will finely and delicately begin to act, to live, to change you. Let the words of Scripture enter into you like the body and blood of Christ to give you warmth and love and life. Let them live at the psychedelic level. Get the kick those Semitic writers are trying to give you. Then you'll find that the Scriptures are food and that they are life.

Doing this, you'll be in good company, because that is the way Matthew, Mark, Luke and John frequently read the Old

Testament. By standards of modern scholarly criticism, these four men were idiots. They turn the Old Testament upside down, applying to Jesus Old Testament words and phrases that no self-respecting scholar in his wildest dreams would use in this way. Jesus himself played fast and loose with the Old Testament. "If you believed in Moses you would believe me – for he spoke of me." I wonder what scholar would agree that Moses was talking about Jesus. You can't believe that Moses spoke of Jesus unless you read the Old Testament with psychedelic eyes as the mystics read it.

Yes, the mystics. The handling of Scripture by John of the Cross, Bernard, and the rest is absurd to the scholar, who smiles patronizingly at their psychedelic dreams. But is it not simply that the mystic has a different approach? He is using different faculties; he is speaking not from the head but from the breast or from the guts; he is speaking from a realm that lies beyond and beneath the superficial discursiveness of the scholar. Yet he is grasping a true message, because the men who wrote the Scriptures were operating at this level. They were *koan*-makers who did not write for scientists and did not want to be taken at the level of rationalization alone.

One more interesting point about the *koan*. Once you solve one, you can solve many. Months of wrestling with the first lead to great facility in running through others. This is because the deep mystical faculties have been opened up by the first breakthrough and now they are in action – now you are capable of identifying with the *koan*. And the same holds true for the Bible. Breakthrough in one passage leads to enlightenment, joy, and enthusiasm in reading the rest. Understanding Paul opens one's faculties to the Apocalypse and to *Job*. In the Zen tradition, one test of the validity of an enlightenment is the ability to solve the *koan*. No real Master will tell you that you are enlightened simply because you have blown your head off with a seemingly big *satori*. Instead, he may ask you to solve a *koan*, and here is the real test. In the same way, the test of an enlightened Christian could be his ability to read the Scriptures with joy, relish, élan, and insight. If he can do this, the chances are that he has had something like enlightenment somewhere along the line, whether he realizes it or not. Somehow, somewhere he has heard the voice of the fair Lady Wisdom who calls out in the streets and raises her voice in the market place. He has consorted with her and he is happy.

Coming to the practical aspect of meditation, if a Christian wants to use the *koan* exercise, let him select from the Bible a *koan* that appeals to him and keep it constantly by him, with faith that it contains enlightenment and that a breakthrough is possible. I have suggested the crucifix as a *koan*, or the word "Jesus". But others are possible. Just as Zen uses the *koan Mu*, so a Christian can use the *koan* God. The author of *The Cloud* suggests words like "love" or "sin" for use in meditation; these too could be *koan*.

Finally I would like to protest that in all this I am not glorifying the cult of irrationality, nor do I want to be anti-intellectual. I believe in reason, and in *The Still Point* I spent a whole chapter trying to prove that the seeming irrationality of the mystics is consonant with reason. Perhaps those pages are not altogether successful, but I would like them accepted as evidence of good will. What I want to say here is that there is more in the Scriptures than words, and that the euphoric joy of digging up pots in the desert should not blind us to the existence of spirit and life. The *koan* exercise may teach us to see into the essence of the Scriptures. Perhaps it is a star from the East, standing in the sky and showing us the place where the child is with his mother.

8

The Body

Anyone interested in meditation has to think about the body, because Brother Ass just won't let himself be ignored. There are few areas of human experience where the interaction of mind and matter is so important and yet so delicate as here. Perhaps Paul himself experienced this. Whether he was in the body or out of the body he just didn't know – God alone knew.

When you come to Oriental religions the attention paid to the body is striking. It is with the body that the whole thing begins, and meditation is an art that teaches the use of eyes, lungs, abdomen, spine and all the rest. Moreover the place of meditation is important, whether it be the neat, dimly-lighted room or the wide open spaces. And then, of course, meditation is good for mental and bodily health. In the temple you may be told that Zen will inure you against cold and flu, and that by constant practice you have a better chance of surviving the threat of air pollution.

I once attended a convention on meditation at a Zen temple near Kyoto. Experts spoke about yoga, about esoteric Buddhism, and about Zen. We all sat silently in the big meditation hall, and we also did yoga exercises – to the best of our ability. These latter were a preparation for entrance into *samadhi*, and I really believe that can be just that. We heard talks about the technique of meditation – how to stretch and relax, how to sit, and so on; and one of the speakers had a large chart of the human body with which he explained the *chakras* (those centres of psychic energy that yoga speaks of), the course of the "breath" through the body, and all the rest. At the end of each meditation we chanted in unison, "Om, shantih, shantih, shantih!"

The surprising thing about the meeting was the lack of any common faith. No one seemed the slightest bit interested in what anyone else believed or disbelieved, and no one, as far as I recall, even mentioned the name of God. It was just meditation, and only the physical aspects were touched upon. These, however, were discussed in great detail, down to the impact of meditation on the sexual life.

I was the only Christian speaker and, quite frankly, I was a bit nonplussed. I felt that whatever I might say would be irrelevant. I couldn't tell anyone how to stand on his head or stretch his biceps, and it was difficult to speak about God at that meeting. But can one speak about Christian meditation without reference to God? I finally took a cue from one of the speakers who had insisted that meditation, far from stopping with the body, must radiate out to the world of the spirit and to the cosmic dimensions of reality. This, I felt, was the best approach to God in such a gathering.

All in all I learnt a lot at that meeting. It was a pleasant and profitable weekend, marred only by the fact that one fellow snored and groaned all night in our communal room so that I didn't get a wink of sleep. The others didn't seem to mind too much. No doubt they were better yogis than I. Or perhaps they had better nerves.

Christians should think more about the role of the body in prayer. After all, there is a lot to be said for beginning meditation where you are. This is particularly true for modern people. Many will call in question the existence of God and the existence of life after death, but only the extremists will call in question the existence of their own body. So why not begin with something they believe in, and through the body go out to the cosmos and to God? In this way, meditation can be taught to people who have little faith – to those who are troubled in conscience or fear that God is dead. Such people can always sit and breathe. For them meditation becomes a search, and I have found, from my little experience in our own place in Tokyo, that people who begin to search in this way eventually find God. Not the anthropomorphic God they have rejected, but the great being in whom we live, move and are. But the body comes first; God comes at the end.

For the fact is that Western prayer is not sufficiently visceral – it is preoccupied with the brain and not with the deeper layers of the body where the power to approach the spiritual is generated. But we can now study the physical aspects of meditation even scientifically, thanks to experiments at such places as the Buddhist Komazawa University in Tokyo. Here are instruments for testing the physical condition of the person engaged in Zen. Students measure the breathing, the heartbeat, the eye movement, the metabolism, the balance, the brain waves, and just about everything. Similar experiments are being conducted in the United States, and eventually these studies may come up with some suggestions about the ideal conditions for meditation in regard to diet, bodily posture, surroundings and so on. Needless to say, all this study becomes a bit ridiculous when you find people wandering around with little gadgets to measure alpha waves. But absurdities exist everywhere and cannot be avoided. Moreover, this scientific study need not lead to crass materialism. While visiting Komazawa University once, I asked the professor in charge if he could judge the depth of people's Zen. "No, we cannot measure Zen," he answered, "because the mind is a mystery. All we can measure is the physical repercussions." I was interested to hear him make such a distinction.

Here I might add in parenthesis that Zen does not go in for the minute control of the body that has made yoga famous. In general, Zen flatly rejects anything that smacks of magic or the extraordinary. There may, however, be some exceptions to this. Once I came across a temple far out in the countryside where it was said that the *roshi* performed miraculous feats such as plunging a sharp sword into his stomach without sustaining injury, or taking on himself the sickness of other people so that they were cured. Furthermore, a person whose word I trust told me that he had seen this sharp sword feat with his own eyes and did not doubt its authenticity. But this particular *roshi* is considered quite unorthodox. Discontented with Japanese Zen, he went to China and India as a young man, and on his return started his own form of *zazen*, which he claimed was a direct importation from China. Other branches of Zen, as I have said, despise such extraordinary phenomena and regard them as dangerous distractions on the way to the imageless experience which is *satori*. Strange phenomena go by the generic name of *makyo*, which literally means "the world of the devil" but is applied to all forms of illusion in Zen. In this respect, Japanese Zen is very healthy and liberates itself from abuses found in other forms of mysticism. The *makyo* doctrine of rejecting strange phenomena is remarkably like that of John of the Cross. Again, it is the "nothing, nothing, nothing". One must not be distracted from the goal by spiritual or bodily phenomena of any kind.

Turing now to Christianity, we find that tradition in the West says more about the body than is generally recognized today. It used to be axiomatic (and in my opinion still is) that if you want to lead a life of meditation you must control your eyes, your ears, your tongue, your hands and your very gait. All this used to go by the general name of modesty, a virtue about which we don't hear much today. It is much stressed in Zen, though the way of describing it is different. In addition to this, however, Christian tradition says that meditation transforms the body and makes it beautiful. The author of *The Cloud* speaks in enthusiastic glowing terms of the beautiful physical reper-cussions of contemplative prayer. Even the most ugly person, he says, will become fair and attractive to everyone: the face will be suffused with joy and a certain grace and peace will accompany every action. This is because the inner glory that comes from prayer cannot but break through and penetrate the body.

One is reminded of Moses descending from the mountain. So bright and glorious was the joy that suffused his countenance that the Israelites could not look at him, and begged him to wear a veil – for the very glory of God radiated from the countenance of the great Israelite. I like to interpret the trans-figuration of Christ as a repetition of this – Christ who is the second Moses, the reality of which Moses is the type. Quite suddenly, in the preserve of those three astonished men, the inner beauty of Jesus broke forth over his whole personality, so that his face shone with an unearthly beauty, and his clothes (yes, the inner beauty extended to his very garments) became dazzling white, with a whiteness no bleacher on earth could equal. In short, his body shared in the inexpressible inner beauty.

Probably most of us at some time or other have met people who share in the bodily beauty of the transfigured Christ. By television standards they may be pretty ugly – no advertiser in his right mind would dream of using their faces to sell toothpaste or soap – but the glory of prayer penetrates their body as it penetrated the body of Moses. I suppose, too, that this is the kind of beauty that monks and nuns should aim at, now that the changing culture makes them change their exterior way of life and dress. It might be a good idea if, instead of looking to London and Paris, they looked to Moses and Exodus for an ideal of beauty that would help modern people in their search for truth.

Be that as it may, while Christian tradition has affirmed the beauty imparted to the body through meditation, it has been slower in using the body as a way to *samadhi*. Here again, then, we can learn from the East; and to illustrate the role of the body I would like to quote from the *Bhagavad Gita*. This classic work is not, of course, Zen nor even Buddhist, though it seems to have considerable Buddhist influence. But it appeals greatly to me. I am further encouraged to use it here after reading a recent book of Professor R. C. Zaehner, who insists that anyone trying to bridge the gap between Zen and Christianity cannot afford to neglect the *Gita*. This, he claims, is one of the great links between East and West.

In the Sixth Part of the *Gita*, the yogi is told to integrate himself, standing apart, alone and in complete renunciation – "devoid of earthly hope, nothing possessing". Then comes a description of meditation.

> Let him for himself set up
> A steady seat in a clean place
> Neither too high nor yet too low
> With cloth or hides or grass bestrewn.

There let him sit and make his mind a single
point
Let him restrain the motions of his thought and
senses
And engage in spiritual exercise
To purify the self.

Remaining still, let him keep body, head and
neck
In a straight line unmoving
Let him fix his gaze on the tip of his nose
Not looking round about him.

There let him sit, his self all stilled
His fear all gone, firm in his vow of chastity,
His mind controlled, his thoughts on Me
Integrated yet intent on Me*

Glancing at the above, I would like to refer briefly to three points. First of all, the stress on place. This should be neat and clean, not too high nor yet too low. In Zen, too, the place is of the greatest importance. How wonderfully Dogen chose the site of his monastery Eiheiji, still far out in the countryside and plunged in deep silence. The Zen temple attaches great importance to proximity to nature, to the sound of the river or the waterfall, to the Japanese garden and all the rest. Meditation, after all, is not performed by a pure spirit but by a human being with a human body.

Now even though there is unending talk today about ecology and environment, the Christian West has made a poor showing in the ecology of religious things. I mean that our Christian churches, especially those recently built, are poor places indeed for meditation. The old Catholic churches had more to be said for them because they at least had a centre – a tabernacle before which hung a red lamp – and this provided a focus for the eyes. And there was atmosphere and warmth. Anyone who knows

*From the book *Hindu Scriptures*, R. C. Zaehner, trans. Everyman's Library Edition (New York: E. P. Dutton & Co., 1966), p. 275. Reprinted by permission of the publisher.

anything about meditation recognizes that you need a place to focus the eyes; if your eyes begin to wander, you are lost. The old tabernacle served this purpose, and nothing has taken its place. I believe that many of the old unlettered people who knelt before the tabernacle for hours, in places like the Carmelite Church in Grafton Street in Dublin, fell quickly into *samadhi*. These people were mystics, as enlightened as any *roshi*, and there have been thousands of such people throughout the world. But I ask myself if they will be able to meditate as well in the churches we have now provided for them. I ask myself if the people who built these new churches thought about meditation at all or had any experience of it. And the same holds true for monasteries and convents. I wonder how much thought is now given to the ecology of the thing – to the relationship between buildings and prayer, between clothing and prayer, between corridors and chapels and prayer.

The second point I would like to note in my quotation from the *Gita* is the magnificent posture. The back is straight, the eyes are fixed on the tip of the nose or between the eyebrows; there is no looking around. Later in the *Gita* the stillness of the mind is compared to that of a flame in a windless place. This is a fine simile, because this meditation has all the power and yet all the stillness of the flame that rises up in a place where there is no breeze. And all this leads to joy and to a great absence of fear. It is supported by the vow of chastity, the vow of the *bramachari*, who is celibate and chaste.

Here I would like to observe, however, that all Christian prayer need not (and indeed should not) be limited to the lotus posture. There are other positions, such as standing, kneeling, prostration, sitting and even walking, and often these are determined by the character of the person or the culture to which he or she belongs. But the posture, whichever it is, is of the greatest importance. Vaguely slouching in a comfortable chair does not lead to depth in meditation.

The third point, the one that makes Zaehner insist that the *Gita* can be a bridge between East and West, is the theocentric character of the passage I have quoted. The gaze is fixed on "Me"; that is, on God. The personality is unified in itself in order that all the faculties may be fixed on God, who is present in the deepest part of the soul – or, more correctly, who *is* the deepest part of the soul, since in man there is a divine spark. In this the *Gita* comes much nearer to Christianity than does Zen.

The yogi seated in magnificent meditation has all the bodily beauty of which the author of *The Cloud* speaks. This beauty is common to contemplatives of every religion, and it is a beauty that the modern world unconsciously seeks.

9

Breathing and Rhythm

It stands to reason that in any kind of meditation control of the mind is of primary importance. Most of us have some idea about control of our body – our arms and legs and the rest – but control of the mind is a more difficult business. And it is in this that the East excels. That this control is no small task, however, is stressed in the *Gita*. "Fickle is the mind," says Arjuna, "impetuous, exceeding strong. How difficult to curb it! As easy curb the wind, I say." To which the Blessed Lord answers, "Herein there is no doubt. Hard is the mind to curb and fickle; but by untiring effort and by transcending passion it can be held in check."* In short, the mind is hard to curb, but the task is not impossible. Control is possible. But how?

One of the oldest ways of controlling the mind is through breathing. Everyone knows from experience how intimate is the connection between breath and the psychic life. When we are excited or jealous or angry, the breath comes short and fast. On the other hand, when we are calm and collected, or deep in concentration or meditation, the breath slows down and even seems to stop. One recalls the beautiful line of Wordsworth: "The holy time is quiet as a nun, breathless with adoration." In the depths of adoration one may become so silent that one is breathless. This happens also in Zen: the breath slows and almost stops, so that one simply hears the beating of the heart.

If the psychic condition affects the breathing, it is equally true that consciousness of the breath can help control the psychic

Hindu Scriptures, op. cit., p. 277.

life. If one is emotionally upset, regular breathing may help to soothe the nerves and calm the mind.

As for meditation, it is recommended in Zen to begin with a deep breath (if the back is straight this will be abdominal) which is held for a moment and then exhaled. I know a Zen master who encourages his disciples to take this deep breath whenever they change their occupation or begin some new kind of work. The breath helps one leave the old and start the new with total concentration.

One way of beginning Zen is by counting the breathing. I myself did not begin this way (I had a different initiation, as I have already said), so I feel a little diffident about describing it. But anyhow, here is how it is taught. One begins by counting each inhalation and exhalation, one on the intake and two on the output of breath, counting to ten. While counting, one concentrates just on the breath. When this has been done for some time (a few days perhaps) one can count simply on the exhalation without counting on the inhalation at all. Again, when this has been done for some time, one counts only on the inhalation. Finally, one stops counting altogether and simply "follows the breath" or is conscious of the fact that one is breathing.

Now this may sound like a gimmick – some Christians react against this kind of thing, and scoff at the idea of calling it meditation at all. But it should be remembered that, apart from calming the emotions, this concentration has the effect of banishing the reasoning and thinking and imagining that go on at the superficial level of psychic life, and thus paves the way for a deeper unification. It, so to speak, silences the upper, superficial layers of the mind so that it becomes possible to concentrate at a deeper level and with a consciousness that is ordinarily dormant. Thoughts and images are brushed aside; one is conscious only of the breathing, and then the deeper sectors of unconscious life surge up into consciousness.

In the *Soto* sect (which uses the *koan* much less than *Rinzai*) concentration on the breath – without counting – is stressed very much even for those who are well advanced. Without it, there is always the danger that one may lose all recollection and unification and simply waste one's time. For Christians, the very sitting and breathing, performed in silent faith, can itself be an act of adoration. Western people, as I have pointed out many times, think that they are not meditating unless they are using their brain. But can there not be a form of meditation in which one sits and breathes and lets the heart beat? Surely total silence can be a wonderful expression of adoration.

Besides, breath rises from the very root of the being, so that consciousness of the breath can lead to a realization of the deepest self by opening up new doors in the psychic life. In the Bible it is clear that breath is identified with the deepest thing in us; it is precisely when breath enters into matter that a human being becomes a human being.

Further, it should be remembered that in Eastern thought breath is not only the little breath in my little body. It is much more than this. It is associated with the breath of the cosmos, so that regulating the breath means regulating one's relationship with the whole cosmos, and bringing about harmony and order. This is true of both Zen and Yoga, where breath plays such an important part. In the Judaeo-Christian tradition, the breath is associated with the Holy Spirit, who is *spiratio* and fills the universe. Hence the symbolism of Jesus "breathing" on his apostles – "Receive ye the Holy Spirit. . . ." Hence also the wind that shakes the building prior to the descent of the Spirit on the apostles. Reflecting on all this, one can see how consciousness of the breath can be truly Christian prayer because it can be consciousness of the Spirit in total forgetfulness of self. I believe that a whole method of Christian prayer associated with the breathing could be developed. But perhaps the time for this has not yet arrived.

Not that consciousness of the breathing is foreign to the Christian tradition. Here are some of the directions to the Hesychasts that we find in the *Philokalia*.

You know, brother, how we breathe; we breathe the air in and out. On this is based the life of the body and on this depends its warmth. So, sitting down in your cell, collect your mind, lead it into the path of the breath along which the air enters in, constrain it to enter the heart altogether with the inhaled air, and keep it there. Keep it there, but do not leave it silent and idle; instead give it the following prayer, "Lord, Jesus Christ, Son of God, have mercy upon me." Let this be its constant occupation, never to be abandoned. For this work, by keeping the mind free from dreaming, renders it unassailable to suggestions of the enemy and leads it to Divine desire and love. Moreover, brother, strive to accustom your mind not to come out too soon; for at first it feels very lonely in that inner seclusion and imprisonment. But when it gets accustomed to it, it begins on the contrary to dislike darting about among external things. For the kingdom of God is within us, and for a man who has seen it within, and having found it through pure prayer, has experienced it, everything outside loses its attraction and value. It is no longer unpleasant and wearisome for him to be within.*

In the tradition to which the above quotation belongs there is not, as far as I know, any counting, but only the repetition of an ejaculation in unison with the breath. This ejaculation can take the form given above or it can simply be the repetition of the word "Jesus". Some writers say that with the inhalation Jesus comes in, and with the exhalation "I" go out, and in this way the personality is filled with Christ. As can be seen from the words I have quoted, the ejaculation purifies the mind of all thoughts and desires and distractions, so that it enters deep down into the psychic life in total nudity of spirit.

The practice of repeating an ejaculation is found especially in the Amida sect of Buddhism where the words *Namu Amida Butsu* (Honour to the Buddha Amida) are repeated again and again and again. Zen does not speak much about this so-called *nembutsu*, but I was surprised once while visiting a Zen temple to hear one of the young monks say that he had made use of the *nembutsu*. He said that at first it was himself repeating the words "*Namu Amida Butsu*", but in time it was no longer "I"

*Writings from the *Philokalia on Prayer of the Heart*, E. Kadloubovsky and G. E. H. Palmer, trans. (London: Faber & Faber, 1951).

repeating the words, but just "*Namu Amida Butsu*" without any subject at all – for the "I" was gone. For him the *nembutsu* was a way to the nonself condition that is so characteristic of Zen. I was interested in this and recalled the thesis of Dr Suzuki, that silent nothingness and the *koan* and the *nembutsu* all lead to the same goal; namely, enlightenment. In all cases, the upper levels of psychic life are purified and cleansed, thus allowing the deep levels of unconscious life to surge into consciousness and give enlightenment.

Be that as it may, the repetition of an ejaculation can enter so deeply into the psychic life that it becomes almost automatic and continues even in the busiest moments. Some Buddhists claim that the rhythm of the *nembutsu* goes on even in time of sleep. A Japanese nun told me of how she once sat by the bedside of a dying sister. This latter had had surgery and was barely conscious; yet she kept repeating the words "*Jesusu awaremi tamae*" (Jesus have mercy on me) in a way that seemed quite effortless and almost automatic. This kind of thing is not, in my opinion, very unusual.

I myself believe that the repetition of an ejaculation or the consciousness of the breathing is somehow linked to a basic rhythm in the body, a rhythm than can be deepened and deepened until it reaches the centre of one's being from which enlightenment breaks forth. Let me try to explain what I mean.

There is a basic rhythm in the body, linked to a consciousness that is deeper than is ordinarily experienced. When human beings were in their natural setting, working in the fields or fishing in the sea, this rhythm was probably easy enough to find, because their rapport with their surroundings was harmonious. And in such a setting they were more open to cosmic forces, less inclined to atheism. Recall that the apostles were fishermen, and that Christianity is closely bound up with fishing. But with the advent of urbanization this rhythm and harmony were lost; we became out of tune with our surroundings. That is where we now stand. Again it is a problem of ecology. We have to cope not only with air pollution but also with a rival rhythm that comes from the Beatles, the Rolling Stones, and a number of forces that jolt our psychic life. Excessive noise, it is well known, dulls not only the sense of hearing but also the sense of smell and of sight. How much more, then, does it dull the deeper layers of psychic life! Small wonder if it deadens the profounder rhythm that should be within us.

But anyone who wants to meditate in depth must find this rhythm and the consciousness that accompanies it. And people find their rhythm in various ways. For some it is through the breathing, and this alone is sufficient. For others it is the breathing linked to an ejaculation. Or again it may be the repetition of an ejaculation without any thought of breathing whatever. Or again, some people find their rhythm by consciousness of the beating of the heart, and not infrequently an ejaculation is attached to this rather than to the breath. I have known people, too, who discover this rhythm simply by walking. A friend of mine goes for a walk every morning before breakfast, repeating an ejaculation. As he walks, the ejaculation becomes automatic (it fits in with the rhythm) and just goes on, to such an extent that he becomes oblivious to his surroundings. He has not yet told me how he copes with the danger of traffic accidents, and I have not asked him. But this is what I mean by saying that an ejaculation fits in with the basic rhythm.

Perhaps all this has something in common with listening to music. Most people have had the experience of being haunted for several days by a beautiful melody they have heard. The music continues within and simply will not go away. In some such way, the Jesus prayer or the *nembutsu* continues in the psychic life of those who are in love with the object to which these ejaculations point. There is, however, one significant difference. Sometimes the haunting music may disturb us. We want to put it away and we can't; it is persistent, even at times tyrannical. Now the rhythmic ejaculation is never like that. Probably this is because it is much, much deeper. The music, I believe, does not enter the deepest layer of psychic life; it remains somehow external to us, and that is why it can jar and even cause discord – because it can be at odds with that other rhythm which is deeper. The ejaculation, on the other hand, wells up from the deepest point of our being and is not external at all. It is the expression of the deepest self.

Formerly many people seem to have found this rhythm through the rosary. Take the case of those old women living near the sea – women who saw their sons mauled and murdered by the cruel Atlantic waves – whose lives were spent in the repetition of the rosary until their fingers were callous with the feel of the beads. These people found their rhythm through the rosary and through suffering. They were deeply enlightened.

For those of us who live in the city, the problem is acute. Life in the countryside in proximity to nature is undoubtedly a great advantage for one who wants to meditate, as the great contemplative orders discovered long ago. Yet I believe that the great noisy cities like Tokyo (which I love) are not an insuperable obstacle. Once the rhythm is found it transcends environment, and place ceases to matter. The ecology problem can be solved at this level too.

As I have said, the rhythm of breath or ejaculation leads to something deeper. All points to the centre of the soul, the core of the being, the sovereign point of the spirit, the divine spark, the true self, the realm from which enlightenment arises. This is the truest thing that exists.

10

Progress

All kinds of people practise Zen or contemplation or *samadhi* at a superficial level, but those who go deep are few. On this point most spiritual traditions agree. The *Gita* states that one in a thousand devotes himself to meditation, and of those who do, one in a thousand goes the whole way. John of the Cross writes his books like a man in a hurry, as if to say, "I don't want to write about the early stages of this ascent because there are plenty of books written about it already. I want to talk about the later stages, almost unknown because seldom experienced." As for the *roshi*, they speak of the kindergarten level to which many arrive, while few carry on to the level of university graduation. In short, many are called but few are chosen. Thousands jostle at the narrow gate but few get through. If you go in search of a just man, you don't find him easily.

It has always struck me as sad that this should be so. After all, the world needs great mystics, not just the small fry, and how wonderful it would be to find a formula for leading people the whole way. Or what on earth stops people from going the whole hog? Why do they stick at the kindergarten or even the highschool stage without going on to graduation?

Yet in my sober moments I know this is a question that should not be asked and cannot be answered. For progress in mysticism is linked with vocation. Most people remain small fry because they are meant to remain small fry. Mother Nature is not prodigal with genius. She seldom gives birth to saints, and when she does, she squirms and wriggles and yells in the writhing agony of parturition. Or she shakes the pillars of the temple till it falls down and crushes everybody. Occasionally, of course, one meets the saint; and then one meets someone who has suffered in the depth of his being, and has tasted the anguish of Gethsemane. Such persons are rare. Usually they are not the people who write books and wander around the world on lecture tours. These latter are often children playing in the sand and looking wistfully towards the rich and teeming bed of the ocean. They are not called to explore it except from afar.

Yet when all is said, it still remains sad that saints are so rare. And it is not impossible that we could have one or two more, if the human obstacles that cross their path were removed. This problem preoccupied me for some time, and I once proposed it for discussion to a group of Buddhists and Christians which had gathered informally to talk about meditation. All agreed that the problem was a valid one, so we talked about removing obstacles and helping people ascend the mountain.

One of the Buddhists remarked that the greatest obstacle is fear. This impressed me quite a lot, and I felt instinctively that it was terribly true. He said that Buddhist art is full of wild beasts that symbolize the terrors of the great descent into the centre of one's being. And he further added, from his own experience, that there comes a time when one simply does not want to sit down on that little cushion to do *zazen*. The very thought of it makes one tremble. Or one wants to run out of the meditation hall (Westerners in Japan sometimes disgrace themselves by doing just this, but Japanese are more long-suffering) and get away. Just to get away. In such circumstances, he went on to say, one is greatly helped by the community or by the system. The order of time obliges one to go to the meditation hall – there is no way out – and it carries one through.

All this threw light on John of the Cross for me. I recalled his words in the *Spiritual Canticle*:

> I will pluck no flowers; I will fear no wild beasts.

To pluck no flowers is to practise the most radical detachment in the face of the seductive beauty of a world that might hinder one's pursuit of the very source of beauty and of love. The fearful wild beasts are those of Buddhist art; they represent the terrors of the mystical descent. Perhaps biblical authors, too,

realize how cramping is fear, because all through the Bible like
a great refrain echo the words,

Fear not. I am.

One most somehow conquer one's fear, one must lose one's
fear. Perhaps the best way is to smile blithely at the yawning
jaws of those romping wild beasts – to look down their gaping
throats and laugh. Because in fact they cannot hurt at all. You
don't have to kill them or fight with them; it is enough to laugh
at them. This is detachment. If you fear them, they smell your
fear (just like your neighbour's dog), and then you get bitten.
My Buddhist friend was carried beyond fear by pressure from
the system; but the Westerner in the seventies is less likely to
be saved in this way, since "system" is a naughty word linked
to an establishment that cramps or persecutes. Yet whatever
way it is done, the seductive flowers and the roaring beasts must
not be allowed to stand in the way of progress.

One might ask, of course, what in God's name there is to fear
and what these beasts are anyway.

First of all I would say that there is fear of the effort involved.
Mysticism is no soft affair. You don't go into the desert to see
a reed shaken by the wind or a man clothed in soft garments.
Everybody shrinks from the inexorable law of renunciation.
Think of what is involved in the shattering Buddhist vow recited
daily in the temple:

However inexhaustible our passions,
We vow to uproot them all.

In Christianity the message is often expressed in terms of death
and life. Unless the grain of wheat falling to the ground dies,
itself alone remains. One must lose one's life. There is no escape
from death. And this death is no breezy metaphor. One must
lose the very grasp upon one's ego (and what a terrible thing
this is), only to find a new ego – and it is then that the joy of
enlightenment fills the personality.

There is yet another reason for fear. In the mystic journey
you go alone into the darkness. Modern man is well aware of the
ghosts and goblins and murky secrets that lurk in the subliminal

sectors of his mind. Good reason to fear them. At the bottom, of course, joy and beauty await us, but other things are released on the way down. I myself believe that within us are locked up torrents and torrents of joy that can be released by meditation – sometimes they will burst through with incredible force, flooding the personality with an extraordinary happiness that comes from one knows not where. This is true of contemplation; it is true of Zen; it is true of yoga (how it is stressed in the *Gita*!); it is found in the *Acts of the Apostles* and mirrored in the Pentecostal movement. One can be suffused with a joy that makes celibacy intelligible and worthwhile. But, and this is the point here, mystics who have penetrated deeply into reality have discovered evil also, evil that has shaken them to the roots of their being, so that they have sweated blood like one who fell on his face in Gethsemane. For deep, deep down at the centre of things is darkness as well as light, death as well as life, hell as well as heaven. The dragons, the beasts, and the whore of the *Apocalypse* speak of something real. If even the LSD trip can have its destructive hell, if it can be a traumatic and hair-raising experience, the same may be said of the mystical descent. The wars and the hatred, the concentration camps and the tortures, the sex crimes and the murders, lurk in the unconscious realms of the mind and in the depth of reality. It would be unrealistic to think of mysticism in terms of unalloyed joy. Evil, alas, is a fact of existence, and I have met people whose mystical experience has been accompanied by horrendous fear.

Again, for Christians there may be another fearful experience, expressed by the kind of old *roshi* who said that God would disappear and only Johnston San would remain. It has happened to Christian mystics that, at times, God has disappeared and they have felt totally abandoned in awful loneliness, clinging only to a faith that is like night. To say this, of course, is not to deny God but simply to say that he cannot be known directly by the natural human powers, and the time may come when he is no longer experienced as present. Perhaps this is because, when experience becomes intense (as in great mental suffering), it seems like no experience at all, because one is completely numbed. And this, too, seems to have happened to the mystics.

Small wonder if those who go deep come up against a crisis or even a breakdown, or become temporary misfits in society. At this moment they may need the help of a director. And this brings me to another point that is crucial for meditation.

Zen is dominated by the towering figure of the *roshi*. When the stars fall and the moon is turned to blood and the mountains tremble, he stands serene and unruffled. He is the granite rock rising up out of the swirling and turbulent waters; the disciple pins his faith on him during the critical period of transition between two lives – between the loss of the old and the finding of the new self. He is not unlike the proverbial psychoanalyst to whom the patient clings for desperate support. In this whole matter, Zen is rather like Catholicism – or it might be more modest to say that Catholicism is rather like Zen.

I mean that Catholic tradition has always stressed exterior authority and direction and the rest. It is true, of course, that Catholic authority became too juridical. So many Catholics are shouting about this today that I need not add my raucous voice to the happy choir. But the clear-cut principle of the director and the directed stands out pretty ruggedly. And then there are Thomas and Albert, Bonaventure and somebody else, Ignatius and his companions, and lots of others. Catholicism, I feel obliged to state, has stressed direction partly from the long-established conviction, born from the accumulated wisdom of centuries, that every potential mystic needs an occasional kick in the pants lest he – or she – fall into conceit, attachments, and all the tomfoolery popularly known as bloody nonsense. Consequently, the fact-slapping, the back-walloping, the nose-tweaking, and the rest are neither out of place nor irrelevant. Yet the role of the Master is not just this; nor is it simply to give information – which in any case you can get from a book – but to steer people through to enlightenment and even to clobber them with a salutary shock that will kill and resurrect.

I believe it is not just fanciful to see this technique put into practice by Christ, the great guru who knocked people into enlightenment with remarkable power. Take the case of the Gentile woman who asked for help. "It is wrong to take the bread of the children and throw it to the dogs", warns Jesus, issuing a slap in the face that parallels anything in Zen. But the woman comes through. She takes it squarely. She dies. "Even the little dogs", she cries, "eat the crumbs that fall from the table of the children." And with this total loss she receives the enlightenment for which she craves. "Go home. The unclean spirit has left your daughter."

The pattern of death and resurrection stands out boldly here, just as it does in the other passages where Jesus asks for total death. Sell what you have and give to the poor. If you do that you'll get enlightenment. But if you prefer to be like the camel trying to get through the eye of the needle . . . Perhaps every religious tradition teaches that you only get enlightenment through the complete loss that is death. Think of Abraham. For him Isaac was everything, and it was only when he was ready to kill his son, his only son, that he heard the tremendous promise that the nations of the earth would be blessed in his offspring. Here again is his enlightenment. And what I say here is true, the main task of the Master is to help you die in order that you may live.

Today, however, we hear the sad complaint that competent gurus just can't be found, and this complaint is voiced not only in the West but also in Japan and India. Alas, the theological market is flooded with Ph.Ds (or is it S.T.D.s?) sauntering around looking for jobs, but if you want a decent guru where do you find him? This lack sometimes prompts people to look outside their own religious tradition, a Christian to a Buddhist *roshi* or vice versa. But I honestly don't buy this idea, and I doubt if it works. While the death and resurrection motif is similar, and a Buddhist can clobber you as effectively as a Christian, the fact remains that the underlying faith is different: it is one thing to believe in Christ and another thing to believe in the Buddha nature. And this has to be faced honestly. It doesn't help to get things mixed up.

It seems to me that Christians must put some effort into forming their own directors or *roshi*. This means fewer Ph.D.s and more gurus; less study and more meditation; fewer universities and more meditation halls. Ordinarily speaking, enlightenment is passed on from Master to disciple and on and on, but when a link is missing in the chain relationship, some people must be driven by the Spirit into the desert to fast and pray and hear the voice of God. And others, then, must stop badgering them about getting into classrooms and teaching mathematics.

On the other hand I have sometimes asked myself, and others also, if it is possible to dispense with the *roshi* altogether and do your dying and resurrecting in another way. I was made to think of this while attending a quiet little *sesshin* in Kyoto, where professors and students practised Zen for seven days without a *roshi*. Instead of *dokusan* they opened their interior life to one another. At a fixed time, when all were sitting in *zazen*, one could choose any of the participants as one's director. He would simply kneel in front of the person of his choice and make a profound bow; then both of them would toddle off to a quiet room where a short chat was possible. Whether or not this method is completely successful I don't know. I merely mention it as a possibility.

There is yet another possibility, and I will refer to it again in my next and final chapter. It is not impossible that in Christianity the role of the guru or *roshi* can be played not by one man but by the community. This came home to me when I saw the Pentecostal movement in the United States. It is not impossible that the imposition of hands, the outward shock, and the charismatic prayer may have an effect rather like the clobbering of the *roshi*. If this is so, it would mean that a Christian Zen needs something like the charismatic renewal for its completion; and similarly, the charismatic renewal may well benefit from the silence of *zazen*. But more about this below.

There are two final points I would like to mention when speaking of progress. The first is that progress in Zen or contemplation is, I believe, linked to age. I mean that, just as Aristotle held that young and emotional people were not good subjects for philosophy, something similar may possibly be said of the higher reaches of contemplative life. It is true, of course, that young people (if they are tough) have some advantages in the gruelling practice of Japanese Zen, but when it comes to the still and silent depths, a certain age is probably an advantage. Jung says somewhere that the middle period of life – thirty-five to forty-five – often sees the beginning of contemplation. Indeed, if I read him correctly, he says that people ought to become contemplative in these years if their psychic life goes well. These years, the psychologists tells us, are often accompanied by violent eruptions and desperation and sexual upheaval. But they are also the years of opportunity, the time of contemplative awakening. Perhaps the traditional Oriental esteem for age is based on the realization that there is a certain level of contemplative wisdom inaccessible to youth and enjoyed by the old if their psychic development has gone well.

And the last point. I believe that celibacy is of great help for anyone who wants to get deep in a thing like Zen. So much has been said and written about celibacy recently that I hesitate to toss off a few half-baked ideas. Nevertheless I hope I will be forgiven for stating my views in all simplicity.

After all, what is the value of celibacy? We have heard that the celibate is more available, or more "open", or that he has more time. Or it is suggested that whoever wants to devote himself to the severe discipline of meditation just cannot get involved in business affairs. Or it is said that the married man is all tied up with his family. All this may well be true. But the ancient Oriental reverence for celibacy does not stem from this. It derives from the belief that the celibate person (if he is truly chaste) has increased spiritual power. Probably this is because his sexual energy is converted into spiritual energy. This gives the celibate a distinct advantage in the pursuit of wisdom and in the practice of contemplative love. It makes him a better candidate for mysticism. Besides, detachment is of the very essence of mysticism, and I doubt if there is any detachment that cuts so deeply into the human fibre as celibacy. It creates an awful loneliness at the core of one's being – and it is precisely from this emptiness that the blind stirring of love takes it origin. This loneliness opens the doors of perception to an inner world that might otherwise be inaccessible. It creates the best soil for mysticism.

If celibacy is little esteemed in modern Christianity, this may be due to a lack of mysticism. The two somehow go hand in hand. Not that all mystics must be celibate – they may well be married – but the celibate has advantages, and a culture that esteems mysticism will not despise celibacy. Perhaps the so-called crisis of celibacy in the Catholic Church is also a crisis of mysticism.

11

Enlightenment

One cannot write about Zen without writing about enlightenment. This is the centre of the whole thing, as it is indeed the centre of all Buddhism. In enlightenment is found great wisdom as well as release from the shackles of suffering; and the enlightenment of the Lord Buddha, from which the rest stems, is one of the great events of history. Though the whole of Zen is geared to enlightenment, one is faced with the interesting paradox that one must never desire it. To do so would be to cultivate an attachment that would vitiate the whole process. It is the old story again; one must desire nothing – and nothing means nothing.

In some Zen sectors in modern Japan, however, there is a certain amount of gossip about enlightenment. "He (or she) did, or did not, get enlightenment." A friend of mine, an assiduous practitioner of Zen, told me that after the *sesshin* in a certain temple the people were more or less divided into those who got *satori* and the also-rans who did not make the grade. This irked my friend not a little, since he was always amongst the also-rans. It was not, he protested, just a question of his bruised feelings – this he could support with philosophy – but righteous indignation about gossip. True Zen, he said, was reticent about the whole business ("he that knows does not speak, and he that speaks does not know") since it was sacred and intimate, and all this talk was a deviation from the pristine and genuine spirit. Most true Zen people would, I believe, support his basic thesis. One the other hand *satori*, being a great interior experience, can tempt the poetic temperament to indulge in melodrama about its soul-stirring repercussions. Even Dr Suzuki cannot be totally exonerated from such touches of melodrama when he writes about enlightenment.

Again it should be remembered that there are various degrees of enlightenment and that some Masters are quicker to recognize and ratify *satori* than others. One hears of stalwarts who have spent decades in assiduous sitting without getting a shred of enlightenment. But this does not mean that they have been wasting their time. Dogen, founder of the Soto sect, insisted that the very sitting is a form of enlightenment, and this again fits in with John of the Cross, who declares that the darkness of contemplation is in itself an enlightenment (for him imageless darkness is faith and faith is enlightenment) even if one never arrives at any soul-stirring experience. And this doctrine is sound. I think it is an error, and no small one, to dramatize the *satori* experience with lurid or beautiful descriptions. It is this that makes Zen look like the kick that comes from drugs. In fact, the important thing is not the sudden shock to one's psychic life but the total transformation that ensues. What matters is the Pauline new man, the new creation that follows the death of the old. I believe that a gradual enlightenment without melodrama should be, and is, possible. The transformation comes slowly but profoundly in people not temperamentally geared to sudden psychic change.

What I want to discuss here, however, is the question of Christian *satori*. If the Christian practises Zen, will he arrive at the same experience as the Buddhist? Or what kind of experience can he be expected to reach? Or is there, in fact, some experience to which constant practice and good direction can lead the well-meaning and determined Christian? I would like to consider three kinds of experience that could be classified as possible Christian versions of *satori*.

First of all I believe that there is a basic enlightenment which is neither Christian nor Buddhist nor anything else. It is just human. Merton was probably referring to this in the letter quoted in Chapter III, where he says that in a certain sense one goes beyond all categories, religious or other. This experience, it seems to me, is found in all cultures, though in modified form, and is an experience of the unity of all things and the loss of self.

T. S. Eliot has written a good deal about this in its relation to aesthetics. I myself have met a Christian monk who told me that before entering the monastery he had a sudden profound *satori* – he didn't know what else to call it – while reading Plato. Later he had other specifically Christian experiences; but this first one struck him as being somehow universal and not specifically Christian, even though it was the thing that prompted him to become a monk. To me this was interesting because I had always believed that Plato was a deeply enlightened man, and that underlying his beautiful Greek is a basic *satori* of great profundity.

The second kind of possible *satori* is specifically Judaeo-Christian. It is the experience of Paul on the road to Damascus, when he fell from his horse in the blinding light and heard the words of Jesus. Or the experience of Moses told to take off his shoes because the ground was holy. Or that of Isaiah and the prophets. Together with this I would classify the transfiguring "wound" of John of the Cross and Teresa and others. Such experiences are deeply interesting, but they are so far removed from the Zen way of speaking that I would hesitate to put them in the same category. They are much more bound up with vocation; they are for few people; no methodology leads to this kind of thing.

The third kind of experience, and the one in which I see the most possibility, is that of conversion or "metanoia". This, I believe, is the central religious experience demanded by the Gospel and expressed in the Baptist's words: "Repent, for the kingdom of God is at hand." The words "conversion" or "repentance" have now, unfortunately, very ethical overtones – "she is converted because she no longer drinks whiskey" – but the original meaning was not this. Conversion was a change of mind and heart, and its most vivid expression is found in the *Acts of the Apostles* and the epistles of Paul, where we read of the baptism of the Spirit that follows the imposition of Christian hands. What a big experience it was! And it is still alive in the world today. Sometimes those who receive it speak in tongues, so deeply are they affected; and it is accompanied by a release of joy not unlike that which floods the personality in *satori*. The most remarkable effect is the proclamation that Jesus is the Lord, and the inclination to praise him. I believe that this conversion experience is found, too, in the Fourth Gospel, where it is a seeing – "whereas I was blind, now I see". It is the opening of blind eyes which now come to see the glory of Christ. "We have seen his glory. . . ."

In the centuries that followed the apostolic age, it was customary to lead people to this deeply-felt experience of metanoia, just as the Zen master leads his disciples to *satori* – though the methodology, of course, was quite different. Metanoia was no exceptional thing. It did not differ from ordinary faith; it was just that this faith could be experienced again and again in a series of "conversions". As late as the sixteenth century we find Ignatius of Loyola with a methodology called *The Spiritual Exercises* for leading people precisely to this great and traditional conversion. He unabashedly expected some people to come to an experience resembling that of Paul on the road to Damascus (as I have said, I myself would not be so ambitious), and he certainly discovered a method for leading people to great depth in the spirit. However, in the period after Trent, the Catholic Church, though it maintained the basic teaching on conversion or metanoia, became suspicious of certain kinds of religious experience, particularly those which seemed to be subjective and emotional, and it was left to some branches of Protestantism to emphasize sudden conversion in its clear-cut Pentecostal dimensions. Now, however, its value is recognized by large numbers of Christians of every denomination, and the so-called charismatic renewal has hit the Church with force.

Now I am not at all suggesting that conversion or metanoia is the same thing as *satori*. What I do say is that the methodology of Zen, if adopted by a Christian, may well culminate in sudden conversion. If Zen is performed in a Christian atmosphere and surrounded by Christian liturgy, it may bring people to this deep and joyful metanoia. Such an experience, I repeat, has in common with *satori* the fact that it is not far beyond the ordinary psychological powers of the human person – it is not like the Damascus experience of Paul or the Horeb experience of

Moses. It should be the ordinary thing of Christian life – at all events that is how I understand the New Testament; and without it, faith is still weak and superficial. Let me say, then, briefly how I came to see the value of the sudden metanoia and its relevance for one who practises Zen in a Christian setting.

When I arrived in the United States in the summer of 1970 I heard for the first time about the Catholic Pentecostals. Some people told me they were crackpots who went in for demonstrative prayer (they spoke in tongues, it was said) and generally gave way to a good deal of emotion in their expression of Christian faith. I accepted the crackpot theory rather uncritically, since by education, though not by temperament, I steer clear of emotion in things religious. I suppose I would have been less prejudiced had the term "charismatic renewal" been used. Anyhow, later in the summer I was staying at a convent on the East Coast and the nuns suggested that I attend a Catholic Pentecostal group. Anyone who has had contact with nuns knows that they are rather persuasive people. So I decided to go to the meeting for the sake of a quiet life.

A large number of people had gathered in the parish hall: young and old, black and white, long-haired and short-haired, bearded and clean-shaven. We sat round in a circle in silence and then, after some time had passed, people would stand up and pray spontaneously or read from the Bible or ask for prayers or share some experience or speak in tongues. The group prayed together and sang together. I was struck by the combination of spontaneity and peace, and began to lose my prejudice. People were not acting according to a fixed plan nor according to a set of rules and regulations – they were following the Spirit. I reflected that people looking for spontaneity often express it in wild revelry, as in the medieval carnivals and in some modern gimmicks; or in sensitivity sessions or what not. But here was a spontaneous expression of deep faith in an atmosphere of peace. Apart from everything else, it must surely be psychologically healthy. After the general meeting, we divided into groups in which some received initial instruction, others asked for prayers and the imposition of hands, others asked for the baptism of the Spirit. I myself received the baptism of the Spirit.

All this may seem ten thousand miles from Zen. How could such a spontaneous, talkative affair have anything to do with the profound silence of *zazen?* Yet I believe there is a connection. Because to think that Zen is all silent sitting is an error. It has another side, an almost irrational side, where people act and shout with Pentecostal spontaneity and fervour – acting, that is, from the deepest centre of their being and not from the cerebral area of discursive thinking. Zen literature is full of amusing anecdotes about people jumping into ponds or tweaking others' noses or saying strange things. It is true, of course, that they don't speak in tongues; but I have seen them do somewhat similar things. I recall how, at a *sesshin* I attended, after some days some of the participants began to shout out at the top of their voices, "Mu ... Mu ... Mu ... MUuuuuuuuuuuuuu!" I took this as way of getting rid of pent-up energy, for it seemed to burst forth from the very depth of their being, and it reminded me of the Christian mystics who shouted out "Jesus!" or "God!" or whatever it may be at tense moments in their prayer. This kind of phenomenon, it seems to me, indicates that deep psychological forces are at work; it indicates that the person's religious experience has touched a profound level of psychic life. But at the same time it is only a by-product and is not of primary importance. This would seem to be the opinion of Paul, who is always careful to put the gift of tongues in the lower grades of spiritual gifts. The principal thing, he says, is charity.

Returning to the Pentecostal meeting, it seems to me that the imposition of hands, the prayers of the people, the charity of the community – these can be forces that release the psychic power that brings enlightenment to the person who has been consistently practicing *zazen*. In the Christian they being metanoia. But to come to this you have to die. And when you kneel to receive the baptism of the Spirit, that is what happens. You die. For me personally the baptism of the Spirit was a great event. It gave me some idea of what the early Christians must have experienced. It gave me some inkling of what *satori* must be like.

So I suppose it is true, after all, that the Pentecostals are crackpots, and I would like to be a crackpot too. Because if you want enlightenment you have to become a crackpot; drugs don't do the trick. This is the lesson of both Buddhism and Christianity – it is the doctrine of death and resurrection.

This, then, is what I mean when I say that in the attainment of enlightenment two factors are necessary: the internal meditation and the external happening. Ordinarily speaking, *zazen* or meditation alone is not sufficient, and the exterior imposition of hands alone is not sufficient either. The external pressure of the *roshi* or of the community brings the interior experience to fruition. I heard this put well by an old Master. Coming to enlightenment, he said, you are like the chicken breaking out from the egg. From within the little thing keeps pushing, pushing, pushing, but it never breaks out unless the mother hen pecks on the shell from outside. And in the same way your meditation may keep maturing, maturing, but it will not reach its climax without pressure from outside yourself.

I have mentioned the Pentecostal experience, yet I am not suggesting that it is the only way to conversion or that it is for everyone. I believe that the sacraments may have the same effect: these can be the exterior signs that carry one to the interior breakthrough. If one speaks to enlightened Christians one will find that often they have had their biggest experience at the reception of baptism or of Communion, or again, at the moment of receiving absolution. In this latter case the confessor is firmly in the position of the *roshi*. He is not there as a friendly counsellor to give good advice (though he may well do this); he may even act as a judge and force the penitent into conversion like any guru in the East, or like that great guru who walked by the Sea of Galilee. And the penitent dies. He loses everything. Then comes resurrection – the release from mental anguish, the joy, the laughter, the sunshine, the enlightenment. . . .

Anyhow, it was through the Pentecostal movement that I came to see the parallel between the Zen *satori* and the Christian conversion or metanoia. From the time of my first contact with Zen I had been struck by its single mindedness. I felt (with something approaching envy) that here were people who knew precisely what they wanted in this world, whereas Christians were often less sure. This was particularly true as far as Buddhist monks and nuns were concerned. They wanted enlightenment, and there were no two ways about it. As I say, the singleness of purpose impressed me greatly; and only much later did I begin to realize that as Buddhism centres around enlightenment, so Christianity centres around conversion. Change your mind and heart, for the kingdom of God is at hand. Change! Turn! This is the perennial call of Christ and the prophets. It is a clarion call, an invitation to rebirth, to a change of consciousness, to become a new person.

This, I now see, is what Christianity is all about; for this is faith. Christianity is concerned with an earth-shaking, soul-stirring revolution as stupendous as anything Dr Suzuki wrote about in his most poetic flights. If we forget this, we end up with a milk-and-water thing that sometimes passes as Christianity but is no more than social respectability.

For me (and, I believe, for many Christians) this basic message could easily have been obscured by rules and regulations and observing the traditions of the elders – the traditions of washing cups and pots and vessels of bronze. My people, rend your hearts, rend your hearts and not your garments. We've been rending our garments too much of late; we've been making too much of the external trappings and of outer changes; it's high time we got to the heart of the matter.

So now, for me at any rate, Christianity is quite as single-minded as Zen. It's just a question of conversion, individual and communal; and the rest follows after that. I suppose the Council was getting at this when it said that exterior changes would be useless without a change of heart. Zen reminds us of all this, and it can do a great service to Christians. And I also believe that we Christians can be of service to Zen, especially to those people who are willing to listen to the voice of the great guru who gave us the Sermon on the Mount. At the great turning-points in history (and who will deny that we are at one today?) the world has always looked for men and women with vision and enlightenment. Perhaps by mutual co-operation Buddhism and Christianity can produce such people, whose lives will be relevant and meaningful for our time.

APPENDIX: POSTURE
(Figures appear on pages 111 and 112.)

It is not good to make a fetish of bodily posture, as though it were the whole of meditation. It sometimes happens, even to people far advanced, that a physical handicap prevents the taking-up of one of the recognized postures. Such people can still meditate in the Zen way. Indeed Zen and contemplation can be, and frequently are, practised on a sick bed. But granted this, the fact remains that the traditional postures are of great value for those who can make use of them.

Figures 1 and 2 show the lotus posture.* This position is very old; it antedates Buddhism in India and has been discovered through archaeological research in ancient Egypt. One places the left foot on the right thigh, and the right foot on the left thigh, sways slightly from side to side and then sits in an upright yet relaxed position. The head may be very slightly tilted forward, and the eyes can be fixed on a point or not focused at all. Some Christians like to fix their eyes on a crucifix placed on the ground a few feet in front of them. This does not mean that they are thinking and reflecting about the meaning of the crucifix – the crucifix is simply there. This posture has great symbolic meaning. As the lotus rises out of the slime and dirt of the pond, so the bodhisattva rises out of the illusion of the world into the serene beauty of truth. For Christians this posture may also symbolize the life of Christ within: "I live, now not I but Christ liveth in me." Self dies and Christ rises up as the centre of all.

In Figures 1 and 2, the left hand is held over the right and the thumbs are lightly touching. However in Figure 3 the hands are held open beside the knees. This posture is not used in Zen

*The author wished to express his gratitude to Miss Miwako Kimura who kindly drew the sketches.

Figure 1

Figure 2

Figure 3

Figure 4

Figure 5

Figure 6

Figure 7

Figure 8

Figure 9

but is popular in India. Some Christians like it because it gives them a sense of openness before God.

For those who cannot practise the full lotus there is the half-lotus (Figure 4). This is quite as good as the full-lotus and is used by some Zen Masters. In this position it is useful to sit on a somewhat higher cushion; otherwise the knees may be slightly raised, and in order that balance be maintained the knees should touch the ground.

Figure 5 shows an easier way of sitting cross-legged. It is not much used in Japan but is widely used in other Asian countries.

Figure 6 shoes the traditional Japanese squatting position called *seiza*, and Figures 7 and 8 show some variations of this. The use of the cushion or small stool makes easier a position which otherwise becomes painful. Even the Japanese are beginning to find difficulty with the traditional postures, so various experiments are being made to find bodily positions that will be reasonably possible for modern people while retaining the advantages of the old postures.

Figure 9 shows how Zen can be practised in a chair. The chair is seldom used in the temple except by Western people who cannot sit in any of the traditional ways. Our Zen-Christian dialogues have often been held in buildings where sitting on the floor is scarcely feasible. On these occasions we have practised Zen in the position here sketched.

Glancing at the above postures one can see some features common to all of them. **The back** is always kept straight. This is of great importance. When the back is straight, the breathing automatically becomes abdominal and slows down. A young Buddhist in charge of a meditation hall told me that he could judge from the back whether or not a person was having distractions. If the back begins to sag, this is a sure sign that the person has lost inner unification. **The eyes** are kept half-closed. If they are completely closed one easily gets distractions or falls asleep. The eyes need not be focused at all; or they can be fixed on a crucifix placed on the ground some distance away. The importance of **the breathing** has already been stressed. One may either count or repeat an aspiration with the breathing. The repetition of the word "Jesus" is a form of prayer that is traditional in the Eastern church and is taught in the *Philokalia* as well as in the famous little Russian classic *The Way of a Pilgrim*. In the *Philokalia* it is said that with the breathing Jesus comes in and "I" go out; and in this way Christ becomes the centre of my life. As progress is made, however, it may not be necessary to count or to use words at all. It is enough to be conscious of the fact that one is breathing – this is called "following the breath". Most people who practise Zen-type meditation need from time to time to fall back on something concrete (either an ejaculation or consciousness of the breathing or a *koan*) lest they get completely distracted. Words may be used just as much as is necessary to maintain unified inner silence without distraction.

POSTSCRIPT

A WAY OF MEDITATION

I

Some people have asked me to write a how-to-do-it book about Christian meditation; and it seems that such a book would fulfill a real need in the modern world. Yet I recoil from this task because I know that meditation is different from cookery, and can only be taught by that great teacher whom Augustine calls the *Magister Internus*, the Master Within. Listen to his voice and you will learn how to meditate.

Granted this, however, it is also true that human guidelines can be given; and so I propose to set down some principles or directives which may be of use to people in search of meditation. In doing so I will rely not on my own experience and wisdom but on the words of the Master himself, who spoke with such authority that the people were astonished. And I will draw inspiration primarily from the Sermon on the Mount which appeals not only to Christians and Jews but also to many Zen Buddhists and fervent Hindus. By taking to heart and putting into practice the terse advice of Jesus in the fifth, sixth and seventh chapters of *Saint Matthew*, we can be introduced to the royal road of meditation and led to the most profound enlightenment.

Consider the words of Jesus: "Therefore I tell you, do not be anxious about your life, what you shall eat or what you shall drink, not about your body, what you shall put on" (Matthew 6:25).

When you sit down to meditate, the first thing is to let go of your anxieties. And when I say anxieties, I include reasoning and thinking and preoccupation and planning and all the rest. Just let them go. Nor is this easy. For, as we all know, the human mind is restless. It looks to the future with fear or anticipation; it looks to the past with nostalgia or with guilt. Seldom does it remain in the here and now. Yet Jesus tells us clearly to drop anxiety about the future in order to remain in the present. "Therefore do not be anxious about tomorrow, for tomorrow will be anxious for itself. Let the day's own trouble be sufficient for the day" (Matthew 6:34).

And so the first thing is to let go of all preoccupation. Of course anxieties may flood into your mind. If so, listen to the practical advice of a great Zen Master: "If you want to obtain perfect calmness in your *zazen*, you should not be bothered by the various images you find in your mind. Let them come, and let them go. Then they will be under control. But this policy is not so easy. It sounds easy, but it requires some special effort. How to make this effort is the secret of practice...."* And again: "When you are practising *zazen*, do not try to stop your thinking. Let it stop by itself. If something comes into your mind, let it come in and let it go out. It will not stay long. When you try to stop thinking, it means you are bothered by it. Do not be bothered by anything."† Yes, do not be bothered by anything!

If you wish you can simply repeat to yourself the words of the Lord: "Do not be anxious", "Do not be anxious".... Or, again, some people like to use the words of Peter at the Transfiguration, "Lord, it is good for us to be here" (Matthew 17:4). Any words of sacred scripture, repeated again and again with relish, can be an excellent form of meditation; and they will succeed in warding off all anxiety and needless thinking and reasoning. Moreover, this simple process brings us into the present moment.

As I have said, you will ordinarily be aware of your thoughts and anxieties, and you will know that they are in your mind. But do not cling to them. The process is not unlike that taught by Carl Rogers when he tells us (and he is speaking in the context of interpersonal relations) to be *aware* of our anger or

---

Zen Mind, Beginner's Mind, Shunryu Suzuki (Tokyo: Weatherhill 1970), p. 28.
†Ibid., p. 30.

frustration or boredom or fear or embarrassment. Be aware of them, he says, and you can handle them. And in the same way, you can be aware of the thoughts in your mind during meditation without clinging to them. As Master Suzuki says, let them come and let them go. Look at them as if they belonged to someone else. This sounds simple: but how difficult it is! For we love our anxieties; we cling to them and wallow in them. We need the advice of Jesus: "Do not be anxious. . . ." His words will gradually teach us the gentle art of letting go.

II

Letting go of anxieties, however, is the negative aspect of meditation. In the same context Jesus continues with a very positive assertion: "Is not life more than food, and the body more than clothing?" (Matthew 6:25).

These words abound in common sense. Look out of the window and you see a world which is crazy about food and clothing and gas and economic progress. Yet all these things, however desirable and even necessary, are peripheral. What matters is life. What matters is the body. Without a body pulsating with life, of what use are the oil and the tin and the copper and the rubber and the other things? And in meditation we come to *experience* our life and our body. We come home to ourselves and get in touch with what is deepest within us. But first let me speak of *life*.

In all the great cultures life is symbolized by breath. It is precisely in experiencing your breath that you experience your life. So just sit quietly with your back straight and *become aware of your breathing*. At first do not interfere with it. Do not attempt to make it short or long or to hold it. In the *pranayama* of yoga such breathing exercises exist; but I do not recommend them here. Only be aware of your breathing as it is; and, if you wish, you can repeat to yourself: "Breathe in: breathe out". That is all. Or you can repeat to yourself the words of the Lord: "Is not life more than food?" The emphasis, of course, is on *life*.

In this context let me quote a classical Buddhist text which is very instructive for Christians or for anyone who wants to learn a simple form of breathing meditation:

A monk who has gone to a forest or the root of a tree or to an empty place, sits down cross-legged, holding his back erect, and arouses mindfulness in front of him. Mindful he breathes in, mindful he breathes out. Whether he is breathing in a long or a short breath, he comprehends that he is breathing in a long or a short breath. Similarly when he is breathing out. He trains himself thinking: "I shall breathe in. I shall breathe out, clearly perceiving the whole body: I shall breathe in, breathe out, tranquillizing the activity of the body". . . . For in breathing in or out a long or a short breath the monk comprehends that he is doing so . . . and he lives independently of and not grasping anything in the world.*

Here, as is evident, one is simply aware ("mindful" is the great Buddhist word) of the natural process of breathing: "I will breathe in: I will breathe out." And this can be done at any time. Sitting in the bus, waiting in a queue, listening to a boring lecture, you can meditate by just breathing in and breathing out. How simple! Yet this practice will give you inner peace, inner strength, inner dignity. It will put you in touch with your deepest self. You may begin to experience in your body the words of Jesus: "Is not life more than food . . . ?"

As time goes on, the breathing of its own accord becomes deep and abdominal. Here let me observe that the abdomen (or *hara* as it is called in Japanese) is the vital centre of the body in all forms of oriental meditation. If certain Western writers have made a huge joke of the so-called navel-gazing of oriental mystics – as though the thing were completely absurd – this does not make it foolish. Oriental mystics do not contemplate their navel in the subject-object sense: but the Sino-Japanese tradition has always taught that life and energy well up from

*See Buddhist Texts Through the Ages, Edward Conze, ed. (Oxford, 1954), pp. 56, 57.

the *tanden*, the point which lies about an inch below the navel – which is expressively called the *kikai* or "ocean of energy". And *tanden breathing* is basic not only to meditation but also to judo, fencing, archery, flower-arrangement, tea-ceremony, calligraphy and the rest.

Let me quote the advice of a Zen Master on this point: "Sit quite still, breathe gently, giving out long breaths, the strength in the lower belly."* And again: "Many of our people breathe through their mouths. But everyone should breathe through the nose and press the breath down into the *tanden*."** Breath, then, is of cardinal importance in Zen. One begins with *tanden* breathing but eventually this breathing seems to extend to the whole body. That is why some masters speak of "breathing through every pore"; and a Chinese proverb states that the wise man breathes from his heels. And another interesting point: observation of the breath enters into spiritual direction. A good master carefully watches the breathing (sometimes his eyes are piercing and hawk-like) and from this he judges the spiritual progress and degree of enlightenment of his disciple.†

*

One does not attain to awareness of breathing overnight. It takes time. But if one perseveres one gradually comes to realize that this breath is not only the life that fills the body from head to toe. It is more. The sanskrit *prana*, like the Japanese *ki*, is *the breath of the universe*, a cosmic force which penetrates all

*See *Hara*, K. Graf Von Durckheim (London: George Allen & Unwin, 1962), p. 178
**Ibid, p. 179.
†It is interesting to recall here that scientists distinguish between the voluntary and involuntary nervous system. There are bodily functions which are voluntary in that we only perform them by an act of will: and there are others (such as digestion, heart-beat, metabolism and so on) which are involuntary or automatic. And breathing stands mid-way between the two. With most people it is involuntary but it can easily be made conscious, regulated and brought under control of the will. When one becomes conscious of the breathing one gradually becomes conscious of the whole body, and even learns to control the whole body. Breathing is the gateway to the unconscious.

things. As for the Hebrews, they believed that their breath was the breath of God whose presence gave them life. For Christians the breath, like the wind, symbolizes the Holy Spirit who fills all things with his love, giving wisdom and joy and peace.

And so, while breathing, you can recite the words: "Come, Holy Spirit", "Come, Holy Spirit", asking to be filled with the breath of the Spirit. And when this happens, you are not only present to yourself, you are also present to God and to a world which is filled with God and in which God is the deepest reality. You may remain quietly in God's presence reciting these words – or without words at all. Your breathing may slow down. Or it may even seem to stop. Or a time may come when the indwelling Spirit prompts you to exclaim: "Jesus is Lord!" Such prayers, welling up from the depths of one's being at the prompting of the Spirit, are frequently mentioned in the New Testament. "Abba, Father!" is yet another.

Furthermore, one who is filled with the Spirit may, and must, communicate this same Spirit to others. Remember how Jesus *breathed on his apostles* with the words: "Receive the Holy Spirit" (John 20:22). Cannot we simply sit and breathe good will and healing power to all men and women, sending them the Spirit? Or we can breathe out love to our friends, imagining that they are present and that we are laying hands on them. Some people like to imagine that they are breathing through their hands, as they communicate the Holy Spirit through this most symbolical action.

Yet another phrase which can be repeated again and again is the Pauline: "For me to live is Christ" (Philippians 1:21). For Paul life was Christ. And we can say the same thing. Yet the profound mystery of these words will not reveal itself to the mere scholar but only to one who is enlightened by the wisdom of the indwelling Spirit. "Come, Holy Spirit."

III

Jesus speaks not only about life but also about the body: "Is not the body more than clothing?" (Matthew 6:25).

Yes. The body is the thing. Any scientist will tell you that the human body is a baffling mystery which no one can fathom. Any theologian will tell you that the body of Christ (a theme that is dear to the heart of Paul) is a mystery of mysteries. And while Sino-Japanese thought will never solve these mysteries, it may teach us a new approach to them: it may teach us to experience and appreciate this precious gift which we call the human body; it may teach us to be present to ourselves and to reality and to God through the body.

Body-awareness can be achieved, as I have already indicated, by breathing from one's heels. But it can also be achieved through posture. And this is one of the great arts of the Eastern world, having its roots in *hatha yoga* with its rich variety of *asanas* or bodily postures, through which one is brought to enlightenment. Chief among these is the lotus, which is called "the perfect posture" and has been widely used throughout Asia from pre-historic times. Perfect indeed it is because, correctly practised, it unites mind and body like two sides of one coin and brings one into a state of total liberation.

To sit in the lotus is an art and an accomplishment which takes time and patience and spiritual training. But once we learn the art of sitting, we discover that the very posture is enlightenment. Here we have a species of *enlightenment through the body*. Listen again to Shunryu Suzuki speaking about the lotus: "To take this posture itself is the purpose of our practice. When you have this posture, you have the right state of mind, so there is no need to try to attain some special state."* And again: "The state of mind that exists when you sit in the right posture is, itself, enlightenment."† It is indeed an enlightenment to sit in the lotus and to realize that the body is more than clothing.

*

But at this juncture let me digress for a moment to make an observation that is of cardinal importance for what I am trying

*Suzuki, p. 22.
†Ibid., p. 24.

to say. We are sometimes told that oriental "techniques" are a marvellous aid to concentration. After all, the nervous and jittery occidental needs to relax, to calm down, to take it easy. And once this is done, he can get on with the real job of praying. In other words, oriental breathing and posture are regarded as warming-up exercises, preparations for the real thing.

Now this is an abysmal misunderstanding. What we can learn from the East is not just preparatory devices but the art of prayer itself. For the Orient can teach us to pray with our breathing, to pray with our body, to pray with our whole being. After all, God created the whole person, not just the mind; and he should be adored by the whole person, not just by the mind. In the past few centuries, prayer in the West has become inexcusably cerebral (though it was not so in the middle-eastern Church where Hesychasm was born) but now at last we are re-learning the art of adoring God with mind and body and breathing. We are allowing faith to fill not only our mind but also our breath and our *hara* and our body. And it is here that the East can help us.

*

As I have already indicated, in Sino-Japanese thought, the centre of gravity of the body is the *tanden*, the point about an inch below the navel which is the elixir of life and the sea of energy. One should breathe from the *tanden* – not in the sense that the breath actually penetrates to that region of the body, but that one imagines that it does. And gradually one gets a sense of the *tanden* together with a balance and harmony and quietude that fill the whole person. An old Zen Master, stating that the *tanden* is the shrine of the divine, asserts that the woes of humanity are caused by lack of balance. He then goes on to divide mankind into three classes.

To the first class belong those who value their heads. Such people develop bigger and bigger heads until they topple over like a pyramid standing upside down. Such people obviously have little power or creativity. How could they possibly maintain balance?

In the second class are those who value their chest. This is the military type that seems to be ascetic and disciplined but is, in fact, easily overcome.

To the third class belong those who value the belly or *hara* and build their strength there. These are the people with calmness, peace and strength. They are (and this is an old Eastern ideal) people who follow their natural inclinations without breaking the law. To sit with the strength in the *hara* is authentic Zen.

*

The men and women who practise the martial arts such as judo, archery, fencing and the like, learn to hold their attention at the *tanden* and to stand with firmness and power.* They, like the practitioners of Zen, wear the traditional *hakama* the sash of which is knotted just at the *tanden*. And there are various forms of "*tanden* practice". Of these an interesting one is the simple art of polishing a table – doing so with large circular sweeps and holding the attention at the *tanden*, not at the polishing hand, until one gradually gets a sense of the whole body and feels fully alive.

And so one learns body-awareness and posture: how to sit, how to stand, how to walk, how to breathe, how to relax. One acts with the whole body. Needless to say, this is not just a prerogative of the Orient. I know of Western pianists and painters and writers who act from the hips and from their whole body, not just from the head. But whereas the West has stumbled on this sense of the body, the East has cultivated it assiduously for centuries.

And yet paradoxically the climax of *tanden* practice is reached when, forgetting one's body and one's self, one allows the universe to act. In traditional archery there is a saying that the action of releasing the arrow should be an action not of the individual but of the universe. And in the same way one who practises Zen for a long time comes to the stage where he does not bother about the *tanden* or the breathing or the body of the

*Note that I say "men and women". All that I say about posture and breathing applies equally to men and women.

self. He comes to experience not that "I am breathing" but that "The universe is breathing". The self has gone.

Yet another result of this training is that one comes to experience a great *wisdom of the body*. One whose mind is attuned to the body finds that the body says when to eat and when to fast, when to sleep and when to watch, when to work and when to meditate. The body is a mysterious and marvellous instrument; it has powers and potentialities which Western science has not dreamed of (though now it begins to suspect their existence) – powers which no computer can possess. But we must train this body, be attuned to it, listen to its wisdom. "Is not . . . the body more than clothing?"

*

Practically speaking, one way of meditating is to adopt one of the postures I have described in this book as a way to bodily awareness. Become aware of your hands and your feet and your whole body, quietly repeating the words of Jesus: "Is not . . . the body more than clothing?" Do not think and reason about these words, just relish or savour them while being aware that this body is more than the clothing. The fact that the words you use are from the gospels puts you in contact with Christ and makes your prayer one of faith. Furthermore the word "body" may speak more and more powerfully if you are aware (but again in a non-discursive way) of the mystery of the body of Christ. This is the body which has become one with my body. "He who eats my flesh and drinks my blood abides in me, and I in him" (John 6:56). This is the body which is "the fullness of him who fills all in all" (Ephesians 2:23). Just as the breath of Jesus is the breath of the universe, so the body of Jesus is one with the universe. "Is not the body more than clothing?" There may come a time when body and breathing and ego are forgotten, and our true self cries out with St Paul: "I live, now not I but Christ lives in me" (Galatians 2:20).

IV

I said that the first step in meditation consists in letting go of anxieties and fears and grasping of all kind. And I quoted the words of Jesus: "Do not be anxious . . ."

Now I can hear someone say: "Well and good! This sounds fine. But is it possible? Can I let go of fears and anxieties? After all, any psychologist will tell you that anxiety is deeply rooted in the human psyche. It is engrained in the memory, going right back to the primal scream which we uttered when we emerged from the womb. As we pass through layers of consciousness in meditation, new anxieties – or old repressed anxieties – will rise to the surface of the mind. And you tell me just to sit and let go! Is it quite so simple?"

This is a very valid objection. And in answer to it I would again quote the Sermon on the Mount which emphasizes one enormously important point: **faith**. "O men of little faith" (Matthew 6:25). Jesus speaks here of the faith which tells you that your Father is looking after you, that he is protecting you – faith that you are loved. Yes, you may be the biggest sinner in the world. You may have committed the most heinous crimes; but you are loved by your Father who "makes his sun rise on the evil and on the good, and sends rain on the just and on the unjust" (Matthew 5:45). And I can let go of anxieties as the conviction of being loved grows and deepens and becomes an unshakable source of strength.

Jesus put it very poetically. "But if God so clothes the grass of the field, which today is alive and tomorrow is thrown into the oven, will he not much more clothe you, O men of little faith?" (Matthew 6:30). Your Father who protects the birds of the air will much more protect you because you are of greater value than they. You are of immense value.

I am loved. I am of great value. To accept this is the great act of faith. For it is well known that many, too many, people despise themselves, find that they are overcome with gnawing guilt and a morbid sense of unworthiness. And to them Jesus says: "Do not be anxious. You are important, You are of value.

If the flowers and the birds are valuable (and they are), how much more value are you!"

Now all this is of the greatest practical importance. When you sit to meditate, recall your personal dignity – remember that you are of the greatest value. "I'm O.K.: You're O.K." To foster this attitude of mind it will help to meditate in surroundings which will create an atmosphere of inner security. It will help to choose a quiet place; to wear suitable clothing. Above all, it will help to adopt a posture that expresses your dignity and gives you a sense of being O.K. And then you can quietly repeat the words of Jesus which I have just quoted. Or you can recite the words from Jeremiah: "I have loved you with an everlasting love" (Jeremiah 31:3). Or the words of Jesus: "Let not your hearts be troubled; believe in God, believe also in me" (John 14:1). Sacred Scripture abounds in phrases which tell us to have faith and not to be afraid. "Do not be afraid. It is I" (John 6:20); "God is love" (John 4:16).

And through the savouring and relishing of these words, faith enters into one's mind and heart and body and breath, becoming co-extensive with one's being. Sometimes there may be moments of great joy and liberation when, freed from anxiety, one can exclaim with Paul: "He loved me and gave himself for me"(Galatians 2:20).

Let me repeat that I am not saying that one should reason and think about faith. Only that one should sit silently, receiving the love of God into the depths of one's being. "And in praying do not heap up empty phrases as the Gentiles do; for they think that they will be heard for their many words. Do not be like them . . ." (Matthew 6:7). Faith does not need a lot of words. Just as a man who knows that he is loved by a woman, or a woman who knows that she is loved by a man, carries this conviction constantly without reasoning about it, so one who believes does not need to think a lot. The principal thing is to receive and to keep receiving the immense love which is being offered, which *threatens* to inundate us and from which we fly as we fly from the hound of heaven.

Perhaps we could say that the basis of Christian meditation is the art of being loved. If someone has written a book called

The Art of Loving, perhaps someone else could write one on *The Art of Being Loved*. It would teach people to open their hearts to love, both human and divine; not to put obstacles in the way. *The Song of Songs* speaks of opening the door to the Beloved. And Jesus says: "Behold, I stand at the door and knock; if any one hears my voice and opens the door ..." (Revelation 3:20). If we are to meditate we must learn the art of sitting silently with the door open.

And let us remember that the love of God, received in meditation, makes us more and more O.K. For it purifies; it redeems; it justifies (if I may use the Pauline term) and makes us holy. Mystics like the author of *The Cloud* tell us that contemplation makes us beautiful not only in the sight of God but also in the sight of men and women who have eyes to recognize this kind of beauty. And Paul calls the brethren "saints".

I have spoken about Christian faith. But what about the role of faith in Buddhist meditation? What about the role of faith in Zen?

No doubt some of my readers will think there is no faith in Zen and little faith in any form of Buddhism. Popular literature on the subject has given this impression. It prefers to emphasize human potential rather than faith – because this is what the West is looking for. Besides, human potential sells better than faith.

But in fact Buddhism is based on faith. This is particularly true of Pure Land Buddhism which arose in North India at the beginning of the Christian era and became extremely popular throughout Asia – the Pure Land is a religion of faith, of pure faith. The Buddha Amida, it holds, has made a vow to save all sentient beings who call upon his name with faith. In other words, one who recites the name (and this recitation of the name is called the *nembutsu*) with faith in Amida will be liberated from bad *karma* and reborn in the Pure Land. And so among Buddhists of this persuasion there exists a form of meditation which consists simply in reciting the name again and again and again, with devotion and trust and faith in the mercy of Amida and in the efficacy of his vow. The resemblance to the Christian "Jesus prayer" is so obvious that I need not dwell on it here.

As for Zen, the masters constantly exhort to *great faith*. This faith is summed up in an incantation which is constantly recited in the temple and runs as follows:

> I put my faith in the Buddha
> I put my faith in the *dharma*
> I put my faith in the *sangha*

Since the *dharma* means the law, and the *sangha* means the community, this triple invocation could be paralleled in the Christian life by the prayer:

> I put my faith in Jesus
> I put my faith in the Bible
> I put my faith in the Church

I believe that without these three elements of basic faith authentic religious meditation is not possible.

My reader will observe the great stress on the holy books: the *sutras* and the Bible. Christians and Buddhists who seriously meditate must constantly recite their holy books with love and devotion. Again there is the stress on community. This community may be a small group indeed (it may even consist of husband and wife) but it is part of the larger group which is the Church. Without it, meditation easily wanders off into the mists of illusion.

Of course the Buddhist way of speaking about faith is often baffling to the uninitiated. Shunryu Suzuki, for example, can write: "I discovered that it is necessary, absolutely necessary to believe in nothing. That is, we have to believe in something which has no form and no colour – something which exists before all forms and colours appear."*

In saying that it is necessary to believe in nothing, Suzuki means (and this is clear from his ensuing pages) that it is necessary to *cling* to nothing – not to say any ideas of God or thoughts of God. But yet it is necessary to believe in something

*Suzuki, p. 112

without form. Suzuki is here proposing something that is very close to the pure or naked faith of St John of the Cross. But I cannot enter into that here because discussion of Buddhist nothingness would take us too far afield.

*

Now obviously Buddhist faith and Christian faith are different, as the Buddha differs from Jesus and the *dharma* from the Gospel. Nevertheless they have something in common. What is the common denominator?

I myself believe that it is the inner conviction that everything is well. Clearly no authentic Buddhist will say that all is well because *God loves the world*; but he will claim inner security based on the conviction that everything is all right – an inner security which stands in the midst of suffering, earthquake, flood, famine and war. It looks all wrong but in fact all is well. "All will be well and all will be well and all manner of things will be well" wrote Julian of Norwich; and her refrain was taken up by T. S. Eliot in *Four Quartets*. It is a refrain that pulsates through the meditation of Christian and Buddhist alike.

And so I suggest that the Christian who wishes to meditate sit constantly with the conviction that all is well, that he is loved by God. Let him advance the pure and naked and silent faith that liberates from anxiety.

V

I am trying to say that when we read the Sermon on the Mount we should do what Jesus tells us to do rather than thinking about the meaning of his words. Just follow his advice! You remember that he says: "Look at the birds of the air . . ." (Matthew 6:26), and: "Consider the lilies of the field . . . (Matthew 6:28). Well, take this literally. Look at the grass; look at the flowers; look at the birds. Just have a good look. Many people have never really looked at anything. While looking at things they are thinking about something else. The result is that they don't really see the beauty that lies around them – the beauty in nature and the beauty in persons.

Now Zen speaks about "just looking", "just listening", "just sitting". This means that you could look or listen or sit and do nothing else. Perhaps we could call it "pure looking". Or Zen will tell us just to listen – to the sound of the river or the waterfall or the rain or whatever it may be. Just listen and do nothing else but listen. And in doing this you become one with the object: you identify with it: you lose your small self and discover your true self.

I have sometimes practised this kind of meditation with students. Smoggy Tokyo is not the best place in the world to look at birds or to relish the beauty of the flowers. But nevertheless Sophia University has a small garden. We go there in silence and each one simply picks up a stone or a flower or some object of nature – and looks at it, touches it, smells it, becomes it. "Look at the birds of the air . . ." (Matthew 6:26). The Greek word *emblepo* which is used in the text does not mean to look in a casual or absent-minded way; it means to have a good look, to penetrate into, to see into the heart of the thing. It reminds me of the way in which a Zen master tells his disciple to look at a *koan*, to look at it with mind and body, to grapple with it, to become one with it. It is in this way that the inner eye is opened and one comes to self-realization.

It is said that the Bodhisattva Kannon got enlightenment by just listening to every sound. The name *kannon*, originally *Kanze-on*, means literally "the one who listens to the sounds of the world". And so Kannon was just listening, totally present to reality and its sounds. What a tremendous *awareness* or *mindfulness* was here! But there is another translation of the name which is even more remarkable. Instead of "the one who listens to the *sounds* of the world", there is a translation which runs "the one who listens to the *cries* of the world". In other words, Kannon listens to the cries of the poor and the sick and the dying. He takes these cries into the depth of his being and identifies with them. This is compassion; and this is enlightenment. If we could imitate Kannon in listening to the cries of the poor in our day how close we would be to the Kingdom of God!

But let me return to the Sermon on the Mount. Jesus tells us to consider the lilies of the field and then to reflect on our own value and dignity. "Are you not of more value than they?" (Matthew 6:26). Now we could take these words in a discursive way, comparing ourselves with the lilies and the birds. We could say that in the scale of evolution we are one step higher and, in consequence, are much more valuable. And then we could reflect on God's great love and care for us, thus becoming conscious of our dignity as men and women. This is the discursive approach to the text.

But can we not approach the same text in a contemplative way? When we do so, we realize that in contemplating the lily we become the lily and realize our true value: in looking at the bird we become the bird and realize our true worth. Again let me return to Zen. In listening to the waterfall I may get a ray of enlightenment: not about the beauty of the waterfall as such but about myself as listening and not separate. Listening, like looking, is thus a way to self-realization. And Jesus, too, is saying that in looking at the lily, in becoming the lily, I realize my true self – I realize that I am loved by my Father and that I am of great value.

VI

All that I have said so far is leading in one direction: namely, towards contemplative prayer. It is upon this that all Christian ways converge. Yet here permit me to recall something I said at the beginning of this Postscript, when I insisted that the Principal teacher of prayer is the *Magister Internus* or Master Within. Now this is particularly true of contemplative prayer. It is not taught by man alone. It is a call, a vocation, an invitation to ascend to a privileged seat in the banquet of love.

The earlier stages of contemplative prayer are characterized by the sense of presence – the sense that God is near, that he loves, that "in Him we live and move and have our being" (Acts

17:28). The author of *The Cloud* speaks of a blind stirring of love that arises in the heart and draws one into the cloud of unknowing beyond all thought and image and ratiocination. One is held by this blind stirring of love (St John of the Cross calls it the living flame of love) in a way that is similar to the silence of lovers who need no words because they are united in intuitive intimacy. And this stirring of love gives birth to a wisdom that guides us, enlightens us, tells us what to do and what not to do in daily life. Under the guidance of love one knows intuitively what to do in concrete circumstances.

When this blind stirring of love arises in the heart, one must follow it with great freedom. One may find oneself forgetting about breathing and awareness exercises just as one forgets about reasoning and thinks of the discursive intellect. All this kind of thing is buried beneath a cloud of forgetting. Now it shows the inner light with complete liberty. Of this stage St John of the Cross writes:

> Here there is no longer any way.
> For the just man there is no way.
> He is a law unto himself.

Here there is no way! It is always a snare to cling to ways and methods. When the time comes, when we hear the voice of the Master who knocks at the door, then we must leave all methodology to open the door to one who comes in and dines with us and we with him.

This inner stirring of love may well up in acts of praise or thanksgiving or petition or trust or love or whatever. But at other times it may be totally silent and wordless. It may consist in loving converse – what the old authors call "intimacy with God", or it may be that, silent and without words, I am "naked of self and clothed with Christ" offering myself to the Father for the salvation of the human race.

Now while this experience of loving contemplation or loving knowledge has much in common with Zen, I do not believe it is the same. In other words I do not think that Christian contemplation and Zen are "the same thing", and I believe that most Zen Masters (and perhaps all authentic Zen Masters) will agree with me here. For one thing, Zen never speaks of love. Some Christian writers, it is true, will say that although there is no talk of love in Zen, still Zen is love-filled and simply uses another terminology. And at one time I myself thought in this way. But when I proposed this theory I never found an authentic Zen person willing to go along with it. For them, sentiments of love for God, even for a God who is my deepest being and my truest self, are a species of illusion or *makyo*. I believe that this comes out in the interview with the Roshi about which I wrote in the first chapter of this book.

Now while it is true that when the Christian contemplative life develops, the sense of presence may become a sense of absence, the light may become darkness and the sentiments of love may wither and dry up – still, this is only towards the summit when one cries out: "My God, my God, why has thou forsaken me?" (Matthew 27:46). Here one is in emptiness and darkness and nothingness and the void. Here all the words of oriental mysticism apply. But still there remains a belief, a profound belief, in a God who, though seemingly absent, *should* be present. Here the blind stirring of love has become very blind indeed and very dark. But love is still there. And the psalm from which these words are taken ends with a cry of joy and praise and thanksgiving:

> I will tell of thy name to my brethren;
> in the midst of the congregation I will praise thee.
>
> Psalm 22:22

These are the words of one who has passed through the desert and has once again a deep experience of the nearness and presence of God.

For me, then, the greatest practical difference between Zen and Christian contemplation is that whereas Zen regards thoughts and feelings and aspirations of love for God as so much *makyo* and illusion, I regard these sentiments as – yes, imperfect and inadequate to express the reality, but nevertheless as true and valid and valuable religious experiences.

And here we are at the crux of the matter: it is one thing to say that sentiments and thoughts of God are inadequate: it is another thing to say that they are illusory. It is one thing to say that thoughts and sentiments must be transcended: it is another thing to say they must be rejected. And it was because of this delicate but important distinction that I myself found it imposs- ible to practise "pure Zen" or "Buddhist Zen" with authenticity. From Zen I can, and will continue to, learn many things. But I am convinced that it is not the same as the Christian contem- plation to which I feel called.*

At one point where the author of *The Cloud* is making a subtle distinction he cautiously observes: "Be careful of errors here, I beg you. Remember that the nearer a man comes to the truth, the more sensitive he must become to error."† I apply this to Zen and Christian contemplation. Precisely because the differences are so fine and subtle we must all the more beware of error.

VII

In the Sermon on the Mount, Jesus issues a solemn warning: "Beware of practising your piety before men in order to be seen by them . . ."(Matthew 6:1). He is speaking, of course, about the hypocrites who stand in the synagogue or at the street corner looking for praise and attention. "Truly, I say to you, they have their reward"(Matthew 6:5).

To look for recognition and praise, to search for success, to glory in achievement – these are very natural human tendencies. But they are the great snare in the things of the spirit. And here is the temptation which besets the meditation movement which has spread throughout the world today. So much of this medi- tation movement is geared to achievement of all kinds – to the development of human potential, to success in interpersonal

---

*St John of the Cross insists that thoughts of God are not God; sentiments and feelings of God are not God; images of God are not God. All these are imperfect and must be transcended. But to say they are imperfect is not to say they are false or illusory.

†*The Cloud of Unknowing*, William Johnson, ed. (New York: Doubleday 1973).

relations, to attainment of enlightenment or illumination – that the great temptation is to cry out in the church or at the street corner: "I got enlightenment; I made the grade. Here is my diploma." And to this Jesus answers: "Truly, I say to you, you have your reward." After all, you are now recognized by men – do you also want recognition from God?

Purity of intention, on the other hand, is a virtue which is stressed throughout Asian spirituality from the time of the *Bhagavad Gita*. One of the main points of the *Gita* (and a point which was dear to the heart of Gandhi) is that we should work without seeking the fruit of our labour. In other words, we devote ourselves to right action without caring about success or failure; and this non-attachment gives us joy and a liberty which is an unlooked-for reward. And what the *Gita* says of action is equally or more true of meditation. You are not trying *to get something*; you are not looking for results. Much less are you looking for recognition. You are engaging in perfect action which is its own reward. In short, the perfection of action in total liberty is the great ideal.

And the same ideal is present in the traditional Sino-Japanese martial arts like archery and fencing and judo. We moderns naturally think that the aim is to hit the bull's eye or to defeat one's opponent. Not so. The aim is perfect action, total liberation, loss of self. The arrow will go straight to its mark; but that is not one's aim. It is just like authentic Zen where one must never look for results. There are early monastic exhortations which tell monks deliberately to do good deeds which will never be seen or recognized by anyone. It all reminds one of the "do not let your left hand know what your right is doing" (Matthew 6:3).

As I have already indicated, Christian teachers also stress purity of intention as something of the utmost importance. This is because Christian meditation is ultimately an expression of love and in its highest form Christian meditation is pure love, disinterested love. If I love because of some gain or profit, then my love is still imperfect. In one of his minor treatises, the author of *The Cloud* speaks about the woman who is not chaste because she loves her husband for his goods and not for himself.

And in the same way if we love God because of the ensuing human potential or inner consolation our love is not chaste.

Perfect love, like perfect action, is its own reward and is for its own sake. That is why Bernard of Clairvaux, that great lover, can cry: "I love because I love; I love in order to love...." How different this is from the cry: "I love because I realize that loving is good for me"! Indeed, there is no reason for love. Love searches for nothing. That is why purity of intention is central to Christian prayer which is an enactment of the commandment to love God with one's whole heart and soul, and to love one's neighbour as one's self.

THE INNER EYE
OF LOVE

MYSTICISM AND RELIGION

FOR MARY

CONTENTS

Preface

Recent years have witnessed an upsurge of interest in mysticism throughout the world. Psychologists and scientists begin to see that here is a phenomenon that cannot be overlooked in the study of the human mind. Religious thinkers like Henri Bergson, Martin Buber and Teilhard de Chardin look on mysticism as the very core of authentic religious experience. Orientalists see it as the key to the understanding of the religions of the East. And, most significant of all, thousands of ordinary men and women, feeling called to a deepening life of meditation and prayer, turn their attention towards mystical experience. All in all, mysticism is in the air we breathe; and it promises to be even more in the air of the new age into which we are moving.

And so I have written *The Inner Eye of Love*. The title, I believe, touches a chord in the great religions of East and West. All are aware that man born of woman is somehow in ignorance but that redemption is at hand. For he has a third eye, an inner eye, the eye of the heart, the eye of wisdom, the eye of love. When this inner eye is awakened man, blind from birth, sees the real glory and beauty and meaning of the universe. "The eye is the lamp of your body. So if your eye is sound, your whole body will be full of light; but if your eye is not sound, your whole body will be full of darkness!" (Matthew 6:22,23). Surely these enigmatic words remind us that the important thing in human life is *to see*, to be full of light, not to walk in the dark.

*

In the opening chapters of this book I have attempted to sketch the background of this difficult word *mysticism*; and then I have given a preliminary description of mystical knowledge. It is possible that some of my readers who would ordinarily shrink from the word mysticism will recognize their own experience in this chapter. If so, let them not be afraid. Let them take courage and embark on the mystical journey which is described later in this book.

In the second section I turn to theology. One need be no great prophet to predict that Western theology of the next century will address itself primarily to dialogue with the great religions of the East. And I myself believe that this dialogue will be a miserable affair if the Western religions do not rethink their theology in the light of mystical experience. In this book I have highlighted the mysticism of Jesus as the key to the understanding of Christianity, just as the enlightenment of Shakamuni is the key to the understanding of Buddhism.

I am aware that for many professional theologians mysticism is a peripheral affair – an esoteric and embarrassing subject which has rightly been relegated to an obscure position in the curriculum of any self-respecting school of theology. I myself have not been able to accept this point of view. And in this book I set myself the task of finding a place for mysticism in the overall discipline which we call theology. I followed the *method* of Bernard Lonergan and found myself drawn to the conclusion that mysticism is the very centre of religion and theology. I discovered that mysticism is the exquisitely beautiful queen before whom the other branches of theology bow down with awe and reverence like lowly handmaids. I also saw clearly that this queen is the Lady Wisdom, for whom all religions search and in whose presence all religions meet.

The third part of my book is entitled "Mystical Journey". I hope that it will enlighten and reassure those men and women (and they are by no means few in numbers) who feel called to this joyful, if arduous, journey. Much of the material in these chapters comes out of lived experience – either my own or that of the many friends with whom I have talked and shared.

Needless to say, I had to deal with questions of nothingness and emptiness and darkness – all this negative terminology which fills the pages of mystics everywhere. And I came to the conclusion that mystical nothingness (and in particular the apparently negative *non-action*) is dynamite. It is the power that moves the universe and creates revolutions in human minds and hearts. For mystical nothingness, properly understood, paves the way for the dynamic action of grace. "When I am weak, then I am strong", cried Paul. And he never said a truer word.

The final section deal with action. Some theologians distinguish clearly, almost radically, between the mystical, passive religions of the East and the prophetic, active religions of the West. I have not been able to accept this dichotomy, as will be clear to the reader of my book. I have tried to say that mysticism, the core of all religious experience, has led to the most dynamic and revolutionary action the world has known. I believe that the great prophets were mystics in action – their inner eye was awakened so that they saw not only the glory of God but also the suffering, the injustice, the inequality, the sin of the world. This drove them into action and often led to their death. And just as the great prophets were mystics, so the great mystics had a prophetic role – even when this was fulfilled through a solitude and a silence and a self-oblation which spoke louder than words and shook the universe.

*

So many people helped me with this book that I feel it is not entirely my own. I cannot here mention the names of all; but I would like first of all to thank Juan and Rich and Dan with whom I live, who gave me constant support and encouragement ("How's the book going, Bill?") and with whom I discussed many of the problems treated here. Also Maureen O'Brien who helped me in innumerable ways; and Izumi Iwasaki who did the typing and editing. And finally there is my friend and colleague Edward Perez Valera, who introduced me to the theology of Bernard Lonergan and kindly read my manuscript with eyes of love and compassion. To him and to many unnamed others I express my sincere thanks.

Institute of Oriental Religions
Sophia University
Tokyo
1977

PART I

MYSTICISM

1

Background (I)

1

It is far from easy to define the word mysticism. Writing at the end of the last century William Ralph Inge cited no less than twenty-six different definitions of this word; and were he writing today he could cite fifty or a hundred. For he would find himself involved with Zen, challenged by Dr D. T. Suzuki, poring over books on yoga, contending with Thomas Merton, Mahatma Gandhi and the Maharishi Mahesh Yogi. Moreover he would have to deal with cosmic consciousness, with sudden illumination, with the occult and even with witchcraft. And he might well throw up agonized hands in despair.

I myself have decided not to do that. Faced with the burgeoning number of definitions and descriptions I will look briefly at the etymology of the word and then take my initial understanding of mysticism from the medieval Western tradition. Using this as a basis I shall try to remain open to modern thought and to the Orient. For while my language and way of speaking is taken from the Christian West I believe that the phenomenon towards which this language points is universal: mysticism is a profoundly human experience found in all cultures, at all times.

In taking Western mysticism as my starting point I may seem narrow-minded and provincial in view of the great encounter of religions taking place before our eyes. Who is not aware of the treasures of mysticism in Islam, in Buddhism, in Hinduism, in Judaism, in all the great religions? But let me be frank. My first intention was to write a book on world mysticism or, at least, on Buddhist and Christian mysticism; but I found, not

without anguish, that this was not possible.[1] Even if I had the
erudition for such a project (and I have not), it would still be
impossible to find a vocabulary or terminology that would cover
all these religious systems. The longer I live in Tokyo the more
I become aware of the enormous cultural gap which still separates East and West. The way of thinking, the words, the manner
of expression of Buddhism and Christianity are so different that
anyone who tries to write a theological book about both is
doomed to superficiality and even to failure. For the fact is that
Christians and Buddhists talk different theological languages.

Now I believe that a time will come, probably in the next
century, when we or those who come after us will forge a
common way of speaking and even some kind of common
theology. But that is the future. At present I think it is only
possible for a Christian to speak from a Christian standpoint
and for a Buddhist to speak from a Buddhist viewpoint while
we work towards mutual understanding, co-operation and love.
Let us, then, write from our respective positions while opening
our minds and hearts to the spirit in others. Let me write about
Christianity as an insider and about Buddhism as a sympathetic
outsider who has learnt very much and wishes to learn more.

II

Historically the word mysticism is associated with the mystery
religions or mystery cults which flourished in the Greco-Roman
world in the early centuries of the Christian era. Eleusinian,
Dionysian and Orphic mysteries attained to great popularity,
attracting thousands of spiritually hungry devotees to their esoteric rites and ceremonies. The mystic (*mustes*) was the initiate
who in an oath of secrecy swore to be silent or, literally, to keep
his mouth shut (*muein*) about the inner working of his new-
found religion. In its original meaning, then, mysticism is associated with mystery and secrecy and the occult.

---

[1] I wrote the first sixty-five pages of such a book; and then, after consul-
tation with two good friends, I threw the whole thing into the waste bin.

The word mysticism (like much of the terminology of the mysteries) passed into neoplatonism where it was associated with secrecy of another kind. Now it meant deliberately shutting the eyes to all external things, a practice which was central to neoplatonic meditation: one excluded the world in order to rise up to the One and to be "alone with the alone". The neoplatonists, Plotinus and Proclus, use the word *muo* of the closed eyes of one who is rapt in profound contemplation. While the eyes of the body were closed, the inner eye was open and was searching for wisdom.

*

The word *mystica* was introduced into Christianity by an anonymous Syrian monk, a Christian neoplatonist of the late fifth or early sixth century AD, who composed several theological treatises, one of which was named *Mystica Theologia*. To his works he quietly affixed the name of Dionysius the Areopagite who is mentioned in the Acts of the Apostles as a convert of St Paul; and the *Mystica Theologia* he fictitiously addressed to Paul's disciple Timothy.[2]

Though little appreciated at first, the works of the so-called Dionysius swept through the intellectual world of Europe after they were translated into Latin by the red-bearded Irishman, John Scotus Eriugena, in the ninth century. Initially some doubts were cast on their authenticity, but "the pious fraud", as Aldous Huxley called it, turned out so successful that Albert, Aquinas, Bonaventure and the schoolmen greeted the author with the enthusiasm and reverence due to one who was close to St Paul and the New Testament. Commentaries on his works multiplied, and even Dante sings the praises of the Areopagite. Only at the end of the nineteenth century was the identity, or lack of identity, of this anonymous monk definitively uncovered. He is now

---

[2] While Paul was at Athens "some men joined him and believed, among them Dionysius the Areopagite and a woman named Damaris and others with them" (Acts of the Apostles 17:34). About this, the real Dionysius, little is known apart from this text. A tradition of doubtful historical value states that he was the first bishop of Athens.

frequently called pseudo-Dionysius but I shall go along with his pious fraud and call him Dionysius.

While the prestige of Dionysius was greatly enhanced by his supposed proximity to St Paul, he was also highly rated because his writings were of value: he had a message: he had something to say. Moreover, he must have been deeply contemplative, and his *Mystica Theologia* was a real contribution to Christian thinking.

It opens with a passage which is important not only for the understanding of the thought of Dionysius himself but for the understanding of mysticism in other religions and cultures. For he describes how the mind ascends to the area of supraconceptuality and interior silence by transcending all images and thoughts, thus entering into darkness. The author, supposedly talking to Timothy, writes as follows:

> Do thou, then, in the intent practice of mystic contemplation, leave behind the senses and the operations of the intellect, and all things that the senses or the intellect can perceive, and all things which are not and things which are, and strain upwards in unknowing, as far as may be, towards the union with Him Who is above all things and knowledge. For by unceasing and absolute withdrawal from thyself and all things in purity, abandoning all and set free from all, thou shalt be borne up to the ray of divine darkness that surpasseth all being.
>
> (*Mystica Theologia* 1, 1)

As can be seen, for Dionysius the word mysticism retains its meaning of secrecy; but now it is a secrecy of the mind which, possessing no clear-cut thoughts and images, remains in obscurity and darkness. A similar state of consciousness is found in Buddhism and in the mysticism of all the great religions, even when the theistic background of Dionysius is lacking. Plenty of Buddhist texts inveigh against concepts as deadly enemies of the great goal which is enlightenment.

For Dionysius, however, concepts are not deadly enemies. He accepts the validity of a theology of affirmation or, in Greek, *kataphatic theology*, whereby one uses concepts to affirm truths about God. But this knowledge which is found by denying concepts and going to God by unknowing – this is the theology of negation or *apophatic theology*. It is precisely here that one finds the most sublime knowledge. Moreover this knowledge, Dionysius maintains, is scripturally based; and he appeals to the example of Moses who climbs the mountain and enters into the cloud of darkness. Moses cannot see God – "You cannot see my face; for man shall not see me and live" (Exodus 33:20) – but he knows God by unknowing; he knows God in darkness. He knows with the inner eye.

The insight of Dionysius is of great importance for anyone who wishes to grasp the meaning of mysticism. For mysticism is nondiscursive. It is not a question of thinking and reasoning and logic, but of transcending all thinking and entering into what modern people might call an altered state of consciousness. Here one is in darkness, in emptiness, in the cloud of unknowing precisely because one does not know through clear images and thoughts nor with the eyes of the body. There is a great inner silence, but it is a rich silence – and that is why we call it silent music. There is conceptual darkness; but the inner eye is filled with light.

III

The *Mystica Theologia* of Dionysius was translated into contemporary English by the anonymous author of *The Cloud of Unknowing* in the fourteenth century.[3] It is interesting, however, to observe that the English translator made some small but significant additions to the text. Speaking of the mystical ascent into the realm of darkness that transcends thought, he says that one is drawn up *by love*. And in his translation of the passages about Moses ascending the mountain, he is careful to add that Moses was motivated and drawn on *by great love*. In making

[3] The English title was *Denis Hid Divinity*. It is interesting to see that *mystica* is translated by the English word "hid". The medieval English translation was almost certainly made from the Latin and not from the original Greek.

this simple textual change he is following a series of medieval commentators who had rendered Dionysius more totally Christian by centring his whole doctrine on love.[4]

So now the mind ascends to a realm of obscurity and darkness under the guidance of divine love. Love is the motivation and driving force behind the mystical journey – it is precisely love that leads one beyond thoughts and images and concepts into the world of silence. The inner eye is now the eye of love. If this seems difficult to understand, it may be helpful to reflect that human love often has the same effect. Profound human love may draw the lovers into a state of deep, unitive silence where thoughts and concepts become unnecessary and even superfluous, yet where the inner eye, the eye of love, penetrates powerfully to the core of the other's being. Such human union is similar to (perhaps in certain cases it is identical with) the mystical loving silence about which the medievals write.

With this in mind it becomes possible to understand some of the classical definitions of mystical theology which were current in the Middle Ages and later in St John of the Cross:

1 Jean Gerson (1363–1429), Chancellor of the University of Paris: "Mystical theology is experimental knowledge of God through the embrace of unitive love." [5]

2 Bonaventure (1217–74): "Mystical theology is the raising of the mind to God through the desire of love." [6]

3 St John of the Cross (1542–91): "Contemplation is the mystical theology which theologians call secret wisdom which St Thomas says is communicated and infused into the soul through love." (*Dark Night*, 2:17,2).

4 Again St John of the Cross. Commenting on his own poem where he has written of "a sweet and living knowledge" he writes: "The sweet and living knowledge is mystical theology,

---

[4] The medievals were much less scrupulous about tampering with venerable manuscripts than our enlightened contemporaries. But do not judge them harshly. A different ethic prevailed at that time.

[5] *Theologia mystica est experimentalis cognitio habita de Deo per amoris unitivi complexum.*

[6] *Est animi extensio in Deum per amoris desiderium.*

that secret knowledge of God which spiritual persons call contemplation. This knowledge is very delightful because it is knowledge through love" (*Spiritual Canticle*, 27:5).

Similar definitions could be multiplied. But let me draw attention to three points.

First of all, it is clear from all the definitions that *mysticism is wisdom or knowledge that is found through love; it is loving knowledge*. This is a central point in my book.

Secondly, my reader will observe that Jean Gerson speaks of "experimental" knowledge. This is important. For knowledge that is experimental is different from knowledge that is abstract. Experimental knowledge can be compared to feeling or touching; and experimental knowledge of God can only be obtained through love. This is the doctrine of the First Epistle of St John;[7] and it is the doctrine of the author of *The Cloud* who writes: "For by love we may find him, feel him and hit him even in himself" (Johnston (2), p. 118). And again he says: "Though we cannot know him we can love him. By love he may be touched and embraced, never by thought" (Johnson (1), ch. 6). Other medieval writers maintain that concepts can attain to God *as he is in creation*, but only love can attain to God *as he is in himself*.

Thirdly, it will be noticed that the definitions make no distinction between mystical theology and mystic experience, and that St John of the Cross identifies mystical theology with contemplation. These are points to which I shall return.

IV

In the thirteenth and fourteenth centuries, schools of mysticism flourished in the centres of spirituality and learning which arose within the great religious orders. There were Benedictine, Cistercian, Franciscan schools, as well as the so-called Victorines, a group of theologians associated with the Abbey of Saint-Victor

---

[7] "... he who loves is born of God and knows God. He who does not love does not know God...." (1 John 4:7, 8)

in Paris. Then there was the famous Rhineland Dominican school (and here the dark Dionysius influence was particularly strong though tempered by Thomist theology), with its big names like Eckhart, Tauler and Suso. There were Flemish mystics, of whom the most famous is Jan Van Ruysbroeck. There was the cluster of English mystics, notably Julian of Norwich, Walter Hilton and the anonymous author of *The Cloud of Unknowing*.

While the voice of Dionysius influences this medieval mystical movement, the main inspiration comes from the gospels, the Epistles of St Paul, the Psalms – the whole Bible. Particularly strong is the influence of the Fourth Gospel, which Dean Inge calls the charter of Christian mysticism and of which he writes movingly: "The Gospel of St John – the 'spiritual gospel' " as Clement calls it – is the charter of Christian mysticism. . . . Perhaps, as Origen says, no one can fully understand it who has not, like its author, lain upon the breast of Jesus" (Inge, p. 45). In short, the Bible is the source of Christian mysticism, as the sutras and the Hindu scriptures are the source of Buddhist and Hindu mysticism.

But there is also the influence of the Church Fathers – of Augustine and Gregory and the rest. Then there is Bernard of Clairvaux (1090–1153), the last of the Fathers, whose sermons on the *Song of Songs* were to have an impact on all subsequent mystical theology. Great, too, is the influence of Thomas Aquinas (1225–74) whose writings have exerted crucial influence not only on scholasticism but also on Catholic spirituality from the thirteenth century to our very day. And in the mysticism which flourished in this medieval period the whole emphasis is on love. This is a time which abounds in lyrical treatises on the grades of love, ecstatic love, the ladder of love; it is a time of discussion and controversy about disinterested love and the chaste and perfect love of God.[8]

In a theological framework, mystical experience was inter-

----

[8] See, for example, *Of the Four Degrees of Passionate Charity* by Richard of St Victor in *Richard of St Victor: Selected Writings on Contemplation*, trans. by Clare Kirchberger (Faber and Faber, London). See also *The Mystical Theology of St Bernard* by Etienne Gilson (London, 1940).

preted briefly as follows: God who is love infuses his gift of love into the soul. When the soul responds to this call she receives the Holy Spirit who is love personified. Writers of the time (including Thomas Aquinas) quote that text of the Fourth Gospel which says that love calls down the Holy Spirit: "If you love me you will keep my commandments. And I will pray the Father and he will give you another Counsellor to be with you for ever, even the Spirit of Truth . . ." (John 14:15,16). Mysticism, then, is based upon the indwelling of the Spirit and the "divinization" of the human person. The Spirit who is love brings the gift of wisdom, which is the special characteristic of the mystical life. But the mystic, possessing not only wisdom but other gifts as well, is described in the beautiful words of Isaiah:

> And the Spirit of the Lord shall rest upon him,
> the spirit of wisdom and understanding,
> the spirit of counsel and might,
> the spirit of knowledge and the fear of the Lord.
> And his delight shall be in the fear of the Lord.
>
> Isaiah 11:2,3

In this way the Spirit is the key to the understanding of mystical theology. The indwelling Spirit transforms us into the body of Christ and makes us cry out: "Abba, Father!" (Romans 8:15). Or the same Spirit enlightens out inner eye and shows us the glory of the Son so that we cry out, "Jesus is Lord!"

But let me say a special word about St John of the Cross, who lives much later but inherits the rich mystical tradition of the Middle Ages. He was a great poet; and for him mystical experience is a "living flame of love". This is how, in one of his beautiful lyrics, he describes the divine love which burns in his breast, paradoxically giving pain and joy, wounding and yet strengthening. And he sings ecstatically:

> O living flame of love
> That tenderly wounds my soul
> *Living Flame*, Stanza I

These words speak of his experience: they come straight from a wounded poetic heart. But when the mystic turns theologian and (at the request of his friends) interprets this experience in theological language, he states clearly: "The flame of love . . . is the Holy Spirit" (*Living Flame*, 1:3). The flame is a person: divine love is personal; mysticism is a love affair and a romance. In centring his mystical theology on the indwelling Spirit and the theme of love, the Spanish Carmelite is in the full stream of traditional Christian mysticism which passes through Aquinas, the Victorines, Bernard of Clairvaux and the Church Fathers to primitive Christianity.

It is precisely this burning love which is the core of the poetry, of the theology and of the life of the medieval, mystical movement. It is precisely this love which guides and points out the way when one is lost in the dark and groping for the light. For there comes a time in the mystical life when love is the only guide. All props have fallen away; all securities have collapsed; the mystic is naked and helpless; and only love is there to enlighten the way:

> With no other light or guide
> Than the one that burns in my heart
>> *Ascent*, Stanza 3

Only love, only the Spirit, enlightens the darkness of the night.

2

Background (2)

I

I have pointed out that the word *mystica* entered the Christian vocabulary in the sixth century and became widely used only from the ninth century. Before that the word used for the phenomenon we now called mysticism was *contemplatio*. This also is a Latin word translating the Greek *theoria* which means "looking at", "gazing at", "being aware of" and has a long history in the Greco-Roman world. Plato writes about the contemplative life which is a search for truth centred on philosophy or love of wisdom; and his disciple Aristotle, that seemingly cold Stagirite, becomes almost passionate and poetic when he writes of the pure joy of the contemplative life and the contemplative moment – that moment when the human exercising the divine element within becomes somehow like God and reaches the pinnacle of human activity.

Within Christianity the word was used by Augustine, Gregory, Bernard (mystics who had no influence from Dionysius) and it is still more commonly used than the word mysticism. Adolphe Tanquerey (1854–1932), whose work on Christian spirituality was once a textbook for students of theology, follows Thomas Aquinas in defining contemplation as "a simple gaze on God and divine things proceeding from love and tending thereto" (Tanquerey, p. 649);[1] and he further quotes St Francis de Sales for whom contemplation is "a loving, simple and per-

---

[1] Tanquerey further quotes Thomas Aquinas: "One delights in seeing the object loved. And the very delight in the object seen arouses a yet greater love."

manent attentiveness of the mind to divine things". As can readily be seen, these definitions resemble those of mysticism which I cited in the last chapter. Both contemplation and mysticism speak of the eye of love which is looking at, gazing at, aware of divine realities. In my book I shall henceforth use these two words interchangeably.

In early Christianity the word is associated with monasticism, with silence, with solitude, with a life devoted to the reading of sacred scripture, recitation of the Divine Office and the pursuit of wisdom. Clement of Alexandria, Origen and Augustine discuss the two lives: the life of contemplation symbolized by the quiet Mary Magdalen and the life of action symbolized by the bustling Martha. At first, Mary the repentant sinner who sits silently, lovingly and mystically at the feet of Jesus, is singled out as the model of Christian perfection while busy Martha is something of a second-class citizen. This tradition is found in *The Cloud of Unknowing* which makes an unfortunate distinction between those called to perfection (and these are the contemplatives) and those called to salvation – and these are the actives. But Thomas Aquinas, himself a Dominican friar, has more esteem for action as it appears in what he calls the mixed life. This is the overflow of mysticism: sharing the fruits of contemplation with others. For Thomas this is the more perfect life for two reasons. Firstly, because it is better for the candle to give light than just to burn, and in the same way it is better to share the fruit of contemplation than just to contemplate. Secondly, this mixed life was chosen by Jesus Christ – who taught and preached and healed and lived an active life.

For Thomas, then, the eye of love gazes not only on divine realities but also on human realities. Or, more correctly, it sees the divine in the human: it sees God in the world. Mysticism overflows into activity.

II

The turbulent years of the reformation gave birth to Ignatius of Loyola (1491–1556), the Spanish soldier saint who founded the Jesuits. And Ignatius, going beyond Thomas, envisioned a mystical life which would not only share with others the fruits of contemplation but would experience God in the hurly-burly of action. It was said that he loved not the desert but the mighty cities. Indeed, he challenged the notion that profound mystical experience could be found only in the silence of a monastic cell or in a hut in the desert. No. One could experience God deeply and joyfully in the anguishing contradictions, persecutions and humiliations which necessarily accompany an active life devoted to apostolate. And so he spoke constantly of the presence of God and of finding God in all things; and he opposed those of his companions who wanted to disappear into solitude for years in preparation for activity. He also talked constantly of the glory of God and of the greater glory of God. Surely this was because his inner eye was enlightened to behold that glory everywhere as well as the glory of the Risen Jesus. For he insisted that his order would be called the Society of Jesus – that and nothing else.

This mysticism of action, far from being a compromise, is extremely demanding. If one looks for a parallel in Eastern thought one will perhaps find it in *karma yoga*, the yoga of action which is splendidly exemplified in the life of Mahatma Gandhi. Here are some words of a Gandhi who experienced God in the midst of social, political and religious action, who saw God in his fellow-man. In his periodical *Harijan* he wrote:

Man's ultimate aim is the realization of God, and all his activities, social, political, religious, have to be guided by the ultimate aim of the vision of God. The immediate service of all human beings becomes a necessary part of the endeavour simply because *the only way to find God is to see him in his creation and to be one with it*. This can only be done by service of all. I am a part and parcel of the whole and I cannot find him apart from the rest of humanity. My countrymen are my nearest neighbours. They have become so helpless, so inert that I must concentrate on serving them. *If I could persuade myself that I could find him in a*

> *Himalayan cave I would proceed there immediately. But I*
> *know that I cannot find him apart from humanity.*
>
>   Griffiths (1), p. 127

Here is a true mystic in action, a true *karma yogi*. Gandhi seeks
union with God through the world, union with God through
mankind. This is different both from a humanism which seeks
only man or from a world-denying flight that seeks only God.
It is a discovery of the world's highest value.

But let me take another example from India, the sub-continent
which constantly gives birth to religious genius. Mother Teresa
of Calcutta relates a story about her sisters:

> "During the mass," I said, "you saw that the priest touched
> the body of Christ with great love and tenderness. *When
> you touch the poor today, you too will be touching the
> body of Christ*. Give them that same love and tenderness."
> When they returned several hours later, the new sister came
> up to me, her face shining with joy. "I have been touching
> the body of Christ for three hours", she said. I asked her
> what she had done. "Just as we arrived, the sister brought
> in a man covered with maggots. He had been picked up
> from a drain. I have been taking care of him, I have been
> touching Christ. I knew it was him", she said.
>
>   Mother Teresa

This is mysticism – and not a watered-down version either. It
conforms to all the definitions I have given in the last chapter:
it is supraconceptual knowledge through love. Moreover it is
experimental knowledge (remember that Jean Gerson insisted
on this) and contains nothing abstract. It is a profoundly incarnational mysticism wherein the eye of love perceives Jesus in
the broken bodies of the destitute poor.

But let me return to Ignatius. The mysticism he envisioned
was a somewhat traditional interpretation of the Gospel and St
Paul; but it had never been formulated as a way of life for a
group of people. Consequently, the notion of a religious order
which did not recite office in choir and was always on the move
created no small stir.

Yet mysticism in action developed within Christianity and is developing still. One of its great champions was Teilhard de Chardin (1881–1955), himself a son of Ignatius. Passionately interested in mysticism throughout his life, Teilhard had a deeply poetic vision of a world vibrating with the presence of the cosmic Christ. He believed that the mysticism of the future (and for him mysticism really did have a future) was that in which the eye of love saw God in the world and Christ Omega as the ultimate point of universal convergence.

And so today we still find mystics sitting in the lotus in Himalayan caves but we also find mystics demonstrating for justice in the streets and suffering persecution in narrow prison cells. Moreover we find mysticism in the lives of simple people who are constantly moved by the Spirit.

III

But let me mention some salient features of this mysticism in action.

First of all, it is not a question of blind fidelity to rules and regulations but of following what Ignatius called "the interior law of charity and love which the Holy Spirit is accustomed to write and imprint on the heart". And this interior law is a person: the indwelling Spirit. It is a fact of experience that as the contemplative life develops one finds oneself interiorly moved by the Spirit to do this and not to do that. Indeed, the great art of mysticism in action is to discern the guidance of the Spirit: to be faithful to the voice of the Beloved who dwells within. "If today you hear his voice harden not your hearts . . ." (Psalm 95). About this discernment I will speak later. Here only let me say that the Spirit does not ordinarily speak in clear-cut words and concepts but only through inspirations and movements which are dark and obscure like the supraconceptual knowledge of which Dionysius speaks – in this sense his communications are real mystical experiences.

I have spoken of Mahatma Gandhi as a fine example of contemplation in action. He did not speak precisely about the

Holy Spirit, but he did talk constantly about the inner truth and the inner light to which he always strove to be faithful. "Devotion to this Truth," he wrote, "is the sole reason for our existence. All our activities should be centred in Truth. Truth should be the very breath of our life. When once this stage in the pilgrim's progress is reached, all other rules of correct living will come without effort, and obedience to them will be instinctive. . . . If we once learn how to apply this never-failing test of Truth, we will at once be able to find out what is worth doing, what is worth seeing, what is worth reading" (Duncan, p. 42). But it was only later in life that the movement of truth became a deeply-lived experience in Gandhi's life and he loved John Henry Newman's hymn: "Lead, kindly light. . . ."

Now for a second characteristic of mysticism in action. In order to be attentive to the promptings of grace which are the voice of the Spirit one must cultivate what the old authors called purity of intention. This means that, liberated from enslavement to intellectual, emotional and spiritual self-interest, one seeks God alone. Here again one could quote liberally from Gandhi, who on innumerable occasions spoke about that "non-attachment" which he saw as the core of the *Bhagavad Gita*. We must act from love: never from desire of success of fear of failure. Nor must we be motivated by anger or hatred or vanity or ambition but only by love, by non-violence, by *ahimsa*.

A third characteristic of mysticism in action – and one which follows from the first two – is the loss of self. Gradually I must pass from an active life in which I am the centre to an active life in which Christ is the centre. This demands a real death; and Ignatius speaks of a life in which one acts constantly against one's ego: *agere contra*. His words here have been misunderstood as a form of self-torture or self-flagellation, as though one always had to do the unpleasant things; and it has often been said that Ignatius preferred ascetics to mystics. Yet this is not entirely true. His *agere contra* was not a rule to be blindly obeyed but was subject to the interior law of charity and love: it was, in short, a mystical grace leading to the loss of self: "It is no longer I who live, but Christ who lives in me" (Galatians 2:20). One who loses self in this way constantly finds himself moving spontaneously and with great compassion towards the underprivileged, the poor, the sick and the imprisoned.

But what about solitude and silence in a life of active mysticism? Again we find Gandhi in his ashram maintaining one day of total silence each week – a day on which the great leader obstinately refused to speak a single word. As for Ignatius his attitude is not completely clear. On the one hand he himself spent long hours and months in solitude and silence. On the other hand he was wary of protracted periods of solitude and maintained that a person with the spirit of *agere contra* would achieve more in fifteen minutes than another in many hours. It seems to me that the time devoted to solitude will be governed by the basic rule: fidelity to the interior law of charity and love. There will be times when the Spirit drives a person into the desert as he drove Jesus into the desert to be tempted by the devil; and there will be other times when the same Spirit will drive the same person into the heart of action. Once again it is a question of discernment; once again it is a question of attentiveness to the voice of the beloved within.

IV

I have spoken about the movement to express mystical experience in scholastic categories which began in the thirteenth century and has continued until our very day.

At the beginning of this century we find a cluster of Catholic theologians who attempt to systematize mysticism, relying heavily on Thomas Aquinas and the Carmelite mystics, particularly St Teresa of Avila.[2] Though these theologians prefer the word contemplation they frequently speak of mysticism and call their discipline mystical theology. Their writings make some distinctions which are probably too tidy to suit the reality but which, nevertheless, are of some interest.

One such distinction was that between *acquired* and *infused*

[2] Auguste Poulain (1836–1919); Adolphe Alfred Tanquerey (1854–1932); Reginald Garrigou-Lagrange (1877–1964); Joseph de Guibert (1887–1942), and others.

contemplation. Acquired contemplation, these theologians held, was not, strictly speaking, mysticism: it could be achieved by one's own effort aided by ordinary grace. Concretely it was a very simple kind of meditation in which one repeats a word or ejaculation again and again effortlessly and with great joy and unction. It was also called the prayer of simplicity or the prayer of simple regard or the prayer of the heart. It is not unlike the more developed forms of the Jesus prayer about which I shall speak later, except that not only the name Jesus but any religious word can be used. In its technique it resembled transcendental meditation where one quietly repeats a mantra or sacred sound; but unlike TM it is the expression of deep religious faith.

Infused contemplation, on the other hand, was equivalent to mysticism and was sometimes called mystical contemplation. It was the next step in the spiritual ascent, a step which could only be taken in answer to a special call. Its initial stages were characterized by a longing for solitude, an inability to think discursively, a profound inner silence and an obscure sense of presence. There were certain signs, very traditional in origin, by which the director or the person himself could judge that the time had come to enter into the void of this so-called infused contemplation or mysticism. About these signs I have written in some detail elsewhere and need not repeat myself here.

(Johnston (3), ch. 9, pp. 94–7)[3]

Yet another important distinction was made between the *concomitant phenomena* of mysticism and the *charismatic phenomena*. These latter were visions, revelations, trances, voices, ecstasies, psychic powers, telepathy, clairvoyance and the like: they were not essential and one must even be wary of them. On the other hand, the concomitant phenomena were inner peace and joy, love, the obscure sense of presence, the gifts of the Spirit. These, it was held, were always present in the experience.

---

[3] It should be noted that some modern theologians, notably Karl Rahner, do not accept the distinction between the *ordinary grace* of acquired contemplation and the *special grace* of infused contemplation. They claim that all grace is "special" being essentially of the same character: the self-communication of God. I have treated this elsewhere. See *The Still Point* by William Johnston ch. 8.

Another interesting question discussed by these theologians was *the universal call to mysticism*. About this there were different opinions. Some maintained that infused contemplation or mysticism was for an elite of specially chosen people. All Christians, they agreed, were called to perfection or holiness ("Be ye perfect as your heavenly Father is perfect" (Matthew 5:48)), but there were two paths to this goal – a mystical path for the few and an ethical path of solid virtue for the many. Theologians who held the latter view based their theory mainly on experience: they claimed that they met many deeply virtuous and pious people who had no trace of mysticism in their lives.

Others held that mysticism was a universal call. Put theologically, it was the ordinary development of the grace of baptism.[4] This theory is very traditional and has its roots in the Church fathers.

I myself believe in the universal call to contemplation, and I write this book in the belief that many of my readers are called to, or already enjoy, mystical experience. Yet in saying this I would like to recall some of the distinctions already made. First of all, while all may be called to the concomitant phenomena not all, obviously enough, are called to the charismatic. Again, mysticism may manifest itself in diverse ways according to temperament, education and culture. For this reason it may be difficult to discern the presence or absence of mysticism in a given person, and certainly it would be disastrous to force everyone into certain patterns like those of St Teresa of Avila or anyone else – there is an infinite variety of ways and mysticism may express itself in the most unusual and surprising manner. Again, while I believe that mysticism is a universal call, I would not be sure about when that call is made. To some it may come in early childhood, to others in adolescence or middle age, to others at the mysterious moment which we call death. But if mysticism is knowledge through love and if love is the great

---

[4] Karl Rahner writes: "Mysticism . . . occurs within the framework of normal graces and within the experience of faith. To this extent, those who insist that mystical experience is not specifically different from the ordinary life of grace (as such) are certainly right." *Encyclopedia of Theology*, editor, Karl Rahner (Burns and Oates, London, 1975, p. 1010).

commandment, can we not say that mysticism is the core of authentic religious experience and that it is for everyone? And when I say for everyone I do not mean just for all Christians but for all men.

This is not mere theory. Later in this book I shall try to show that the most profound encounter of world religions takes place at the level of mysticism.

3

Mystical Knowledge

I

In order to understand the nature of mystical knowledge it is helpful to reflect on the human psyche as seen by some modern psychologists. With them we can picture the mind as a huge iceberg, of which only the tip rises above the water, while underneath lies a whole world of wonder and terror, of light and of darkness, of good and of evil. Or we can see the psyche as composed of many layers of consciousness, one superimposed upon the other. Or we can reflect on the mind as a huge polyphony in which there are higher and lower voices. In our waking states ordinarily it is the higher voices that dominate and lead; but our conduct is all the time influenced by the lower voices too. In this way of thinking the word unconscious is, strictly speaking, a misnomer: nothing is unconscious in the psyche.

Whatever way we envisage it, the microcosm or inner universe is investigated by psychologists and explorers in consciousness from Jung to Aldous Huxley and from D.H. Lawrence to Timothy Leary. What precisely it contains we do not yet know but one thing is clear: the deep forces of the so-called unconscious are profoundly stirred by love. Love of man for woman or of woman for man, love of mother for child or of child for mother – this is the power that moves the inner universe and stirs mysterious, unknown, uncontrollable forces within us.

But there is a human question which psychology never asks and which leads people to religion; namely, what is at the deepest realm of the psyche? What is the basis or centre or root of all? Put in Jungian terms I might ask: When I go beyond the ego, beyond the personal unconscious, beyond the collective unconscious, beyond the archetypes, what do I find? And in answer to this all the great religions speak of a mystery which they call by various names: the Buddha nature, Brahman and Atman, the divine spark, the ground of being, the centre of the soul, the kingdom of God, the image of God and so on. They use different terms; but all, I believe, are pointing towards a single reality.

Coming now to mystical experience, we find ourselves confronted with the most powerful love of all – divine love, infinite love, unrestricted love; and this force shakes the so-called unconscious to its very foundation. The hidden layers of consciousness, normally dormant, are awakened; the inner eyes come to see; the inner voices begin to talk. But in particular it is the Holy Spirit who awakens within us; and it is to his voice that we must be attuned and attentive. Nor is this easy. We must learn the art of discernment in order to recognize his peaceful stirrings in the midst of the great chorus (sometimes a cacophonous chorus) which sings within. But about discernment I will speak later in this book. Here only let me stress the point that mystical knowledge arises from a deep level of the psyche which is ordinarily dormant. It is a different kind of knowledge from which we ordinarily enjoy. Mysticism does not mean that we learn new things but that we learn to know in a new way.[1]

This same thing is expressed by the scholastics in a different psychological framework. For them all ordinary knowledge comes through the exterior senses, the windows of the soul, the interior senses and then to the intellect. "There is nothing in the intellect which was not previously in the senses" ran the old scholastic tag; but to this general principle mysticism was an

---

[1] St John of the Cross describes how mysticism leads one into what we would now call an altered state of consciousness: "Besides its usual effects, this mystical wisdom will occasionally so engulf a person in its secret abyss that he will have the keen awareness of being brought into a place far removed from every creature. He will accordingly feel that he has been led into a remarkably deep and vast wilderness, unattainable by any human creature, into an immense unbounded desert, the more delightful, savorous and loving, the deeper, vaster, and more solitary it is"(*Dark Night II*, 17:6).

exception. For mystical knowledge was not ordinary; it was directly infused into the soul bypassing, so to speak, the faculties. Technically they spoke of "infused species" and said that God communicates himself "by pure spirit" without any admixture of image or concept. Remember that I quoted St John of the Cross speaking of "the secret wisdom which St Thomas says is communicated and infused into the soul through love" (*Dark Night*, 2:17,2). And elsewhere he beautifully describes this divine communication saying: "In contemplation God teaches the soul very quietly and secretly, without its knowing how, without the sound of words, and *without the help of any bodily or spiritual faculty*, in silence and quietude, in darkness to all sensory and natural things. Some spiritual persons call this contemplation knowing by unknowing" (*Spiritual Canticle* 39:12). Knowing by unknowing! Here St John of the Cross looks back to Dionysius. He means that one layer of the psyche knows and another does not know; or that one layer of the psyche (the sensory and intellectual) does not know what is happening at the other (the mystical). The left hand does not know what the right hand is doing. This is knowing by unknowing.

All this leads to the conclusion that mystical knowledge is totally different from the conceptual, imaginative knowledge that comes through the senses. It belongs to a different layer of consciousness; and for this reason it is ineffable and can never be described or adequately talked about. Again let me quote St John of the Cross: "Not only does a man feel unwilling to give expression to this wisdom; but he finds no adequate means or similitude to signify so sublime and understanding and delicate a spiritual feeling. Even if the soul should desire to convey this experience in words and think up many similitudes, the wisdom would always remain secret and still to be expressed."

(*Dark Night*, 2:17,3)

II

To give a more adequate picture of mystical knowledge I would like to discuss some of its characteristics taking as my starting point the perceptive insights of the eminent psychologist William James (1842–1910).

His first characteristic I have already mentioned; namely, *ineffability*. James very simply and very wisely, attributes this ineffability to the fact that mystical states are more like states of feeling than states of intellect. "No one can make clear to another who has never had a certain feeling, in what the quality or worth of it consists. One must have musical ears to know the value of a symphony; one must have been in love oneself to understand a lover's state of mind" (James, p. 371).

Indeed, mystical experience is ineffable because it is an affair not of the head but of the heart; and from time immemorial lovers remind us that the things of the heart defy all expression. The mystics love to quote those words of the Song of Songs:

> I slept, but my heart was awake
>
> Song of Songs 5:1

Here the mystics, interpreting these words quite differently from the exegetes, declare that the mind is asleep, the mind is silent, reason and imagination and sense are quietly lulled to rest; but the heart is alert and awake. What conceptual language could express such loving awareness?

It was precisely because of the ineffability of the experience that the medievals welcomed the negative theology of Dionysius, with its vocabulary of darkness, nothingness, emptiness and unknowing. Taken in the ordinary sense these words are negative and world denying, but when applied to the deeper states of awareness they are profoundly meaningful.

*

William James's second characteristic is a *noetic quality*. By this he means that mystical experiences are not simply blind inner movements but have a definite cognitive content. "They are states of insight and depths of truth unplumbed by the discursive intellect. They are illuminations, revelations, full of significance and importance, all inarticulate though they remain; and as a rule they carry with them a curious sense of authority for aftertime" (James, p.371).

In other words mystical experience gives real knowledge. yet, as I have pointed out, the cognitive content of mystical knowledge is non-conceptual and belongs to a different state of consciousness from that which we ordinarily enjoy. For this reason the greatest caution must be taken when one attempts to interpret mystical experience in conceptual language. Here great mystics have had pitiable mistakes. Let me quote from *The Cloud of Unknowing* a very powerful illumination which, the author claims, cannot be interpreted at all. The mystic is quietly and silent in the cloud of unknowing and then:

> Then perhaps he may touch you with a ray of his divine light which will pierce the cloud of unknowing between you and him. He will let you glimpse something of the ineffable secrets of his divine wisdom and your affection will seem on fire with his love. I am at a loss to say more, for the experience is beyond words. Even if I were able to say more I would not now. For I dare not try to describe God's grace with my crude and awkward tongue. In a word, even if I dared I would not.
>
> Johnston (1), ch. 26

Here we are back to the ineffability of mysticism. Yes, it is cognitive; it is true knowledge; but it cannot be adequately formulated in words.

*

The third characteristic of William James is *transiency*. "Mystical states cannot be sustained for long. Except in rare instances, half an hour or at most an hour or two seems to be the limit beyond which they fade into the light of common day" (James, p. 372).

This is only partly true. The peak experiences are transient; but underneath is a permanent state, a deep peace which is compatible with joy or suffering, a sense of presence or a sense of absence, dryness or longing, boredom or monotony. All this is most undramatic; but it is truly mystical; it is the work in those deeper layers of consciousness. Indeed, it is the ground and basis of the transient, ecstatic moments.

For mystical experience extends over a whole life. As the author of *The Cloud* says, it goes to bed with you at night and it gets up with you in the morning. It is a permanent awareness which can exist in a very busy and active life.

*

The fourth characteristic is *passivity* – "the mystic feels as if his own will were in abeyance, and indeed sometimes as if he were grasped and held by a superior power" (James, p. 372).

This again is true in that the mystics will say that they are moved by a power which is deeper than themselves. And yet this word "passivity" must be used with the greatest caution. For while it is true that one layer of consciousness is passive and empty and dark, it is also true that a very powerful activity is going on at a deeper layer of the psyche. This is an activity which may continue for nights and days without fatigue to mind or body.

I consider the active dimension of mysticism very important and am wary of the word "passive". This is because there have been in all religious traditions schools of so-called quietism, and their voice can still be heard today: "Be absolutely still! Empty your mind! Erase all thoughts from your consciousness! Blot out everything! Stop thinking! And this is mysticism."

But this is not mysticism, oriental or occidental. This is nonsense.

III

The mystics of the Dionysian tradition speak frequently about the "secrecy" of mysticism – mystical knowledge is "hidden" in the depths of one's being. This is quite understandable in view of the fact that it belongs to a layer of consciousness which is hidden from, and inaccessible to, the intellect and the sensible

faculties. "Ordinarily," writes St John of the Cross, "this contemplation *which is secret and hidden from the very one who
receives it*, imparts to the soul an inclination to remain alone
and in quietude" (*Dark Night*, 1:9,6).

Secret from the one who receives it! How strange and how
different from the popular conception of the mystical trip! So
often mysticism is associated with lights and bells and incence
and ecstasy; whereas ecstasy, pertaining as it does to the realm
of sense, is a sign of superficiality. The deepest mysticism is more
like the still small voice which spoke to Elijah. Yes, mysticism is
secret from the person who receives it. And it is interesting to
reflect that in Buddhism also the most enlightened person is
often the one who does not know that he is enlightened: his
enlightenment is hidden even from himself.

Now this point is very important and very practical. Not
infrequently one meets people who have spent years in dryness,
in inner suffering, in darkness. Their meditation is sleepy and
uncomfortable and seems like a waste of time: they think they
are doing nothing. But the tiny flame of love is burning quietly
in the depths of their being; the loving knowledge is there in
secret; their experience is profoundly mystical. This will seem
less strange if we reflect that human love is often just the same.
It grows secretly at night when no one is watching like the seed
scattered upon the ground. Then one morning we wake up –
and there it is! Quite often it is only in moments of separation
and death that we advert to the depth of our own love. Or
again human love may at first be filled with rapturous joy; but
the lean and fallow years have to come.

And in the same way mystical experience may at first be
delightful and filled with froth and joy; but eventually the call
comes to go deeper and (wonder of wonders!) this going deeper
in all the great mystical traditions is *a passage to the ordinary*.
Remember how Zen keeps speaking of "your ordinary everyday
mind". No longer the first exciting silence of discovery but an
almost boring silence of penetration and familiarity, a "becoming at home" as the author of *The Cloud* would say. And I
wonder if it does not take yet another enlightenment from the
Spirit to recognize this seemingly humdrum experience as a real

God-experience and to be faithful to the time of the fallow ground (which may mean years of perseverance) until the right time, the *kairos*, arrives.

But instead of patiently waiting, some modern people join in the frenetic search for new experiences, for oriental meditation of all kinds, for the soul-stirring illumination that will revolutionize their lives. If they only knew that they are leaving the fruit to go back to the rind! No one in their right mind would do this; but the problem is that *the fruit is not recognized as fruit*: it is secret: it is hidden. That is why discernment is so important; that is why it is so necessary that contemplatives should meet someone who can understand their experience or, at least, read some book with which they can resonate. Otherwise they may not know what is happening in their lives and may become discouraged.

But if they persevere, they come to love the darkness and the dryness; they come to see its beauty; or they come to recognize that the darkness is no longer dark and the dryness is no longer dry. They come to see that mystical knowledge is, so to speak, an acquired taste. At first one does not like it at all; one recoils from a bitterness which is so distasteful to the palate. Yet in time it becomes so sweet and delicious that one would not exchange it for all the world. Again St John of the Cross: "If in the beginning the soul does not experience this spiritual savour and delight, but dryness and distaste, it is because of the novelty involved in this exchange. Since its palate is accustomed to these other sensory tastes, the soul still sets its eyes on them. And since, also, its spiritual palate is neither purged nor accommodated for so subtle a taste, it is unable to experience the spiritual savour and good until gradually prepared . . ." (*Dark Night*, 1:9,4).

In short, mysticism opens up a new layer of psychic life which is bitter and unpleasant because of its unfamiliarity. But when the eye of love becomes accustomed to the dark, it perceives that the darkness is light and the void is plenitude.

IV

Finally, let me say that many of those endowed with profound mystical knowledge are very active people: the inner light has driven them into the mighty cities and the maelstrom of a whirling world. In such cases "the obscure sense of presence" of which the mystics speak may become dynamic. I become conscious not only of the Spirit *present in me* but of the Spirit *working in me*, not only of Christ being in me but of Christ dynamically alive in me and driving me to union with his members and with the cosmos.

Such active people, it is true, need periods of silence and of solitude; but it is also true that they carry around in their hearts a great solitude which is also a great love – and this solitude continues in the midst of activity. Indeed, it is a solitude which is deepened by the hurt, the criticism, the disappointment, the betrayal, the human friction, the humiliation and the ordinary pain of living. Just as the beating with the stick or *kyosaku* deepens the Zen experience, so the ordinary contradictions of life (with much less pomp and ritual and solemnity) deepen contemplative experience. Indeed, without this kind of suffering it is difficult to see how one can die to self in order to live to one who rose from the dead. Frequently it is through the suffering of action that the inner eye is opened and we truly come to see.

PART II

MYSTICISM
AND THEOLOGY

4

Mystical Theology

I

From what has been said it will be clear that there is a distinction between mysticism and mystical theology. Mysticism is the experience: mystical theology is reflection on this experience.[1] The medievals did not make this distinction clearly, as can be seen from my earlier quotations in which they identify mystical theology with mystical experience and call contemplation mystical theology. But the distinction is completely necessary today if we are to build up a theology that will speak to contemporary men and women and promote dialogue between the world's great religions at the level of mysticism.

I am aware that some people will maintain that only experience matters, and that mystical theology with its theory and words and concepts is a useless accretion. While I would agree that mystical experience is the basic thing, that it is ineffable and that all efforts to formulate it are totally inadequate, I cannot accept the anti-intellectualism which would reject all reflection. No. We need to interpret mystical experience and to find its meaning. We need to distinguish the authentic from the inauthentic. Then there is the practical need to guide people, to protect them from mistakes, from illness, from illusion – to help them understand what is happening in their lives and save them from unnecessary suffering. Besides, must we not learn all we

[1] Theology was traditionally defined as "the science of God". More recently, however, Bernard Lonergan defines it as "reflection on religion". Following this I understand mystical theology as reflection on mystical experience. See Lonergan (I), p. 267.

can, even conceptually, about the action of the divine in the human?

In the East we find something akin to mystical theology in the great religious philosophers and thinkers like Sankara and Nagarjuna. We also find numerous commentaries on Buddhist sutras and Hindu scriptures – for every religion has its holy books which are the source of its mysticism. But the practical aspects are incarnate in the living master or teacher. Here is a man who guides and who has the practical knowledge to do so. He knows what he wants; he knows the nature of the experience towards which he leads; he is quick to detect error. The Oriental master has a fund of conceptual knowledge culled from his own enlightenment, from the enlightenment of others and from his assiduous reading of his own scriptures.

In the West also a great deal of practical knowledge was handed down orally, particularly in the great religious orders. At the basis of this is the Bible, particularly the Gospel, St Paul and the Psalms. But a science of mystical theology also evolved, a science which still exists but is in drastic need of updating. For every age must have its own mystical theology; and we need something new in view of the peculiar problems which confront us today. As Bernard Lonergan says in a slightly different context; "There are real problems of communication in the twentieth century, and they are not solved by preaching to ancient Antioch, Corinth or Rome" (Lonergan (1), p. 140); and in the same way there are real problems of mysticism in the twentieth century and we will not solve difficulties about the drug culture and Oriental mysticism just by quoting Augustine and St John of the Cross. Assuredly the works of these mystics are of inestimable value, and I quote them abundantly; but we must advance, and we must do for our generation what they did for theirs, remembering that we are children of an age which has made outstanding advances in psychology, neuro-physiology, brain research and all aspects of inner space – to say nothing of biblical research, archaeology and ancient history.

If we wish to construct a modern mystical theology, however, there will have to be a much greater division of labour than in the past. Some people will reflect on mysticism from the aspects of psychology and medicine while others, working and collaborating with them, will devote themselves to the strictly religious aspects. It is about these latter aspects that I myself will speak.

II

If mystical theology is a science it must have data. Such data will be found in the experience of mystics living and dead, in the experience of mystics past and present, in the experience of mystics East and West. All the great religions already have their mystical theology, even though they may not use this term. They reflect on the seers and prophets of the *Upanishads* or upon the experience of great Buddhist mystics like the Zen masters Dogen and Hakuin. Even further there is reflection (and this is basic) on the experience of the Buddha himself when he found enlightenment sitting cross-legged beneath the Bodhi tree at Bodh Gaya. As everyone knows, Buddhism aims at nothing less than a repetition of this enlightenment of the Buddha: if I am a Buddhist, my aim is to re-enact within myself the experience of Sakyamuni and to become a Buddha.

Coming to a specifically Christian mystic theology, we must again ask about the data and the sources. Many books written on this subject have expounded the doctrine of the Rhineland mystics, the Spanish Carmelites, the medieval English mystics, the Fathers of the Church – and we have the diaries of holy people and biographies of saints. Undoubtedly all this is of great value; but I would like to point out that the source of all Christian mysticism is – and must be – the Bible, and in particular the Gospel. This is because the Christian mystical tradition states clearly that the aim of the Christian life is to become "another Christ" (*Christianus alter Christus*) and in the process of becoming another Christ the Gospel is obviously the central inspiration. If, then, there is to be an updating of Christian mystical theology the first step is a return to the Gospel.

In saying this, however, I am immediately faced with a formidable objection. There are scholars who hold that the Bible contains no mysticism whatever: that mysticism is basically an

oriental and non-Christian trend. This way of thinking stems
from their understanding of the word mysticism (remembering
I spoke of fifty or a hundred different definitions) which they
associate with a monism or pantheism that is incompatible with
belief in a personal God. At the risk of making a brief digression
I would like to consider their viewpoint, simply selecting one
scholar who seems to be representative.

*

The well-known scholar Friedrich Heiler distinguishes between
prophetic or biblical religion and mysticism. This latter he
defines as: "that form of intercourse with God in which the
world and self are absolutely denied, in which human personality is dissolved, disappears and is absorbed in the infinite unity
of the Godhead" (Heiler, p. 136). Obviously if the world and
self are denied, and human personality is dissolved, there is not
much mysticism in the Bible or in any theistic religion which
speaks of a relationship between man and God. But how valid
is this definition?

No doubt Heiler understands mysticism in this way because
of the phenomenon of "undifferentiated consciousness" which
is so central to oriental thinking and is found also in many
Western mystics. This is the consciousness of one who transcends subject and object to enter into a state of pure oneness.
Bede Griffiths describes it well:

> There is an experience of being in pure consciousness which
> gives lasting peace to the soul. It is an experience of the
> Ground or Depth of being in the Centre of the soul, an
> awareness of the mystery of being beyond sense and
> thought, which gives a sense of fulfilment, of finality, of
> absolute truth. . . . It is an experience of the undifferentiated
> ground of being, the abyss of being beyond thought, the
> One without a second.
>
> (Griffiths (2), p. 137)

Bede Griffiths is writing from the Indian scene but, as I have
said, a similar form of pure consciousness is found in some
Western mystics, and something analogous exists through East

Asian culture where one hears of the non-self or no-mind condition called in Japanese *muga* or *mushin*. This state of consciousness is found in an intense form in the sudden illumination
or *satori* of Zen. But I believe that it admits of degrees and is
found in a simpler form in the Sino-Japanese arts such as the
flower arrangement, archery and the tea ceremony. Here one
identifies with the object (I *become* the flower or the bow) and
one loses self. The experts tell us, however, that to attain to this
state of consciousness takes years of discipline and training.[2]

Confronted with this consciousness in its various forms, Western philosophers (who feel happier when they can put labels on
things and apparently control them) have freely used words like
pantheism and monism, applying Hellenistic words to Oriental
experiences. And a few scholars have made this oneness the
kernel of all mysticism and the supreme achievement of the
human mind.

But surely it is gratuitous to limit mysticism to this kind of
thing. And surely it is equally gratuitous to decide that this is
the "highest" or supreme experience. It is true, of course, that
all mysticism leads to oneness or unity; but there is a union of
love in which far from losing my personality I become my true
self, hear myself called by name and cry out: "Abba, Father!"
This is the experience in which I become the other while remaining myself. Or, more correctly, I become the other and become
myself. Paradoxical, you will say. Yes. Mysticism is full of
paradox.

And one more important point. This undifferentiated consciousness can only be labelled pantheism or monism if the
subject passes from the psychological inner experience to the
outer world, affirming that in the objective order the self and
the world do not exist. And I am not at all convinced that many
mystics have done this. They were more subtle than that – and
scholars are still divided in their interpretation of the most
radical monists like Sankara.

As for the Western mystics, they wrestled with this problem,

[2] This consciousness is frequently called the *non-discriminating consciousness* because no distinction is made between subject and object and there
is no reasoning or thinking or conceptualization in the mind.

for they experienced both the unity of all things and the father-hood of God. But they were greatly handicapped by the Hellenistic psychology in which they were educated. This psychology speaks of intellect and will, or of memory, understanding and will – it speaks of the senses and the spiritual faculties. With such a psychology it is not easy to reconcile the unity and diversity of being.

In a modern psychology, however, which speaks of states of consciousness the problem is more easily solved. For here we can recognize a consciousness which sees unity (and such a consciousness undoubtedly exists) and a consciousness which sees diversity. These states of consciousness can exist at different times in the same person. Or (and this is significant) they can exist concomitantly in the same person in such wise that one sees unity and diversity simultaneously. I have written about this in *Silent Music* and need not repeat myself here (Johnston (3), ch. 7).

This has been something of a digression; but I think it was necessary because the notion that mysticism is "pantheistic" or "monistic" and in consequence non-biblical is widespread. Let me now return to the Bible.

*

First of all there, is prophetic experience. The scripture scholar John L. McKenzie, after discussing the various theories about the nature of prophecy, comes to the conclusion that "the prophetical experience is . . . a mystical immediate experience of the reality and presence of God". Indeed, he compares it with that of the great Spanish mystics:

> *The only satisfactory parallel to the prophetic experience is the phenomena of mysticism* as described by writers like Teresa of Avila, John of the Cross and others. They affirm that the immediate experience of God is ineffable; like the prophets, they must employ imagery and symbolism to describe it, with explicit warnings that these are used. They describe it as a transforming experience which moves one to speech and action beyond one's expected capacities. It

grants them profound insight not only into divine reality but into the human scene. Thus the prophetic experience is such a mystical immediate experience of the reality and presence of God.

(McKenzie, p. 697)[3]

If we accept this thesis we can see the most profound mysticism in that chapter of Exodus where Moses hears his name called: "Moses, Moses!" and is overwhelmed by the presence of God and the sense of the holy. "Do not come near; put off your shoes from your feet, for the place on which you are standing is holy ground" (Exodus 3:5). Or again in Jeremiah: "Before I formed you in the womb I knew you" (Jeremiah 1:5). Here also the prophet hears the inner voice and is liberated from fear (and this, be it noted, is a common characteristic of mystical experience): "Be not afraid of them, for I am with you to deliver you, says the Lord" (Jeremiah 1:8).

In these experiences we find union with God, the sense of being loved, of being chosen, of being sent; and we also find a profound sense of personal uniqueness and unworthiness. I am a person loved by God, but yet I am far distant from him, unworthy to stand in his presence. "And Moses hid his face, for he was afraid to look at God" (Exodus 3:6).

[3] Some theologians, notably, A. Ritschl, N. Söderblom, E. Brunner, and K. Kraemer, distinguish between Oriental mystical religion and biblical prophetic religion, claiming that these two types are mutually exclusive and irreconcilable. In an excellent article in *Concilium* (123, 1977) Peter Nemeshegyi shows that these two types are not incompatible but complementary. I myself maintain that mysticism, as I have understood it, is the core and climax of all religious experience and that it expresses itself sometimes in a life of solitude and at other times in a prophetic life of powerful activity. Karl Rahner writes: "the prophetic element can (it does not have to) be connected with mystical experience" (*Encyclopedia of Theology*, edited by Karl Rahner, Burns and Oates, London 1975, p. 1010). St John of the Cross takes it for granted that the great prophets had mystical experience and constantly appeals to their example.

III

Keeping in mind that mysticism is the supraconceptual wisdom that comes from love, we can find such experience throughout the pages of the New Testament. In particular we find it in the great contemplative prayer taught by Jesus: "Our Father."

"Mysticism in the Lord's prayer?" you will say. "How simple can you get?" Yes. But the greatest Christian mystics have written commentaries precisely on the "Our Father". Origen, Cyprian, Teresa of Avila have found in its simple phrases treasures of mystical experience.[4] Thérèsa of Lisieux, great contemplative that she was, sat quietly in the chapel reciting the "Our Father", her heart sometimes filled with dryness and inner suffering. Yes. It is all very simple; but remember I said that mysticism is a journey towards the ordinary; remember that I quoted Zen about your ordinary everyday mind. Christian mysticism reaches its peak when, as another Christ in utter simplicity and trust, I allow the words of Jesus to well up from the depth of my being and cry out: "Abba, Father!"

And there is mysticism in the Sermon on the Mount. This is the mysticism of the present moment – a moment that is lived without anxiety about the future or fear about the past, without preoccupation about what I shall eat or drink. My Heavenly Father knows what I need before I ask. The Sermon on the Mount has (and very justly I believe) been compared to Zen in that it describes the undifferentiated consciousness of one who lives in the here-and-now with joy and without care: "Therefore do not be anxious about tomorrow . . ." (Matthew 6:34).

One could go on to speak about the parables and the various aphorisms or *logia* of the Gospel of St. Matthew – for these indeed strike a chord in the Buddhist heart. Or one could speak about the opening of the eyes of the blind (what a great enlightenment!) and how the inner eyes came to see the glory of God:

---

[4] Many of the Church fathers commented on the "Our Father": Tertullian: *De Oratione*; Cyprian: *De Dominica Oratione*; Origen: *Perieuches*; Gregory of Nyssa: *Five Homilies on The Our Father*; Ambrose: *De Sacrementis*, lib v; Peter Chrysologus, *Sermones* 67–72.

"But blessed are your eyes, for they see . . ." (Matthew 13:16). But let me say a word about *Jesus the mystic*.

Again, if mysticism is the wisdom which comes from divine love, can we not see Jesus as the mystic *par excellence*? Because love for his Father was the dominating passion of his life: "Abba, Father!" And the whole Gospel relates the drama of how Jesus loved the Father, how he was loved by the Father and how he offered himself for the world, praying for his disciples "that the love with which thou has loved me may be in them, and I in them" (John 17:26).

Jesus, we can presume, being truly human, grew in the knowledge of his divine sonship and in the realization of who he was. And one of his great mystical experiences takes place at the time of his baptism:

And when he came up out of the waters, immediately he saw the heavens opened and the Spirit descending upon him like a dove; and a voice from heaven: "Thou art my beloved Son; with thee I am well pleased".

(Mark 1:10, 11)

Mark observes that *Jesus saw*. It was the inner eye, the eye of love that saw; and Jesus realized in the Spirit that he was the Son of the Father.

We know little of what happened when Jesus went alone into the mountains to pray; but the Gospel story leads me to believe that those nights were spent in loving communion with the Father in the Spirit and in intercession for the world. Perhaps his prayer was sometimes like that of Gethsemane and at other times like that of Mount Tabor; but in either case it was dominated by love for his Father, a love which reaches a climax in those mystical chapters of the Fourth Gospel where Jesus speaks of the indwelling of the Son in the Father: Jesus is dwelling in his disciples and his disciples dwell in him and all are dwelling in God and God is dwelling in all. These are remarkable chapters. If we read them again and again we may find in ourselves that consciousness which is at the same time differentiated and undifferentiated, the consciousness which grasps unity and diversity at the same time. For Jesus prays "that they may be one; even as thou, Father, art in me, and I in thee, that they also may be in us" (John 17:21). They are to be one, perfectly one, as Jesus is one with the Father. And yet they are not one, for the Father and the Son are different persons. I myself believe that this experience of unity in diversity and of diversity in unity is the core of the Christian mystical experience. And it can only be attained through love.

And so the life of Jesus is the working out of this relationship with the Father at whose command he lays down his life. It is a loving relationship which passes through its final stage in a dark night of the soul when Jesus cries out: "My God, my God, why hast thou forsaken me?" (Matthew 27:46). After this comes the resurrection and the sending of the Spirit.

IV

The conclusion, then, is that in the updating and modernizing of mystical theology the first step is a return to the Scriptures and, in particular, to the Gospel. Here we will find the mystical experience and the mystical teaching of Jesus of Nazareth. On this the whole structure of Christian mysticism is built. This was the food which nourished the Christian mystics; this was the fountain from which they drank. Mystics like St John of the Cross read and reread and reread the Scriptures until Christ began to live his life in them.

For, as I have already indicated, Christian mysticism is nothing else than the process of becoming Christ – of living with him, of dying with him, of rising with him. Or of allowing him to live in us, to die in us, to rise in us. Jesus of Nazareth, who lived and died in that little colony of the Roman Empire called Palestine, wishes to relive his life in us – in Japan, in America, in India, in Europe, in Africa – in another time and another culture. For the mystics this was not just theory. They knew and deeply experienced that their lives were gradually dominated by the power of the resurrection (if I may borrow Paul's phrase) and that they were being transformed into Christ. Augustine in a different context will say that Peter baptizes but, in fact, it is Christ who baptizes: he is the principal agent in all we do. Others will say that Christ prays to the Father in me, suffers in me, dies in me – he sees through my eyes, listens through my ears, loves through my heart, blesses through my hands. "It is no longer I who live but Christ who lives in me" (Galatians 2:20). Now the eye of love is no longer my eye but the eye of Christ who sees through my eyes and looks with compassion on the world.

Obviously, a mystical theology based on the Bible will be specifically Christian. As such, it will be the basis for dialogue with the mysticism of non-Christian religions. For, as I have already pointed out, Buddhism has its mystical theology based on the experience of the Buddha and on the Buddhist scriptures – based on the experience of becoming a Buddha. When Jesus and the Buddha meet in their disciples, real mystical dialogue will have begun.

At the same time, I believe it is also possible to sketch the beginnings of a mystical theology which will be common to both Christianity and Buddhism. About this I will speak later in this book.

5

Mysticism in Theology

I

I have spoken about mystical theology. But theology is broader than just mystical theology; and in this chapter I would like to discuss the role of mysticism in the vast and complex discipline which we call theology today. My contention will be that mystical experience is, and has to be, the very core of authentic theology. So it was in antiquity when theology was, in the wise words of Anselm of Canterbury, "faith searching for understanding" (*fides quaerens intellectum*). The great theologians of primitive Christianity (that is to say, those who built Western civilization and whose works are vibrantly alive today) were men of faith, living faith, mystical faith. While their outer eyes pored over tomes and manuscripts and sacred books, their inner eye "beheld his glory, glory as of the only Son from the Father" (John 1:14). In other words they were deeply enlightened people; and they tried to express – inadequately and imperfectly as they well knew – the wisdom they perceived with the inner eye. They knew, of course, that this vision could never be satisfactorily expressed in words; yet they did their best. As for Thomas, that wise and enlightened man, he finally protested that all his writings were as straw compared with the vision he perceived with the eye of love.

II

Let me start with St Paul. His mystical experience began on the road to Damascus when he fell in love with the Risen Jesus: "Saul, Saul, why do you persecute me?" (Acts of the Apostles 9:4). Prior to this Saul had held the garments of the young men who stoned Stephen. He had seen that face which was like the face of an angel; he had heard that voice which cried: "Lord, do not hold this sin against them" (Acts of the Apostles 7:60). Divine love, no doubt, was working in his unconscious before that flash of light which brought about the epoch-making conversion on the road to Damascus. This is the *metanoia*; this is the great turning-point; this is the death and resurrection – when Saul becomes Paul. Later he is to look back on this experience and see what an earth-shaking revolution took place in his life. His whole value system changed. Whereas he had been proud to be a Pharisee, a Hebrew of the Hebrews, a meticulous observer of the law, a persecutor of the Church, now all this is loss. "Indeed I count everything as loss because of the surpassing worth of knowing Christ Jesus my Lord" (Philippians 3:8). For Paul to know Christ is to love him, to be united with him – to be united with him not in a static but a dynamic way: "That I may know him and the power of his resurrection, and may share his suffering, becoming like him in his death, that if possible I may attain the resurrection from the dead" (Philippians 3:10).

And so Paul's mysticism is one of action. There is no evidence that he spent long hours on his knees and I cannot imagine him sitting in the lotus – though he doubtless had lengthy periods of silence, of inner silence, in his journeys by sea and land as well as in the quiet of a prison cell. But Paul's union with Christ is dynamic in such wise that he suffers with Christ and dies with him. All through his letters the same idea recurs: with Christ I am nailed to the Cross. The whole drama of the life of Christ is not only a historical event, it is also an event which is taking place in Paul. "It is no longer I who live, but Christ who lives in me" (Galatians 2:20). Indeed, the words "in Christ" appear one hundred and sixty-four times in the Pauline writings. They are no mere metaphor but describe a real experience: the Church Fathers compare Paul's, and our, immersion in Christ to the drop of water which falls into the wine or the glowing iron or coal which becomes part of the fire. But I believe that Pauline mysticism reaches its zenith when the great apostle realizes that he is a son and calls out "Abba, Father!"

The point I wish to make here, however, is that while Paul heard about Christ and "received" the good news from apostles and eye-witnesses, he also met Christ, he was involved with Christ, he lived the good news in his busy life. And this shines through his theology: it is a theology which wells up from the depths of his powerful, inner experience. He writes about original sin as one who experiences original sin; he writes about redemption as one who experiences redemption; he writes about the death and resurrection of Jesus as one who experiences the death and resurrection of Jesus within himself; he writes about the Spirit as one who has received the Spirit; he calls God Father, knowing that the Spirit of Jesus within is calling out: "Abba, Father!"; he speaks of love of Jesus as one who experiences the love of Jesus. In short, the theology of Paul is based not only on a historical event in the past but also on a living mystical experience in the present. This is what I mean when I say that mystical experience is the core of authentic theology.

III

Now as centuries pass new problems arise within Western Christianity, and great theologians appear to solve them. Their task is to explain the Gospel in the language of their times and in the new culture which is being formed. And so a new theological vocabulary is forged and fresh insights are obtained. For the first time theologians use Hellenistic words like *Trinity, essence, nature, person*. These words are not found in the New Testament but they are necessary, even indispensable, in the new age. The theologians who use them know very well, like Paul, that they are dealing with mystery, they are trying to express the inexpressible, they are speaking about a reality which transcends formulations of any kind. But the Gospel has to be restated; a new theology has to be formed.

The question I wish to ask here, however, is "How did the great theologians of antiquity come to elaborate the new theology? Where did they get their knowledge? Whence came the inspiration and wisdom of Clement and Irenaeus and Gregory and Athanasius and Augustine? Did they just learn their theology from books?

Well, of course they studied. They read and reread the Bible, they knew the tradition of their forebears, they absorbed the culture of their times and studied the works of their adversaries. They were men of great learning. But they were also mystics and saints. And the secret of their great theological achievement was not their learning but their contemplation; not their outer eye but their inner eye. Through their mystical experience, through their contemplative reading of the Bible, through the inner revelation which we call grace (does not Augustine speak of "the master within", the *magister internus*?) they came to meet the Risen Jesus in a personal way just like Paul. They, too, travelled their road to Damascus; they, too, were united with Christ; they, too, died and rose. As I said about Paul so I can say about them – if they wrote about sin and redemption this was because they experienced these things in their lives. If they wrote about the love of God it was because they experienced the love of God as a living reality. Their theology reflected their faith, the living faith, the mystical faith that burned in their hearts – out of the fullness of their hearts they spoke and wrote.

But they wrote and spoke for contemporary people. It is indeed a characteristic of great religious personalities that they reflect the conflicts and sufferings, the joys and the anguish of the world in which they live. That world vibrates within them; they breathe its air; they feel its frustrations; they carry its cross. In our own times this has been true, I believe, of Mahatma Gandhi and Teilhard de Chardin and Thomas Merton. It was also eminently true of Augustine and Gregory and Bernard and Thomas. Their enlightenment was not just biblical; it was the Gospel experience lived out and made incarnate in the new culture and the new world. Consequently it was profoundly relevant for the men and women of their day.

Their theology, I have said, welled up from their mystical experience. But (and this is very significant) it also led to mystical experience. In this sense it can be called a spirituality. For the Fathers of the Church and the early Christian writers had no mystical theology apart from their ordinary theological writings: they had no separate discipline to which they could attach the label "spirituality". Their theological treatises, even when they were apologetic in nature, were calculated to lead the reader to a relishing of the great mysteries of faith. Take, for example, the doctrine of the Trinity. Later generations, alas, looked on this as an attempt to reconcile the seemingly contradictory teaching of three persons in one nature. Not so Augustine and Thomas. For them the Trinity is the key contemplative experience in the Christian life: it is the experience I have when, divested of self and clothed with Christ, I offer myself to the Father in the Spirit for the salvation of the world. These words may sound complicated but the experience itself is simple: God is my Father, I am his son: the Spirit dwells in me, and I cry out: "Abba, Father!" In this experience I have a consciousness which is at once undifferentiated and differentiated. It is undifferentiated in that there is a total unity, identification with Jesus and through Jesus with the Father; and, on the other hand, it is differentiated in that I am not Jesus and Jesus is not the Father. The experience of the Trinity was very real for Thomas (as it has been very real for all the Christian mystics) but a sad situation was created some centuries after his death when unenlightened scholastics repeated his Trinitarian words without enjoying his Trinitarian mysticism. They grasped the conceptualization but not the enlightenment which inspired it.

For the great temptation of theology has always been to divorce itself from mystical experience and to wander off into irrelevant speculation. That is why we find writers like Thomas à Kempis somewhat lugubriously warning ambitious clerics that it is better to have compunction than to know its definition, and asking what is the value of speculation about the Trinity if one is not pleasing to the Trinity. This was a very real problem in the Middle Ages; and it a very real problem today. Particularly so, since in the last few centuries theology has been greatly preoccupied with controversial issues, has become extremely academic and has largely divorced itself from spirituality. Contemplative experience has been relegated to the pious writers of pious books while theology proper has addressed itself to more academic questions. This is scarcely a healthy situation; for a theology which is divorced from the inner experience of the theologian is arid and carries no conviction.[1]

IV

And now at the end of the twentieth century we again find ourselves at a great crossroads in the history of humankind. Such an age demands a new theology, a re-statement of the Gospel message, and answer to the peculiar problems that confront us. Yet the construction of such a theology is an extremely difficult and delicate task because we are aware that the old culture is dying but has not yet died and the new culture is coming to birth but has not yet been born. Caught in the middle and not knowing what will come next we wonder where to turn. For my purposes here, however, it is enough to recall two aspects of this new culture. First of all it will be, and already is characterized by what Bernard Lonergan called "the shift to interiority". That is to say, the whole emphasis is, and will be, on the inner world, the world of the mind, the human consciousness. Secondly, the new culture will certainly be a world culture profoundly influenced by all the great religions: Hinduism, Islam, Buddhism, Judaism as well as Christianity. In such a situation one of the great challenges to a new Christian theology will be mysticism, particularly Oriental mysticism. How to meet this challenge?

From all that has been said in this chapter one might draw the conclusion that the primary need is for Christian theologians

[1] Let me add that Buddhism has precisely the same problem. The scholars are not always enlightened.

who are also mystics. It might be said that now, if ever, we need men of the stature of Paul and Augustine – we need men and women who will speak not only from a wealth of sound scholarship but also from a wealth of personal experience. It might be said that we need theologians who, while vibrating in unison with the modern world, have met Christ on the road to Damascus – only such people, it might be said, can build the new theology, speak to the modern world, speak to the Orient.

All this is very true and very fine. Yet I will refrain from drawing any conclusions of this nature. The reason is that from the time of Thomas à Kempis better men than I have been attempting to convert the theologians – and they have been conspicuously unsuccessful. The theologians remain unregenerate. Consequently I will confine myself to a more practical suggestion.

Is it not possible to elaborate a theological method which would put greater emphasis on *reflection on mystical experience*? Over the past two or three centuries, as I mentioned in the previous chapter, such reflection was relegated to a discipline of somewhat minor importance called *mystical theology* or *spiritual theology*; and while it is certainly useful to have such a separate discipline to treat of the practical problems of spiritual direction, the actual mystical experience should, it seems to me, occupy a more central position in the overall theological picture. In particular the mystical experience of the Trinity should be a central theme for theological reflection – for the doctrine of the Trinity comes out of the mystical experience of Jesus himself and looms large in the inner life of Paul and all the great Christian mystics. As I have said, the word "Trinity" was not always used but the experience was always there.

Now I see the possibility of placing mystical experience in such an honoured position within the *method* elaborated by Bernard Lonergan. Here importance is given to research, interpretations of texts, history, doctrines; but when Lonergan comes to the foundation of theology he speaks of *reflection on conversion*:[2]

This conversion has a threefold nature: intellectual, ethical and religious. But here I need only mention religious conversion which is compared to the experience of a man falling in love with a woman or a woman falling in love with a man. The converted person is totally in love – "in love without limits or qualifications or conditions or reservations" (Lonergan (I), p. 106). Here is how Lonergan speaks of religious conversion:

> Religious conversion is being grasped by ultimate concern. It is other-worldly falling in love. It is total and permanent self-surrender without conditions, qualifications, reservations. But it is such a surrender, not as an act, but as a dynamic state that is prior to and principle of subsequent acts. It is revealed in retrospect as an under-tow of existential consciousness, as a fated acceptance of a vocation to holiness, as perhaps an increasing simplicity and passivity in prayer. It is interpreted differently in the context of different religious traditions. For Christians it is God's love flooding our hearts through the Holy Spirit given to us. It is the gift of grace. . . .
>
> (Lonergan (1), p. 241)

Now it can easily be seen that what Bernard Lonergan means by religious conversion and what I mean by mystical experience are very similar. There are, however, differences because while conversion involves a repudiation of the past or of some elements of the past, I do not see that mystical experience necessarily does so. But I do think that reflection on mystical experience together with reflection on conversion could be a foundation and basis of a theology of the future.

If this were so, pride of place would be given to the mystical experience of Jesus himself which, as I have repeatedly said, was primarily Trinitarian. Christianity indeed stems from the mystical experience or self-realization of Jesus, a self-realization

---

[2] "As conversion is basic to Christian living, so an objectification of conversion provides theology with its foundations" (Lonergan (1), p. 130).

which reaches a climax in his resurrection from the dead. That is to say, Jesus came to realize who he was. He saw that he was truly Son, the only-begotten Son, and that filled with the Spirit he could in a literal sense call God his Father and cry out: "Abba, Father!" He realized that all things had been delivered to him by his Father and that "no one knows the Son except the Father, and no one knows the Father except the Son and any one to whom the Son chooses to reveal him" (Matthew 11:27). From the experience of his divine sonship came his vocation to reveal the love of the Father and to pray that "the love with which thou hast loved me may be in them, and I in them" (John 17:26). That is, that the Spirit of love who was in him might be in them.

After the experience of Jesus we must reflect on that of Paul (again a Trinitarian experience), of the Fathers of the Church and of the whole Christian community. I believe we will again and again find the same Trinitarian experience even in the hearts of the simple people who dare to say: "Our Father . . ."

Such a theology with its foundation in the mystical experience of Jesus and the Christian community is eminently suited to enter into dialogue with a modern world moving rapidly into the realm of interiority as well as with the great mystical religions of the East. For although Buddhists do not use my terminology, I believe that their whole philosophical reflection is founded on a consideration of the enlightenment of the Buddha, enlightenment attained beneath the Bodhi tree in Bodh Gaya and repeated in the lives of Buddhist patriarchs through the ages to the present day. A Christian theology which reflects on the mystical experience of Jesus and his disciples and the Christian community will be eminently suited to enter into dialogue with contemporary Buddhism.

6

Mysticism in Religion

I

I have spoken about a specifically Christian theology; and no doubt my readers, or some of them, are growing restless and asking: "But what about Islam and Hinduism and Buddhism and Judaism? Surely these great religions have their profound mystical tradition which cannot be overlooked or omitted in any modern discussion of this subject. What about them? How do they fit into the mystical picture?"

Here let me recall my first chapter, where I said that the great religions have as yet no common vocabulary or theological way of speaking and that this makes it necessary to take a stand within the framework of one religious tradition. Consequently I have spoken out of the Hebrew-Christian tradition of the West. And now while continuing to maintain this stand (and hoping that a Buddhist will approach this subject from a Buddhist standpoint and with a Buddhist vocabulary) I would like to sketch the beginnings of a mystical theology that will be universal in scope – that is to say, a mystical theology that will include the mystical experience of believers in all the great religions and, indeed, of those people who belong to no specific religion but have been endowed with profound mystical gifts. Such people there are. For mysticism is a human experience limited to no one religion: it is, I believe, the high point in man's search for fulfilment, authenticity and self-realization.

II

Let us, then, consider human life as a movement towards self-transcendence and authenticity through fidelity to the transcendental precepts:

> Be Attentive
> Be Intelligent
> Be Reasonable
> Be Responsible

It is by following these laws that one becomes fully human in one's thinking and in one's activity. Yet there is a more crowning precept which gives beauty and joy and fullness to human life. This is the precept:

> Be in love
>
> (Lonergan (1), p. 13)[1]

Now it is my contention that a very radical fidelity to this last precept leads to mystical experience. And I draw the conclusion that as love is the most human of human activities, an activity for which the human heart was made, an activity in which men and women transcend themselves and become authentic, so mysticism, which is a question of love, is the most profoundly human activity. It is not a transcending of the human condition, as some authors have suggested, but a becoming more totally human. That is why it is a universal phenomenon and that is why one can speak of "the universal call to mysticism".

Assuredly mysticism is not achieved by human effort alone. Just as no sane man sits down and decides to fall in love with a woman, so no authentic human being calculatingly decides to fall in love with the infinite. Just as a man's love is elicited by the good in a woman, so unrestricted love is elicited by the footprints of the ox or the glimpse of the treasure hidden in the field. The call must always be there, And it *is* always there – because God shows no partiality. He wishes all men to be saved.

[1] See also p. 268 where Lonergan speaks of "total surrender to the demands of the human spirit: be attentive, be intelligent, be reasonable, be responsible, be in love".

He offers grace to everyone. It is in answering this call that men and women become truly human.

*

But before speaking about love, which is my main point here, let me discuss each of the transcendental precepts in its relationship to mysticism.

Be attentive! In Oriental meditation this attentiveness or awareness is of the utmost importance and there are many "awareness exercises". One can practise meditation simply by being aware of one's body or of one's breathing or of all the sensations that are going on inside oneself, a practice which sounds very easy but is extremely demanding. Or one can be totally aware of all the sights and sounds that are present here and now.

A variation of this is found in Zen. I can sit in the lotus posture just listening (that is, being totally attentive) to the flow of the river or the thunder of the waterfall. Here I am, sitting in total attentiveness or awareness. This in itself may bring profound interior peace and unification. But I can go one step further and, as I listen to those outer sounds, I can focus my attention inwardly by asking the question:

"Who is listening?"

Quietly sitting, I let go of all discursive reasoning, all thinking, all concepts and images; I keep asking myself this question, endlessly asking this question, with my attention focused not on the exterior object but on *myself as listening*.

Now it may happen that, if I practise this meditation for many hours or even for many days and weeks, I will come to a shattering enlightenment which fills me with joy and exaltation, liberating me from craving and anxiety. I may experience a timeless moment of illumination. *This is an experience not of the river nor of the waterfall but of my true self*; and it has come while I am faithfully practising the first two transcendental precepts: **Be attentive, be intelligent**. What a wonderful thing! I have broken out of the confines of my little ego. I have burst the bonds that imprisoned me in myself and have emerged from a habitat to a universe. Zen literature speaks enthusiastically about such experience: we hear of people who reach deep enlightenment just by listening. It is all very wonderful. But is it mysticism?

The answer is: No. For it is not knowledge that comes from love. It is, of course, a great triumph of the human spirit. One should never belittle such illumination. But it is no more than the first step on the road to authenticity.[2]

After having had this illumination, however, I may go one step further and make an affirmation or judgement. If I am Occidental, I may say: "Being is!" If I am Oriental, I may say "Not a thing is!" But in either case I have now transcended myself by making an objective judgement that reality exists or does not exist independently of myself. This may sound dull and drab and commonplace; but philosophers agree that the profound realization that *being is* can be an earth-shaking experience. It can be an intellectual conversion – "a personal philosophical experience of moving out of a world of sense and arriving, dazed and disorientated for a while, into a universe of being" (Lonergan (2), p. 79). Aristotle speaks of such experiences of contemplation when man is like God and rises to the heights of spiritual attainment. This has come about from fidelity to the third transcendental precept: **Be reasonable**. Again, it is a great experience, but not mysticism.

But let us go one step further. Besides judgements about being there are judgements of value, when I affirm that something is good in itself irrespective of the pleasure or satisfaction it gives me. And perhaps I make this affirmation at the cost of liberty or life. I follow the voice of conscience rather than the lure of money and success; I choose duty rather than personal satisfaction. Here is the noble judge of ancient Rome who out of loyalty to country sentences his son to death. This is moral self-

---

[2] Let me add, however, that the person who practises this kind of meditation may happen to be a mystic; he may well have in his heart an unrestricted love – which will then flower and develop through this exercise. What I am saying here is that *in itself* this great illumination is not mysticism as I have defined the word.

transcendence; it is fidelity to the fourth transcendental precept: **Be responsible.**

This again is a triumph of the human spirit. Here one transcends self even more than before and at much greater cost. Here one moves even closer to self-realization and authenticity. This may entail a great ethical conversion which brings immense joy in the midst of suffering. But is it mysticism?

Again the answer is: No. In itself it is not mysticism unless (as will frequently happen) the man who makes such a great decision is also drawn on by love. But in itself it is a moral, and not a religious, achievement.

III

The fifth transcendental precept is: **Be in love.** For besides striving to be attentive and intelligent and reasonable and responsible, men and women fall in love. They fall in love with one another and they fall in love with the infinite: that is to say, they fall in love without reservation or restriction. "Being in love with God, as experienced, is being in love in an unrestricted fashion. All love is self-surrender, but being in love with God is being in love without limits or qualifications or conditions or reservations" (Lonergan (1), pp. 105, 106).

This is authentic religious experience (I do not yet speak of mysticism proper) and it only arises in answer to an invitation or call from the Spirit who floods our heart with his love. The Hebrew-Christian tradition formulates it very clearly as the core and centre of religious experience: the Gospel looks back to Deuteronomy when it says: "You shall love the Lord your God with all your heart, and with all your soul, and with all your strength, and with all your mind; and your neighbour as yourself" (Luke 10:27) Yet such unrestricted love is not limited to Judaism and Christianity.

But let me select some significant characteristics of this religious, unrestricted love.

First of all, it is a universal love from which one's enemies are not excluded. Moreover, it is incarnational in that it is not love of God divorced from love of the world. Rather it is the love about which I spoke in connection with Mother Teresa of Calcutta and Mahatma Gandhi and Ignatius of Loyola. It is the love which prompts good Samaritans everywhere to pick up the destitute and dying in the streets, to help the underprivileged, to give a glass of water to the little one. And yet at other times this same love may drive a person to leave everything for a life of solitude in a cave in the Himalayas or a hut in the desert.

And yet it should be noted that when I say unrestricted love I do not mean perfect love. I simply mean a love that goes on and on and on, just as man's knowledge and questioning go on and on and on. But, I repeat, it is never perfect in this life: authenticity is never fully achieved. The person with this unrestricted love has conflicts and struggles, imperfection and anguish, neurosis and fear. He or she has moments of betrayal and failure and sin. All this is part of that human adventure which is a love affair with the infinite. It is part of the experience of being in love.

Yet another aspect of this love (and one which is of supreme importance for the understanding of mysticism) is that it has eyes which see. In other words it is a love which necessarily brings enlightenment. And *the knowledge born of religious love* I call faith (Lonergan (1), p. 115). This is an obscure knowledge which dwells in the heart of the simplest person who loves God.

Such is the unrestricted love and such is the faith which lie at the heart of authentic religious experience.

But now let me come to mysticism.

This inner light of faith, this knowledge born of religious love, leads one to the outer revelation, the outer word of scripture and sacrament and community. Here it is nourished, here it develops and grows until eventually it enters a cloud of unknowing or a dark night. Now, while it continues to be nourished by the exterior revelation it *turns into naked faith, dark faith, pure faith. And this is mysticism.* It is naked because it is no longer clothed in thoughts and images and concepts; it is dark because it does not see clearly; it is pure because it is unmixed with concepts which (when applied to the divine) always contain an element of imperfection. It differs from ordinary faith only in the intensity of its nakedness, its darkness and its purity.

The Western mystics speak constantly of this naked faith. Especially valuable here is *The Book of Privy Counselling*, that little gem composed by the anonymous author of *The Cloud*, which opens with an exhortation to abandon all thoughts, good thoughts as well as evil thoughts, and continues with the words: "See that nothing remains in your conscious mind save a *naked intent* stretching out towards God" (Johnston (1), ch. 1). And later in the same first chapter the author writes:

> This awareness, stripped of ideas and deliberately bound and anchored in faith, shall leave your thought and affection in emptiness except for a naked thought and blind feeling of your own being.
>
> (Johnston (1), ch. 1)

And so this English author continues to exhort his disciple to remain naked, even when his faculties clamour to be clothed in thoughts, because only in naked faith is found security and freedom from error.

Now the point I wish to make here is that this naked faith is found in all the great religions. In Islam, in Hinduism, In Buddhism, and in Judaism we find people who love without restriction; who are filled with this exquisite wisdom which flows from religious love. They all speak of nakedness and darkness and emptiness and silence. And mystics of the great religions understand one another very well: they grasp intuitively, sometimes in a flash, the naked faith and the mystical solitude which dwells in the heart of the other.

Be it noted, however, that I am not saying that the naked faith in the heart of a Hindu and a Buddhist and a Christian is always the same. This no one can say; this no one knows. What we can say, however, is that there is a recognizable similarity between the naked faith of the Hindu and the Buddhist and the Christian, and that it is the gift of the same God. Hence it is the very best basis for ecumenical, if silent, encounter between the members of the great religions.

Having said this, however, I am aware that this whole matter may make some of my readers uneasy (some people rightly fear an oversimplified syncretism) so let me elaborate first on the question of love, then on the question of faith, and finally let me state my views on the role of Jesus Christ in this mystical process which exists in all the great religions.

IV

I have spoken of unrestricted love as the heart of authentic religious experience in all the great religions. But I can foresee that some of my readers may object that Buddhism says little or nothing about love. Or they may object that being in love without restriction implies the existence of a personal God. After all, it will be argued, if I am in love I must be in love with somebody. If I am in love without restriction I must be in love with a transcendent God. But, as everyone knows, Buddhism does not talk about God, much less about a personal God. So I may be asked: "Are you excluding Buddhism from the mystical, and indeed from the religious, experience which you call universal?"

In answer to this I would first of all agree that a Buddhist would not ordinarily use my terminology: he would not speak about God nor would he say much about love and about mysticism. But, as I have repeatedly said, I am forced to use this terminology because we have no theological way of speaking that applies to both religions.

If, however, we get beyond terminology and look carefully at the reality towards which it points, then we will see that the Buddhist mystics were what Westerners would call men and women in love. It is true, of course, that they were not at all clear about the object of their love. While Jews and Christians give a name to the object and source of their love, Buddhists resolutely refuse to name it. Hence they will speak about "nothing", but this nothing does not mean that "no thing is there" as I shall point out in a later chapter.

Furthermore, it is important to remember that if Buddhist mystics are not clear about the object of their love, Christian mystics are not clear either. For them God is not a clear-cut object but a loving presence which they obscurely sense. They feel that they are in a cloud of unknowing, crying out to a God whom they love but cannot see. And at times even this loving presence is withdrawn and they are left crying out in the night of naked faith. Only from revelation can they say that the emptiness in which they find themselves is the love of a benevolent Father who wraps them in His tender care.

There can be no doubt: the Buddhist mystic, like his Christian counterpart, is passionately and unrestrictedly in love. In the history of Japanese Buddhism we find saints, and plenty of them, who braved the stormy seas to go to China in search of enlightenment. They tramped from temple to temple in search of a master. They sat for days and nights in the lotus posture. They endured heat and cold, hunger and thirst, scolding and beating. And this they did with joyful hearts. What can we say except that they were in love? They were drawn by someone or something they did not know. They loved without clear knowledge of the object of their love. And once enlightened, they had a limitless compassion for all sentient beings. Read the Buddhist sutras, read the *Lotus Sutra* and you will find tremendous and overflowing compassion in the heart of the bodhisattva – and this is not a vague and formless love but a great spiritual passion which is direct towards the tiniest and most insignificant being who crosses his path. The bodhisattva is in love with everyone he meets. This is unrestricted love. This is mysticism.

V

A second objection which may arise is that I have spoken about faith without differentiating sufficiently between Buddhist and Christian and Hindu and Jewish faith. How can one say that faith is the basis for ecumenical dialogue when there are, in fact, so many different kinds of faith?

And in answer to this I would like to distinguish between faith and belief (Lonergan (1), p. 118ff).

In religious experience it is possible to distinguish between a superstructure, which I shall call belief, and an infrastructure, which I shall call faith. The superstructure is the outer word, the outer revelation, the word spoken in history and conditioned by culture. The infrastructure, on the other hand, is the interior word, the word spoken to the heart, the inner revelation. It was of this that Jesus spoke when he said to Peter: "Blessed are you, Simon Bar-Jona! For flesh and blood has not revealed this to you, but my Father who is in heaven" (Matthew 16:17). Here the Father speaks directly to the heart of Peter. Or again Jesus says: "No one can come to me unless the Father who sent me draws him" (John 6:44). Read the Gospel and you find Jesus bumping into faith in the most unexpected places – people have faith without knowing clearly the object of their faith, like the blind man who exclaims: "And who is he, sir, that I may believe in him?" (John 9:36). Such is the inner word uttered by the Holy Spirit who floods our hearts with his love.

Now this inner light of faith is not the prerogative of Christians alone, for God loves all men and women and desires them to be saved (1 Timothy 2:4). Consequently this inner light shines in the hearts of all men and women of good will who sincerely search for the truth, whatever their religious profession. And it is precisely this which binds together Jew and Gentile, Hindu and Buddhist, Christian and Muslim. This is an inner gift which at first is, so to speak, formless – that is, prior to any outer cultural formulation – and which often lives in the hearts of the most unsuspecting people who could never formulate it in words.[3]

At the risk of digressing for a moment, let me say that this distinction between inner faith and outer belief throws light on our contemporary religious plight. We constantly hear talk about the crisis of faith in the modern world. But in the terminology which I have chosen our crisis is not one of faith but of belief. What is called into question today is the cultural superstructure with its myriad of beliefs. But there is plenty of evidence to support the view that the inner light of faith is as

[3] Although formless, this is not the naked faith or mysticism of which I have spoken. It is the seed from which the flower of naked faith is eventually born.

strong as ever in the modern world. Perhaps more than at any time in history men and women today are searching for the authentic superstructure, for the outer belief that will satisfy their inner longing for the infinite. But to return to my main point.

I have indicated that while the great religions differ in their beliefs their members can be deeply united in faith. But one should not conclude from this that the outer word of belief is unimportant. Not so. For the inner gift of faith always seeks outward expression. In itself it is imperfect and incomplete. Again let me quote Bernard Lonergan on the bridegroom and the bride:

> One must not conclude that the outward word is something incidental. For it has a constitutive role. When a man and a woman love each other but do not avow their love, they are not yet in love. Their very silence means that their love has not reached the point of self-surrender and self-donation. It is the love that each freely and fully reveals to the other that brings about the radically new situation of being in love and that begins the unfolding of its life-long implications. (Lonergan (1), p. 112)

The inner light, then, leads to the outer revelation and is nourished by it. Put concretely in a Christian context, the inner prompting of the Spirit leads us to the Word so that we cry out: "Jesus is Lord" (Romans 10:9) with the realization that the God who speaks to the heart also speaks through history. And in other religions also the inner light of the Spirit (again I use the Christian term) leads people to recognize the working of the same Spirit in their history. And when this happens there is an interplay between the inner faith and outer belief – there is a marriage and a fullness of religious experience. It is through this that the naked faith about which I have spoken is finally born. Mysticism could never mature and develop without the exterior word.

*

Finally I promised to say a word about the role of Jesus Christ. Let me, then, state briefly my own belief.

I have spoken of an inner revelation, a gift of faith, an interior word offered to all men, and I have said with Paul that God does not show partiality. This I believe is true. Yet I also believe that this inner grace is offered to all, thanks to the death and resurrection of Jesus Christ who is "the true light that enlightens everyone" (John 1:9). In other words, the inner light of faith is not unrelated to Christ but is his gift to all. "For there is one God, and there is one mediator between God and men, the man Christ Jesus, who gave himself as a ransom for all . . ." (1 Timothy 2:5, 6).

I am aware that in taking this position I may sound unecumenical in that I give to Jesus Christ a unique role which I cannot accord to the founders of other religions, even when I esteem them profoundly. But, after all, this is my belief, and ecumenism can only grow and develop when the members of the great religions are honest and faithful to their deepest convictions. Perhaps the matter could be stated more positively by saying that the Risen Jesus who sits at the right hand of the Father belongs to all men and to all religions. No one religion, even Christianity, can claim to understand "the unsearchable riches of Christ" (Ephesians 3:8). That is why we need one another, so that by dialogue and mutual help our partial knowledge may become more complete.[4]

More could be said about the relation of Jesus Christ to the founders of other religions but this must be postponed to a later time. Let me now speak more concretely about the Christian encounter with Buddhism.

[4] It should also be noted that there are two senses of the word meditation. There is the traditional doctrine according to which all graces are *mediated* through the death and resurrection of Jesus Christ. On the other hand, in the theology of Bernard Lonergan mediation is usually *a mediation of meaning*. And in this sense Christ is hardly the mediator for non-Christians since he mediates no meaning, or at least not the fullness of Christian meaning, to them. Hence Lonergan writes: "What distinguishes the Christian, then, is not God's grace, which he shares with others, but the mediation of God's grace through Jesus Christ our Lord" (Lonergan (2), p. 156).

7

Encounter with Buddhism (1)

I

More than a millennium has elapsed since Christian Nestorian missionaries met Pure Land Buddhists in central China. How much mutual influence was then exerted is an open question to which scholars have not yet found a satisfactory answer. But since that time there has been constant contact (sometimes friendly but more often unfriendly), until today the two religions face one another like two great giants. What will happen next?

In this historic situation two attitudes of mind are apparent. The first is dominated by the question: *Who is going to win*? After all, Christian missionaries have ardently carried the Gospel to the East, while Buddhist missionaries have equally ardently carried the *dharma* to the West. Now the two religions, already worldwide communities with followers everywhere, look like two *sumo* wrestlers quietly confronting one another in the ring. Who is going to win? This kind of question preoccupied even the great soul of Teilhard de Chardin, who confidently predicted the victory of the West. It is also broached by Mircea Eliade who indicates that the West is being slowly dominated by the East. Alas, poor Yorick! And does the West again need three hundred Spartans to stand in the pass of Thermopylae and save it from destruction?

I do not think so. For a second attitude of mind is possible. We can view the encounter of religions in the wider context of a human race searching for world unity and desperately realizing that it must find unity or perish. In such circumstances the challenge confronting the two wrestlers is not to throw one another out of the ring but to join hands, to give the lead, to show the way, to become the centre of a movement towards unity and peace. Assuredly this is no easy task (it would be much easier to fight) but is it not particularly the challenge thrown down before that wrestler who owes allegiance to one who prayed for unity – who prayed that his disciples might be one, perfectly one, and that this unity might be a sign of the unity of all mankind?

II

In Japan (the Asian country with which I am most familiar) the relationship between Christianity and Buddhism was somewhat stormy until recent times. In the 1890s, it is true, some orthodox Buddhists met in friendly, if uneasy, dialogue with a group of orthodox Protestant Christians; but for Catholic Christians no deep encounter took place until the late 1960s, when the Second Vatican Council had already ushered in a new age.

Preoccupied with problems of international peace and world unity, the Council could not fail to see that dissension between religions was a scandal whereas unity would be a beacon light to the whole world. And so we find stress on unity: "For all peoples comprise a single community and have a single origin . . . One also is their final goal" (Abbot, pp. 660–1). And this was followed by the clear assertion that the Church rejects nothing that is good, that she honours and respects the great religious traditions, that she recognizes the Spirit of God working in ancient cultures prior to the preaching of the Gospel. And this is rounded off by an exhortation to "acknowledge, preserve and promote the spiritual and moral good found among these men as well as the values in their society and culture".

At first it all sounded revolutionary, even scandalous. "Are we not encouraging people in their error?", it was asked. Yet the Council's message was nothing less than an answer to the prayer, the toil, the research of many missionaries and theologians who for long had been impressed by the undeniable goodness and truth and beauty of the indigenous religions in their adopted countries. Moreover, it was the continuation of an even older tradition which held that Yahweh made a covenant not only with Israel but with the whole human race when he pointed to the multi-coloured rainbow and spoke to Noah: "Behold I set my bow in the cloud, and it shall be a sign of the covenant between me and the earth" (Genesis 9:13). Such an appreciation of the inherent goodness of the human race is also found throughout the Gospel of St Luke and in the Church Fathers, notably Gregory of Nyssa, who claims that the collective human race, not just the individual soul, is created in the image of God.

From this it is not difficult to conclude that there is a revelation to all authentic religions and to all people. No one is deserted by God; no nation is without its divine gift; and in this sense every nation is a chosen people. With this we can also definitively bid farewell to the outside-the-church-no-salvation way of thinking as well as to exaggerated ideas about the ravages of original sin and the *massa damnata* which sits in outer darkness. We can have a more optimistic view of God's grace offered to all men and women.

And so now, it seems to me, the authentic Christian position is to encourage good wherever one finds it – even if it exists in an apparently rival camp. If something is good it is the gift of the same Yahweh who set his bow in heaven as a sign of his covenant with the human race. If something is good it belongs to the Christian. That is why Paul can tell the Corinthians that everything belongs to them. "For all things are yours, whether Paul or Apollos or Cephas or the world or life or death or the present or the future, all are yours; and you are Christ's; and Christ is God's" (1 Corinthians 3:23). That is why he can tell the Philippians to enjoy everything good in life: "Finally, brethren, whatever is true, whatever is honourable, whatever is just, whatever is pure, whatever is lovely, whatever is gracious, if there is any excellence, if there is anything worthy of praise, think about these things" (Philippians 4:8)

How far this is from the anguishing who-is-going-to-win frame of mind! No. Let those two *sumo* wrestlers shake hands. Let them work together in service of mankind. It would be no fun to watch one throw the other out of the ring while the excited crowd roared with thunderous applause or lifted hands of despairing grief.

III

Over the past few decades dialogue has flourished in the modern world and has taught us some worthwhile lessons. In particular dialogue between Christians has taught us three lessons which I would like to mention before applying them to the wider dialogue with Buddhism.

First of all, we see the immense wisdom of Gamaliel who, when the apostles were dragged before the Sanhedrin, prudently counselled the group: ". . . keep away from these men and let them alone; for if this plan or this undertaking is of men, it will fail; but if it is of God, you will not be able to overthrow them. You might even be found opposing God" (Acts of the Apostles 5:38, 39).

Underlying these words is an enormous faith in the ultimate victory of truth. We do not need to hound error or to persecute those whom we consider erroneous. Neither need we feel threatened by others. The truth will prevail since it is of God. If only Christians had appreciated the wisdom of these words a few centuries ago! How much suffering would have been spared!

A second point we have learnt is that unity is achieved more quickly and more deeply by common prayer than by discussion. This latter frequently leads to bitterness, controversy and anger, whereas prayer unites. Prayer in common reminds us all that union is a gift of God and cannot be achieved by human effort alone. Furthermore, prayer is closely associated with forgiveness. "And whenever you stand praying, forgive, if you have anything against anyone; so that your Father also who is in heaven may forgive you your trespasses" (Mark 11:25). And Matthew's Gospel adds: "But if you do not forgive men their trespasses, neither will your Father forgive you your trespasses" (Matthew 6:15). Do not take these words as a threat, as though the Lord were warning those who do not forgive. They are no threat but a statement of the intrinsic nature of things. Lack of forgiveness renders prayer totally impossible because it erects a barrier between ourselves and others, between ourselves and God. While, on the other hand, prayer leads us to forgive and to receive forgiveness. The wounds of the past are healed – those deep wounds that have lived for centuries in the unconscious. The healing power of prayer has to be experienced to be understood.

A third lesson we have learnt is that common action unites. In famine and in earthquake, in flood or in fire, when Christians have united to fight against injustice or to help the poor they have experienced a bond of union and a friendship which has made them realize that they are one in Christ. It is indeed and interesting fact that any kind of common action, even sport, unites; and we all know that cracks appeared in the bamboo curtain when the ping-pong team went to China.

These three points, with necessary adaptation, are valid in Christian dialogue with Muslims and Jews. But what about Hindus and Buddhists? Here the problem is more delicate since the gap which separates us is much greater. Yet I believe that we can work towards union with these same points as guidelines.

About the statement of Gamaliel I need not speak since it is clear that in dialogue Christians and Buddhists must recognize one another's position. But there is the question of prayer. Can Buddhists and Christians pray together?

If by prayer we mean intercession or thanks or praise to a Father who loves us, orthodox Buddhists are slow to accept any such practice since it seems incorrigibly dualistic and contrary to the sense of oneness on which their religious experience is built. Even Pure Land Buddhism, which constantly calls on the name of the Buddha Amida, ends up by saying that Amida is your own mind. That, at least, is what orthodox Buddhist scholars say – what precisely is in the mind of the simple people who invoke the name of Amida is another story – and they cannot accept the kind of intercessory prayer which exists in Judaism, Christianity and Islam.

I myself believe, however, that this difference is less formi-

dable than appears at first sight. For the highest form of intercession is not simply dualistic. I invoke the God with whom I
am one. It is like the prayer of Jesus who calls, out, "Abba,
Father!" and yet claims that he and the Father are one. So we,
through Jesus, are one with the God whom we invoke. I will
speak about this in a later chapter and deal with its Trinitarian
connotations. Here only let me say that at our present stage of
dialogue this is still a hurdle; Buddhists do not accept prayer of
intercession: I know of no case in which Buddhists and Christians pray together in this way.

However, even if common prayer of intercession is impossible,
Christians and Buddhists can still have a *religious experience in
common*. For example, we can sit together in silent and wordless
meditation. And in such a situation we can feel not only the
silence in our hearts but the silence of the whole group. Sometimes such silence will be almost palpable and it can unite people
more deeply than any words.

Now you may ask: What precisely is this silence which is
uniting you – Christians and Buddhists?

And I would answer, first of all that it is our common human
nature. When we sit together in silent meditation, just being,
we are experiencing our true selves at the existential level. We
are all doing the same thing: just being. And this gives birth to
a powerful unity.

But going one step further I would say that we are united at
the level of faith. Remember that I distinguished between the
superstructure of belief and the infrastructure of faith, and I
said that this infrastructure is a formless inner light. Here we
have it in practice. For here we have a situation in which the
eyes are turned away from words and concepts and images to
remain in empty faith. And do not think that such faith is the
prerogative of Christians alone. Buddhists of all sects, including
Zen, speak constantly about faith and its necessity. And when
this faith flowers and develops into the naked faith which I have
called mysticism then the union is deepest. This is the union of
people who are in love without restriction or reservation, and
whose love has entered the cloud of unknowing. They are one

at the centre of things; they are one in the great mystery which hovers over human life and towards which all religions point.

Here I have been speaking of Christian dialogue with those forms of Buddhism which concentrate on wordless meditation. But equally interesting is the dialogue with Pure Land Buddhism.

I have already spoken of the invocation of Amida. *Namu Amida Butsu*, meaning "I take refuge in the Buddha Amida" or "Honour to the Buddha Amida", is repeated again and again and again with the faith that through the merits and mercy of Amida one will be released from bad *harma* and reborn in the Pure Land. This form of Buddhism, little known in the West, was extremely widespread in Asia and was at one time the most popular form of Buddhism in Japan. Anyhow, a friend of mine, a committed Christian, has entered deeply into dialogue with Pure Land Buddhists by praying with them (I think prayer is the only word I can use) and by speaking to groups of young Buddhists on the beauty and power of faith. Her faith is in Jesus (she constantly recites "the Jesus prayer") and their faith is in Amida. And this is quite clear to everyone. While with joy and gratitude they pray, "I take refuge in Amida", she with equal joy and gratitude prays, "I take refuge in Jesus". It is almost an amusing situation. But here there is a beautifully-shared experience. A close bond of unity and love is established.

Here again is a situation which can be explained by distinguishing between faith and belief. There is profound union at the level of faith even when the belief seems completely different. This is the level at which we can all be in love without restriction, all possessing the wisdom which flows from love.

IV

Finally there is the question of common action. This brings us back to the two *sumo* wrestlers. Are they going to expend their energies in fighting one another or are they going to join hands to serve the world?

Let us remember that the aim of a religion is not to increase its own numbers but to serve the world and to promote the salvation of humankind. If we look back in history we can see that both Buddhism and Christianity (in spite of their defects) have always served their people by giving spiritual values to the culture of the time. In this way Christianity served and gave inspiration to the Hellenistic world, the medieval world, the renaissance world – a glance at the art and music and poetry of these times makes this clear. And anyone who passed through Asia getting even a superficial view of its ancient culture sees the great spiritual and cultural achievements of Buddhism. In both East and West the inner eye, the eye of love, has always been active, has always been beautiful, and without it the cultural achievement would have been nil, or almost nil. "So, if your eye is sound, your whole body will be full of light; but if your eye is not sound, your whole body will be full of darkness" (Matthew 6:22, 23).

But now we are entering a new world which has largely rejected both Christianity and Buddhism. It is a world which, in spite of its incredible progress, is acutely aware of its spiritual poverty, its rootlessness, its insecurity, its superficially. It is a world which is unable to handle problems of nuclear energy, peace and war; unable to cope with social injustice, racial discrimination, marital breakdown and fear of the future. It is a world which, for all its talk about democracy, needs leadership and looks for guidance. For it is a world from which despair is not absent. Who is to guide such a world? Who is to give it spiritual values?

Surely this task must be undertaken by Christians and Buddhists and the believers of all the great religions. This is the challenge to the wrestlers. No one religion can answer the needs of modern man. We must pool resources and insights so that together the great religions can offer the values of meditation, interiority, compassion, non-violence, justice, peace, fidelity. Through co-operation in this great venture sincere believers of all religions can form friendship and community; they can travel the path of union.

8

Encounter with Buddhism (2)

I

I have said that believers of the great religions can best meet at the level of faith even when their beliefs are vastly different; and I have said that the deepest encounter will take place in the area of mysticism where we go beyond thoughts and concepts and images to a state of silent love. Here the conceptual super-structure is reduced to the minimum; here people remain in wordless union; here spirit meets spirit. Jews and Christians, Hindus, Buddhists and Muslims believe in the existence of a "hidden power which hovers over the course of things and over the events of human life" (Abbot, p. 661). And when this infinite power is not just recognized but deeply experienced union is indeed profound.

But all this is not to say that discussion and exchange of ideas is useless. Far from it. We must eventually talk to one another with friendship and true desire to help. Let us remember that dialogue of some kind has existed between religions from the earliest times. There is no religion in the world which has not been influenced by other religions. Even Old Testament Judaism which was extremely careful to preserve its own unique insight was greatly influenced, we now know, by the surrounding religions. No need to speak here of Hindu influence of Buddhism or of how Christianity was influenced by Hellenism (the Diony-sian story is one example of this), and how today all modern religions have received influence from Marxism, Existentialism and the culture of our time.

Between the Reformation and the Second Vatican Council, it

is true, Christianity in both its Protestant and Catholic form insulated itself carefully from outside influence – with the consequence that growth ceased. But now dialogue and exchange of opinion has developed into an art and we are faced with a period of tremendous progress: dialogue with science, dialogue with Oriental religions. We have learnt to meet and mutually explain our beliefs without thought of proselytizing, without exerting pressure on others, with complete equality and inner freedom. In dialogue both parties are free to take what they want and leave what they don't want.

Furthermore, exchange of ideas and mutual sharing can take place in many areas: through liturgy, through spiritual literature, through conversation. Whereas at one time Christians were insulated from the holy books of other religions now they can discerningly read the *Bhagavad Gita*, the *Tao te Ching* and the Buddhist sutras. If these works contain a genuine insight into the nature of reality and the mystery of life, is it not legitimate and desirable for educated Christians discerningly to avail themselves of this insight? And is it not also desirable that Buddhists and Hindus should avail themselves of the treasures and insights of the Christian classics? Indeed, one interesting example of this is found in Mahatma Gandhi. Here was a Hindu with remarkable insight into the Sermon on the Mount, which he brilliantly applied to social and political life. How many Christians have understood as profoundly as Ghandi the precepts to forgive one's enemy, to turn the other cheek, to give away one's cloak? How many Christians have understood as well as he did the power of suffering and of non-violence, of truth and of seeking first the kingdom of God and his justice? Gandhi confessed openly and frequently his debt to the Gospel; but he remained a Hindu. Similarly some modern Christians have had remarkable insight into the practice of Oriental meditation; they have seen in Buddhist and Hindu scriptures treasures which have astonished Buddhists and Hindus. Yet they remain Christians. And so the process of cross-fertilization goes on. I myself believe that the sharing of the Gospel, the sharing with others of "the unsearchable riches of Christ" (Ephesians 3:8) is as relevant and imperative as ever. Only it must be done in a context of dialogue and never with force or constraint.

Obviously all this exchange of ideas has its problems and difficulties and dangers. At an ecumenical meeting I once attended, a Japanese Buddhist observed smilingly that we all feel the religious and cultural danger: we all feel threatened. And his remark was a bit like that of the little boy who observed that the emperor was wearing no clothes. For if we dialogue we must be prepared to change (otherwise why dialogue?), and for some people this change entails a profound psychological shock. They are sadly jolted. They feel that the rug has been pulled from under their feet or that they are adrift on a sea of insecurity. This is particularly true if the change affects not only outward things like structures and the externals of liturgy, but the very way of thinking about God and Christ and redemption and original sin. And such violent change is taking place today not only because of the meeting of East and West but also because East and West are both facing the birth of an entirely new culture in the whole world. All this revolutionizes our society and our religious way of thinking until we begin to ask: "But what are the limits of change? Can we go on changing for ever? Will we lose our identity as Christians or as Buddhists?" Is there a point at which we can face the movement towards change with the words: "Thus far shalt thou go and no further?" This is a point to which I would like to give some consideration.

II

All authentic religion originates with mystical experience, be it the experience of Jesus, of the Buddha, of Mohammed, of the seers and prophets of the *Upanishads*. The founders speak of a realm of mystery that lies beyond the reach of thinking and reasoning and concepts of any kind, a realm about which one can only speak stammeringly and indirectly. They use expressions which they or their followers translate into words like Yahweh and God and Brahman and the Tao and the Buddha nature or whatever it may be. No one can have a clear and distinct idea of what these words mean: the reality to which they point lies hidden in a cloud of unknowing. "No one has ever seen God" (John 1:18).

But being human we must try to express this great mystery in words and phrases and holy books as well as in liturgy and drama and dance and art of all kinds. This we do; but however rich and beautiful the words and descriptions, they never contain the reality. "Eye has not seen nor ear heard, neither has it entered into the heart of man to conceive what God has prepared for those who love him" (1 Corinthians 2:9). The mystics are keenly aware of the inadequacy of words and phrases which try to formulate the mystery of life. That is why they are so often silent and say nothing. It is not that the formulations are wrong but that they are hopelessly inadequate to express this great mystery of which the mystic has had the tiniest existential glimmering.

Furthermore, any conceptual system or formulation in words is culturally and historically conditioned. That is to say, it takes on the cultural patterns of the society in which it was written. The Bible was written mainly by Jews with a Jewish way of thinking and a Jewish mode of expression. Augustine wrote from within a Hellenistic framework: he explains the Trinity and the Redemption to suit his age and to answer the questions of his day. So also does Aquinas. And so we have several formulations of the Christian message. Only today are we beginning to understand the full implications of "historicity". Now we realize that we can only understand Paul or Augustine or Aquinas or the theologians of the Reformation by studying the historical background out of which they wrote. It is useless to quote Augustine as a spokesman for modern Christianity without examining his cultural background. It is also impossible to come up with one formulation of Christianity which will last for all time. We may (and hopefully we shall) find a formulation that will speak to the men and women of our age; but the next century will look for something different. They will not say our formulation was wrong; but they may say that it does not suit them and has to be modified or changed.

Viewed in this way we can see that in the area of formulation and conceptualization of doctrines, as well as in the area of rites and structures, change is constantly taking place. Anything can change. There will always be reformulation, new insights, progress, new understanding of the great unchanging mystery which hovers over human existence.

And the moral from all this is that we must not become too attached to words and letters. Yes. There is a fine Buddhist saying that words and letters are like a finger pointing to the moon. If you want to see the moon, don't get too attached to that finger. Don't be attached to words and letters. Look out into the night for that reality to which they point.[1]

But the question, the sometimes agonizing question, remains: Is there anything I can cling to?

III

If we read the Bible we quickly discover that one thing is unchanging: the steadfast love of God. "For the mountains may depart and the hills be removed but my steadfast love shall not depart from you, and my covenant of peace shall not be removed" (Isaiah 54:10). It is precisely here that the Jews find their security. The bride may play the harlot; the people may turn to the fleshpots; the heavens may collapse and the rivers run dry; but Yahweh will always love his people. And Paul is profoundly conscious of the fidelity of God. "Let God be true though every man be false" (Romans 3:4). But for him this love of God is "in Christ Jesus Our Lord" (Romans 8:37). Nothing can separate us from this.

Now the steadfast love of God is a mystery. It can never be adequately described or delineated through any conceptual system. Moreover, its expressions are always changing – no one is more unpredictable than the God of Israel. In short, *the mystery of God's love can only be grasped through faith*. If we want to cling to anything we can only cling to faith. This is the

[1] All this is not to deny that the formulations contain the truth, but only to point out that in true propositions there are relative elements. See Lonergan (2), pp. 11ff.

message of Paul in Romans and he appeals to the example of Abraham.

*

I myself belong to a little dialogue group consisting of Buddhists and Christians of various denominations. One of our Japanese Christian members maintains strongly that our patron saint must be our father Abraham. Here is a patriarch who goes forth from his home and from his kindred. Where he is going he does not know; but he has faith, faith in the promise: "I have made you the father of many nations" (Romans 4:17).

But the promise is a mystery of which Abraham's understanding is very imperfect. In fact he is quite baffled by the whole thing. It looks ridiculous yet "he did not weaken in faith when he considered his own body, which was as good as dead because he was about a hundred years old, or when he considered the barrenness of Sarah's womb" (Romans 4:19). The promise seems even more absurd when he is ordered to kill Isaac. Surely the death of his only son will nullify everything! Yet "no distrust made him waver concerning the promise of God, but he grew strong in his faith as he gave glory to God, fully convinced that God was able to do what he had promised" (Romans 4:20, 21).

And so Abraham has great faith in a mystery which cannot be adequately formulated. If it is formulated the wording is imperfect and the reality is hidden. "And I will make you a great nation, and I will bless you and make your name great . . . and by you all the families of the earth shall bless themselves" (Genesis 12:2, 3). This promise is very mysterious and we do not yet know its full meaning and its implications. Some light is shed on it by the Mosaic covenant and by the new covenant predicted by Jeremiah and by the words of Jesus at the Last Supper. But it is still a mystery. The promise; the love of God; the old covenant; the new covenant – this is the great unchanging mystery which lies at the core of the Hebrew-Christian tradition.

Because of his faith Abraham had to abandon all security of any kind. Not only did he leave his home and kindred and country but he had to relinquish attachment to his only son.

More than that, he had to be detached from the promise itself – because if Isaac was dead how could the promise be fulfilled? Abraham was left with nothing, with absolutely nothing. And this is pure faith, naked faith. This is mysticism.

Nor is it by accident that Paul cites Abraham as his model. Because Paul, too, has to abandon all security and all formulations of the law to carry the Christian message out of its Jewish framework into the Hellenistic world. What was Paul's old security? To be "circumcised on the eighth day, of the people of Israel, of the tribe of Benjamin, a Hebrew born of Hebrews, as to the law a Pharisee, as to zeal a persecutor of the Church, as to righteousness under the law blameless" (Philippians 3:5). How important all this was for the young Paul! His religious adherence to the law and his cultural background were everything to him. But he had to give up all – "for his sake I have suffered the loss of all things" (Philippians 3:8) – in order to move forward with faith in only Christ: "that I may know him and the power of his resurrection" (Philippians 3:10). And so for Paul the whole Jewish framework of circumcision and the law collapsed, but his faith in the promise remained. He was a true son of Abraham.

*

All this may seem like a digression. But what I want to say is that our situation today is not unlike that of Abraham and of Paul, and we must emulate their faith. We, too, have the promise. This time it is the promise of Jesus: "I will be with you all days even to the end of the world" (Matthew 28:20). What precisely this promise entails we do not know. We will only know from day to day as it is revealed to us by the Spirit. Quite certainly we will get severe shocks because just as the promise to Abraham was fulfilled in a way he could never have imagined, so will be fulfilled the promise to us. But of one thing we can be sure: it will be fulfilled in a more mysterious and wonderful and beautiful way than we can imagine. As with Abraham; so with us.

Let us remember, too, how at the Last Supper Jesus told his disciples that they could not understand his whole message immediately but that the Holy Spirit would guide them day by day and would direct and comfort and strengthen them. "But the Counsellor, the Holy Spirit, whom the Father will send in my name, he will teach you all things and bring to your remembrance all that I have said to you" (John 14:26). Day by day as each new situation arises the Spirit will direct us.

And so I reach the conclusion that the very question: "What are the limits of change?" may even be an indication that we are clinging to words and letters, to plans and false securities; and all this may distract us from the important work of listening to the daily inspirations of the Spirit.

*

We live in an age which asks for faith, pure faith, naked faith, mystical faith. It is an age in which we accept the formulations but see their inadequacy; we believe in the doctrines but do not cling to the words; we respect the teaching of the past but are not attached to the modes of expression. This means that we are open to change. It means that there will be times when we must sing with St John of the Cross:

> With no other light or guide
> Than the one which burns in my heart
>
> (*Ascent*, Stanza 3)

Like Abraham we are going on a journey into darkness. In order that we may go to a place that we do not know we must go by a way that we know not. We do not know the place and we do not know the way. This may mean that we suffer some of the insecurity of Abraham and we may be visited by some of the dread which fell upon him: "As the sun was going down, a deep sleep fell on Abram; and lo, a dread and a great darkness fell upon him" (Genesis 15:12). Like him we have faith in the steadfast love of God which lasts for ever.

IV

But there is one practical problem of dialogue which must sooner or later be confronted. Let me put it this way: Is it possible for a Christian, a committed Christian, to experience another religion from inside? Can dialogue go to such lengths?

This question could not have been asked twenty years ago but now with the new thinking about non-Christian religions it is not irrelevant. We know that Thomas Merton spoke of (shall we say soliloquized about the possibility of?) practising Oriental meditation in a Buddhist temple and under the direction of a Buddhist master; but death tragically intervened. He was, of course, misunderstood; and some people spoke foolishly of Merton's "conversion to Buddhism". Yet other Christians, committed Christians, ask if confronted with Buddhism one is in an either-or situation. Can Christians avail themselves of the treasures and wealth of Buddhism from inside?

To this I would answer that quite certainly Christians can experience *some of the values of Buddhism* from within. If the Spirit is at work with Buddhism it would seen legitimate to enter discerningly and find his action. If in Buddhism there is an experience of the Absolute (and I believe there is) why cannot a Christian experience the Absolute through Buddhist categories?

The question usually asked, however, is: "What about the role of Christ?" Or, as someone facetiously put it, do you leave Christ at the door of the temple with your shoes?

And to this I would answer with Paul that no authentic Christian can be separated from the love of Christ. If he enters the Buddhist temple he does so as a member of Christ – to grow in the Christ experience and to search for Christ who, he believes, is there in another way. This may mean that he leaves his thoughts and concepts and images of Christ at the door (just as a Buddhist leaves his thoughts and concepts and images of the Buddha at the door) but he does so to find Christ through other cultural categories, to meet the Risen Jesus, the universal man who belongs to all cultures. In fact, one of the great challenges confronting modern Christians is that of experiencing

Christ in a non-Christian culture. Precisely because Christianity claims to be a universal religion we cannot shirk this challenge.

And yet, having said all this, I would quickly add that such a venture is for a few people who feel within themselves the vocation to a delicate path which demands much prudence and discernment. For the fact is that just now we do not know how much of Buddhism can be accepted by Christians; we do not know if there is incompatibility or, if there is, where it lies. We are at the beginning of a long, long journey. Consequently this pioneering work is not something to be undertaken lightly and in cavalier fashion. It may be the calling of some who have experienced Christ profoundly in their own culture and are willing to accept the cultural cross, the anguish and the conflict which necessarily accompanies any attempt to reconcile seeming contraries. This is the vocation of a few who have already seen the glory of Christ with the inner eye of love.

PART III

THE MYSTICAL
JOURNEY

9

The Call

I

Mystical experience begins with an invitation. It is never something that we strive for by personal effort – or if we strive we must remember that our very striving is a gift. It is a call from beyond oneself. Sometimes this call is dramatic, as were the great inaugural visions of the prophets Isaiah and Jeremiah, or the flash of light that blinded Paul on the road to Damascus. At other times it is a secret and quiet call, a still small voice like that which spoke to Elijah, a voice that may have been alive in the heart since early childhood. Then this invitation is so delicate, so subtle, so unobtrusive that the recipient does not even realize that he has been called and has to be reminded: "You did not choose me, but I chose you . . ." (John 15:16).

The futility of human effort and the necessity of a call is a note that is sounded in the mysticism of all the great religions. It is strikingly presented in the *Upanishads* where the Ultimate, called the Self (Brahman and Atman), is the one who chooses and calls: "That Self cannot be attained by the study of the scriptures, nor by the intellect, nor by learning. He whom the Self chooses, by him, the Self can be attained" (Griffiths (2), p. 103). Assiduous study of the scripture, faithful practice of virtue, constant devotion to learning, practice in breathing, sitting and awareness – these things have value; but in the last analysis what matters is grace.

In Christianity, as we have already seen, mysticism begins and ends with the experience of being loved. "We love, because he first loved us" (1 John 4:19). The secret of the energy and fire of Paul and Bernard and Teresa was not so much that they loved (this was secondary) as their conviction of being loved. So also the prophets. They are called from their mother's womb – that is to say, they are called without any merit on their part. "Before I formed you in the womb I knew you . . ." (Jeremiah 1:5). This call is purely gratuitous. It does not come because Jeremiah is good but because God is good. And so the principal thing in the mystical life is not to love but to receive love, not to love God and man but to let yourself be loved by God and man. Don't put barriers in the way; don't put up a defence mechanism; let love come in – because human love is a response to divine love. This is the message of the First Epistle of St John. This is the key to mysticism.

Yet if there is a call and if we hear it, then ordinarily we answer. "Then the Lord called, 'Samuel! Samuel!' And he said, 'Here I am!' " (1 Samuel 3:4) And so in the mystical life. But the answer (as I have already indicated) is also a gift. It is moreover a living and burning reality that arises in the human breast and can only be described in symbolical language. It is what St John of the Cross powerfully calls a "living flame of love"; it is what the author of *The Cloud* calls a "blind stirring of love"; it is a dark night and a cloud of unknowing; it is a quiet movement in the depths of one being; it is a passionate being in love without restriction; it is the urgent longing which motivates the whole mystical journey:

> One dark night
> With anxious love inflamed
> – Ah, the sheer grace! –
> I went out unseen.
> (*Ascent*, Stanza 1)

And so here we have an inner light which guides and directs. This light is the Holy Spirit.

*

All this is difficult to express in ordinary language, and the mystics usually resort to symbols. Here let me refer to twelve symbolical pictures which describe the mystical journey as it was envisaged in ancient China. I choose these pictures because I believe they have universal validity and can apply equally well to Christians or Buddhists or anyone who is called to this mystical journey. I believe they illustrate the point I made earlier, that mysticism is a deeply human experience found at all times and in all cultures.

The first picture depicts man lost in the woods and searching for a way out. This is life; this is the human condition; this is the situation in which we men and women find ourselves – we are lost in the woods and looking for a way out. (I might add, however, by way of digression, that one could draw a picture antecedent to the first; and this would be of the man who is lost in the woods without knowing that he is lost. This is the most pitiable condition of all: the condition of the blind man who thinks he sees. The blind man who knows he is blind has already made progress. But, anyhow, no such picture exists in the Chinese series: it begins with man lost in the woods and desperately trying to get out.)

In the second picture, which is the one I wish to speak about here, he sees the footprints of the ox. This is a great experience which fills him with hope and joy. Here he is:

(*By kind permission of Kobori Nanrei, Daitokuji, Kyoto*)

This is the invitation. This is the call. He did not put those footprints there by his own efforts. He found them. Perhaps he had been looking at them every day for some time; but now he sees them with his inner eye. They are a gift. They are grace.

And his life changes. Powerfully motivated, he is determined to follow those tracks even if it costs him his life. He will follow and his eye of love will see that ox (what an enlightenment) which symbolizes true wisdom.

The remaining pictures describe his journey with its conflicts and sufferings and surprises. This need not concern us just now. Only let me say that the man is archetypal: he represents the mystic.[1]

Indeed this man following those tracks is not unlike that other man who caught a glimpse of the treasure hidden in the field and with great joy gave up everything (and everything means everything) to buy that field. Or like the man who sold everything to buy a pearl of great price. He is not unlike our father Abraham, who went out from his kindred and his father's house to a land that he did not know. In his tremendous sacrifices that man is even like those of whom it is written: "They were stoned, they were sawn in two, they were killed with the sword; they went about in skins of sheep and goats, destitute, afflicted, ill-treated – of whom the world was not worthy – wandering over deserts and mountains, and in dens and caves of the earth." (Hebrews 11:37,38).

For the vital question is: What motivated that man? What was burning in his heart?

I have said that it was the living flame of love or the blind stirring of love or unrestricted love. But now I would like to put it in theological language and call it *faith*. Mysticism is a journey of faith – deep, dynamic, awe-inspiring, naked faith. This flame of faith, this infrastructure in religious experience, is found everywhere, and the path along which it leads is always similar. Of course the superstructure of belief is very different. Indeed, a great Chinese commentator on these pictures observes that the man caught sight of the footprints *while reading the*

---

[1] For other pictures see Johnston (3), pp. 80–1.

sutras. A Christian, on the other hand, might well see the foot-prints *while reading the Gospel.* But nevertheless one can scarcely deny that the powerful Buddhist faith which drove that man to search for the ox, and the unshakable Jewish faith which burned in the heart of Abraham when he left his country, and the joyful Christian faith which impelled the man to buy the field in which lay the hidden treasure – that all these have something in common. This is what I call the infrastructure where the mystics of all religions meet, where they recognize one another and feel united.[2]

II

The oxherding pictures are highly symbolical. Now let me try to say more practically how men and women enter into the mystical life.

There are in fact many paths and I have spoken about them elsewhere (Johnston (3), ch. 5). Here let me select another which developed within Eastern Orthodox Christianity and is now popular throughout the world. This is the beautiful Jesus prayer wherein one recites the formula: "Lord Jesus Christ, Son of God, have mercy on me a sinner"; or just the name "Jesus"; or "It is the Lord" (John 21:7), or one of the several variations. In Japanese one version is the word *Shu* meaning Lord or Kyrios; and some Japanese Christians sit in the lotus and repeat this word with the exhalation of the breath; *Shuuuuu.* In this way it resembles the use of *mu,* meaning nothing, which is used frequently in Zen. It need not, however, be recited with the breathing, and some people prefer to repeat the word naturally in accordance with their own body-and-spirit rhythm. In fact, this prayer seems to arise spontaneously, without help or direction from a teacher, in Christian hearts throughout the world.

[2] Let me again emphasize that I am not saying that the superstructure is unimportant or that any superstructure will do. The same God who speaks to the heart speaks through the superstructure in history. I am stressing that what all the mystics have in common is the grace or inner gift of the same God.

What is important is the name – it is precisely here that the power resides – and it is claimed that this prayer goes back to New Testament times and even, in a sense, to the Old Testament where there was profound reverence for the name of God.

It should be noted that the prayer must be recited with faith in Jesus who is Lord. This is of the utmost importance. For the modern world we hear of the mantra or sound constantly repeated to deepen awareness. One simply recites a meaningless sound or counts the breathing – "one, two, three" – to clear the upper layers of consciousness in order that the deeper forces of the psyche may be brought into play. Now the Jesus prayer may have something in common with this in that it also empties the upper layers of consciousness to allow the deeper forces to work; but it is not only this. Incomparably more important is the faith of which it is an expression. This faith is not only in Jesus who lives in my heart but also the Jesus who lives in the whole universe, especially in the poor and suffering and afflicted. Consequently, one who truly recites this prayer with faith is never locked up in the little ego but is opened up to a unity with Jesus who is Lord of all.

*

At first the prayer may be recited aloud like any vocal prayer: it may be formulated with the lips or harmonized with the breathing. On the other hand, it may also be recited interiorly. But in either case it may initially demand effort and persever-ance. As times goes on, however, it becomes interiorized to such an extent that it acquires its own rhythm within us. Theophane the Recluse[3] writes charmingly that after the initial effort the prayer becomes like a brook that murmurs in the heart: "At first this saving prayer is usually a matter of strenuous effort and hard work. But if one concentrates on it with zeal it will begin to flow of its own accord like a brook that murmurs in the heart. This is a great blessing; and it is worth working hard to obtain it" (Ware, p. 117). On and on goes the Jesus prayer

---

[3] Theophane the Recluse (1815–94) was an Orthodox bishop who trans-lated the *Philokalia* from Greek into Russian.

of its own accord and without effort on our part, even in the midst of work and activity. "The prayer takes a firm and stead-fast hold when a small fire begins to burn in the heart. Try not to quench this fire, and it will become established in such a way that the prayer repeats itself; and then you will have within you a small murmuring stream" (Kadloubovsky and Palmer, p. 110).

The small murmuring stream! It continues to flow in the depth of one's being, altering one's whole countenance, dominating one's whole person so that every word and action spring only from it. Its rhythm may identify with the beating of the heart, becoming an endless source of joy and gratitude and inner freedom. "And I live, now not I; but Christ lives in me" (Galatians 2:20). Through the Jesus prayer man is divinized becoming another Christ. He comes to the "prayer without ceasing" (Luke 18:1) which was the ideal of the famous Russian pilgrim and is now the ideal of thousands of men and women who believe.

A similar pattern is found in Pure Land Buddhism where one recites the name of Amida with faith and trust in his infinite compassion and love. For Amida, teaches Pure Land Buddhism, has made a vow to save all those who take refuge in him and call upon his name.[4] After some time believers find that the name repeats itself. It is no longer "I" who call upon the name of Amida: the name is reciting itself within me. And there exist today believers in Pure Land Buddhism whose hearts are filled with boundless trust in Amida – his sacred name is always on their lips with gratitude and joy. Most of them are simple people who have never heard the word mysticism nor its Japanese equivalent; but the small fire and the murmuring stream live within them.

In this process one abandons thinking and reasoning. The recitation of the sacred name brushes aside all thoughts and one enters a cloud of unknowing. "When you notice thoughts arising and accosting you," writes the *Philokalia*, "do not look at them even if they are not bad; but keeping the mind firmly in the heart, call to Lord Jesus and you will soon sweep away the

---

[4] The formula used in Japanese is *Namu Amida Butsu* meaning "I take refuge in the Buddha Amida" or "Adoration to the Buddha Amida". This is called the *nembutsu*.

thoughts and drive out their instigators – the demons – invincibly scorching and flogging them with the Divine name" (Kadloubovsky and Palmer, p. 81).[5] And in this way one comes to the sacred emptiness and detachment from thinking which characterizes the mystical state. There may come a time when even the word Jesus is no longer necessary because a total unitive silence reigns in the heart; and here again one is in nakedness and darkness with no other light than that which burns in one's heart.

III

I have used many words to describe mystical experience which in the end is ineffable. I have used all kinds of symbols. I have called it a small flame of love, a determination to follow the ox, an infinite trust in Amida. But perhaps in the last analysis it is best described as a being in love. For being in love is different from plain loving. I may love many people; but if I am in love with a woman the thought of my loved one is always in my mind and heart like the small fire or the murmuring stream. She dwells in me and I in her.

Mysticism is like that; and the mystics are men and women in love, in love without restriction. That is why contemplatives from Origen to Bernard of Clairvaux and on to St John of the Cross have sung passionately about the man who loves the woman and the woman who loves the man. Their erotic language has embarrassed the pious; their interpretations of the Song of Songs have dismayed the exegete; their sexual symbols have intrigued the psychologist. But when all is said and done, is this not a good way to express it? A profound love which consumes the whole person. Earlier in this book I spoke of the secrecy and hidden quality of this mystical love. I will not deny this now, but let me say that it is not always secret and hidden. It may become all-consuming and surge to a ravishing climax

[5] See also p. 280. "Attention is unceasing silence of the heart, free of all thoughts. At all times, constantly and without ceasing, it breathes Christ Jesus the Son of God and God and him alone. . . ."

as St John of the Cross declares: "Because the enkindling of love in the spirit sometimes increases exceedingly, the longing for God becomes so intense that it will seem to a person that his bones are drying up in this thirst, his nature withering away, and his ardour and strength diminishing through the liveliness of the thirst of love. A person will feel that this is a living thirst" (*Dark Night* 1:11, 1 319).

Such a thirst also consumed the psalmist who longs for God as the hart longs for flowing streams. And again he thirsts for the infinite as one in a parched land thirsts for water:

> O God, thou art my God, I seek thee,
>   my soul thirsts for thee;
> my flesh faints for thee,
>   as in a dry and weary land where no water is.
>
>   (Psalm 63)

Such is the cry of the mystic.

*

I have said that the mystical life begins with an invitation. But it is an invitation which is repeated many times. "Friend, go up higher" (Luke 14:10). "If today you hear his voice, harden not your hearts . . ." (Psalm 95).

10

Journey into the Void

I

Once called, the mystic starts out on a journey. And what a journey, this going forth into the desert and into the void!

First of all, it is filled with conflict from the very start. The man who sees the footprints feels called to follow them, but he also wants to stay in the forest. After all, he knows the forest; it is familiar territory; it has its crude and sensual joys. Why venture out into the night? And even if he conquers his fears and tears himself away from his clinging to the forest, he will find the same conflict at every stage of his journey. He will always have to keep moving on, leaving what is familiar to enter a terrain that is unfamiliar. At times he may get discouraged and decide that he has had enough. "What a crazy journey! Let me stay in this outhouse at the fringe of the forest. . . . But no, I must go on and on and on, always following the call of love which I hear in the distance."

When I say he leaves the forest, however, do not take me too literally. If he is employed in the bank of Tokyo he may stay in the bank of Tokyo. But then he will make an inner journey into the unknown. He will travel into ever new states of consciousness, passing through successive stages of the psyche and moving towards the ground of being where dwells the great mystery which we call the Spirit of God. And in this process he will be changed, radically changed, in such wise that he will come to think and feel in a new way – and he may see things in a way so different from the other executives in the bank of Tokyo that he finds himself in the midst of conflict and friction once again.

Yes, the person who embarks on this journey is asking for trouble; for he may come into conflict not only with executives in the bank of Tokyo but with ecclesiastical authority in his own backyard. This can be a painful affair.

Yet follow the call he must, even when it leads him to leave everything. For on this journey one must travel light, getting rid of superfluous and burdensome paraphernalia. This is precisely what the Lord said to his disciples:

> Take
> no gold,
> nor silver,
> nor copper in your belts,
> no bag for your journey,
> nor two tunics
> nor sandals,
> nor a staff
> (Matthew 10:9, 10)

In short, take nothing! All your security must rest in faith alone. Dom Helder Camara puts it well:

> You want to be,
> excuse me,
> First get free
> of that excess
> of goods
> which cram
> your whole body
> leaving no room
> for you and even less
> for God[1]

As I have already indicated, one may not literally leave these things (just as one need not leave the bank of Tokyo) but one must learn to live without them; one must leave attachment and clinging. Non-attachment is here the big word.

[1] *The Desert is Fertile* by Dom Helder Camara (Orbis Books, New York, 1976, p. 23.)

This non-attachment could be, and has been, analysed in considerable detail; but here let me just mention two practical points.

The first is: let go of anxieties. This is the message of the Sermon on the Mount and it is of cardinal importance in the mystical journey. For amidst all the useless and superfluous baggage the most useless and superfluous things are fear, anxiety, scrupulosity and the like. So don't be anxious about your life, what you shall eat, or about your body what you shall put on. Look at the flowers of the field: they are not anxious and yet our Father clothes them. Above all, don't be anxious about the future, for the future will look after itself. And don't look with anxiety or guilt or nostalgia into your romantic past. Let go of those anxieties. They don't help. Live in the present.

Beautiful, you will say. Yes, but how difficult! Because we love our anxieties; we cling to them and, what is more, they are buried deep, deep down in the psyche. That means that we are always being liberated from subliminal anxieties in this great journey. We are constantly liberated from fear. "Do not be afraid. I will be with you."

The second practical point is closely related to this and it is: Surrender all attachment to thinking – that is to say, to discursive thinking, to images and concepts and knowledge of any kind. (But let me again stress that one does not give up knowledge: one gives up attachment to knowledge.) And this is difficult because, as wise Aristotle says at the beginning of the *Metaphysics*, man naturally desires to know and to use his rational faculties. But it is only by abandoning rational knowledge that one can enter into the silence of faith and the night of supraconceptuality – it is only in this way that one can move towards the ray of darkness about which Dionysius speaks so eloquently.

And yet renunciation of discursive thinking is only the first step. One must not cling to the joys of mystical silence or to the rapture of enlightenment or the consolations of passive love. One must cling *to nothing*: this is the void. One must not even cling to noble thoughts and feelings about God, for these thoughts and feeling are not God. If you wish, you may cling to God as He is in Himself. But this is not very helpful because in this life God is the void, God is the nothingness, God is the cloud of unknowing. He is fullness and everything and wisdom in Himself; but He is like nothingness and emptiness and the cloud to us. For no man ever sees God.

Renunciation of clinging is the negative aspect. But let us not forget the positive. Let us recall that this man is led and drawn by the power of love that burns in his heart and the pillar of fire that goes ahead. And it is precisely this love that makes him relinquish all. His love makes him detached. And it is precisely his love which renders him joyful in his nudity of spirit: he can throw everything away with great *élan* – with a smile and a song.

And so the journey is one of great insecurity and of great security. It is desperately insecure because he has no money or copper (and which of us does not like to rattle the money in our pocket?) to give him human security; it is secure in that he relies on faith. "No other light to guide me than that which burns in my heart."

For as he journeys along, a great love is welling up within him and he is being transformed by the fire of love that burns in his breast.

Let me attempt to explain this phenomenon in terms of the non-action or *wu-wei* which is central to Asian thinking.

II

It is principally in Taoism that we hear of non-action. We are told that there are two aspects of human conduct and human growth: *the way of conscious effort* and *the way of non-action*. The way of conscious effort is particularly important in the first part of life and in the pre-mystical stage. Quite simply it is the way of the person who thinks, asks questions, deliberates, weighs the evidence and makes decisions. And if such a person happens to be a politician or a big businessman or a leader of some kind, then his decisions may build or destroy the lives of millions of people. But more than that they will build or destroy his own life. For through his decisions he creates his character and makes himself.

But there is another way: that of non-action, and this pertains usually (but by no means exclusively) to the second part of life. Here I am less preoccupied with doing things and more able to let things happen, less intent on making decisions and more able to allow the true decision to well up from the depths of my being. "Truly, truly I say to you, when you were young you girded yourself and walked where you would: but when you are old, you will stretch out your hands and another will gird you and carry you where you do not wish to go" (John 21:18). These words addressed to Peter might well be addressed to all of us. When we are young, particularly when we are young in the things of the spirit, we walk the path of conscious effort; but when we are mature we are carried along the path of non-action.

Of course, the word non-action is easily misunderstood. For this reason and to avoid misunderstanding, some people prefer to emphasize the active dimension of this process by calling it non-interference or active inaction or creative quietude. Yet others speak of "doing nothing", and this is all right provided we remember that while we are doing nothing a deeper force within us is doing something or doing everything. I myself like to speak of the great art of *letting things happen* in one's psyche and in the world. The man of Tao is the one who can let the Tao act (and the Tao is the great unnameable mystery that hovers over human life) without putting any impediment in its way. This means that he can follow his deepest spiritual instincts without breaking the law. Confucius is reported to have said that at seventy he could do anything at the dictates of his heart without violating any rule of conduct. Yes, at the age of seventy – not before!

I have said that this non-action is found all over the East. There is more than a hint of it in Gandhi's non-violence: his belief in the power of suffering and fasting and imprisonment. For underlying this is a conviction that Truth will win out. Gandhi spoke constantly of the force of truth: *satyagraha*.

Again this non-action is found in Zen:

Sitting, only sitting
And the grass grows by itself.

I sit in the lotus and allow the Tao to act: I do not interfere: I believe that the Tao will act benevolently in me and in the whole world.

Again, there is something of the *wu-wei* in transcendental meditation. Here I quietly recite a mantra without understanding its meaning. In this way I bind the discursive intellect in such wise that the deeper powers within me begin to work: these deeper forces are a source of creativity and human potential. More examples could be given. The principle simply is that if we can learn the gentle art of doing nothing, of letting things happen, of not putting obstacles in the way, then the forces of nature will act powerfully and beautifully in the universe and in human life.

III

I have spoken about non-action because it is of cardinal importance in the mystical journey. Beginners, of course, will ordinarily meditate according to the way of conscious effort. That is to say, they will think about the Bible or they will make lengthy prayers to God with fervour and devotion or they will repeat the Jesus prayer with considerable effort, and they will make resolutions to do good works; but there comes a time when they must cease from discursive meditation and active effort in order that those realities which lie deeper in the psyche may begin to talk. In other words they must pass from conscious effort to non-action: they must let the Spirit act, they must not put impediments in his way. This means that they pass from action to a non-action, which is paradoxically a new level of even more powerful action.

Practically, this entails the abandonment of reasoning and thinking and of any effort whatsoever. Let things happen! Let the Spirit act! God is a great artist and you are the model. If you keep jumping around, the artist cannot paint a masterpiece.

So keep quiet. "Be still and know that I am God" (Psalm 46:10). Listen to the wise advice of St John of the Cross:

> The attitude necessary . . . is to pay no attention to discursive meditation, since this is not the time for it. They should allow the soul to remain in rest and quietude, even though it may seem very obvious to them that they are doing nothing and wasting time, and even though they think this disinclination to think about anything is due to their laxity. Through patience and perseverance in prayer, they will be doing a great deal without activity on their part. All that is required of them here is freedom of soul, that they liberate themselves from the impediment and fatigue of ideas and thoughts and care not about thinking and meditating. They must be content simply with a loving and peaceful attentiveness to God, and live without concern, without effort, and without the desire to taste or feel Him. All these desires disquiet the soul and distract it from the peaceful quiet and sweet idleness of the contemplation which is being communicated to it.
>
> (*Dark Night* 1:10, 4)

How difficult this non-action is for some people! It is particularly difficult for Westerners or for Orientals who have received Western education. They feel that they are being lazy, that they are wasting their time, that they ought to get busy in the way of conscious effort. This is a time when they must somehow learn to understand their own situation – to understand what is happening in their lives. But if at this time they meet an incompetent director (and such directors abound) then they are in trouble.

This state is sometimes called passive, though for reasons which I have stated earlier I am wary about this word. But whatever you call it, it grows. It may even happen that one seems to become more and more helpless. At first one was aware of an obscure sense of presence but eventually even this may go – and one is just listening, waiting, and nothing seems to happen. The whole situation may be painful as one's experience becomes more and more "secret" and "hidden". It is now most of all that the mystics use words like emptiness, darkness, obscurity and the void. Some people object to these negative words; but how else can one describe the experience? Most mystics, East and West, find these words useful. Only one must remember that they are descriptive. The experience itself is far from negative: one has given up walking in order to be carried, carried in the arms of God.

*

The fact is, let me repeat, that in giving up thinking and reasoning, in letting go of those anxieties, I am allowing myself to be loved by God. And isn't that the main thing in life? Not that we love God but that God first loves us. He is taking care of me; he is clothing me and nourishing me just as he nourishes and clothes the birds of the air and the flowers of the field. He is loving me through other people (often their love is His love made incarnate) and why should I struggle against it by my conscious efforts? Why should I obscure it with my anxieties? Why should I fight against this love? Remember the words of Isaiah:

> Woe to him who strives with his maker
> An earthen vessel with the potter.
> (Isaiah 45:9)

When in empty faith I am doing nothing, a limitless divine love is welling up within me and taking over my life. The emptiness, the void, the darkness – this is infinite love dwelling in the depths of my being. The important thing is that I surrender to this love and allow it to envelop my life.

But this is not easy. Even Paul fought and struggled and kicked against the goad. The problem was that he did not recognize love when he saw it. And so he fights and begs to be delivered from the sting of the flesh that torments him, until the answer comes: "My grace is sufficient for you for my power is made perfect in weakness" (2 Corinthians 12:9). It is precisely when we are beaten down and helpless and weak that the deepest power within us, the real Tao of endless love, rises to the surface. Paul now understand this. Overflowing with joy he cries out:

> For the sake of Christ, then,
> I am content with weaknesses, insults,
> hardships, persecutions and calamities;
> for when I am weak, then I am strong.
> (2 Corinthians 12:10)

Yes. When Paul is weak the power of Jesus begins to act in him. And this has been true of so many people. It was precisely when their health collapsed and their work failed and their reputation was sullied – it was precisely then that the power and the glory and the love of God surfaced in their lives. This point is beautifully worked out by Graham Greene in *The Power and the Glory*. When I am weak, then I am strong. Something analogous appears in the mission of the disciples to which I have already referred. It is precisely when they have no gold or silver or copper in their purse, when they are rejected by men and dragged before governors and kings, when they give up reasoning and thinking and anxiety about what they will say – it is precisely then that the Spirit rises up and speaks within them – "for what you are to say will be given to you in that hour; for it is not you who speaks, but the Spirit of your Father speaking through you" (Matthew 10:19, 20). Here non-action reaches a powerful climax of supreme action.

IV

I have tried to describe the journey. And what a journey! It is the journey of one who is in love without reservation or restriction, who has an endless thirst, whose love goes on and on and on and on as he searches for the ox or crosses the desert. It is a journey that has its conflicts, its failures, is disappointments, its compromises, its temptations, its neuroses – for this unrestricted love (as I have already pointed out) is not perfect love, even though it is the most human of human loves.

But in this path, I have tried to say, it is much more important to receive love than to love, much more important to be loved than to love. This is *wu-wei* in a mystical setting. It is the situation of one who tries to drop defences and clinging and selfishness so that this immense love may inundate the whole person and take over life. And when this happens the love with which one loves others is not one's own but the divine love which is a gift. Only such love can go out to one's enemies as to one's friends, only such love can go sincerely and authentically to the poor, the sick, the underprivileged and the imprisoned.

Of course we fight against love. And no wonder. Because it transforms us, changes us into another person – and we don't like to be changed: we like to stay where we are. because to be changed is to die and rise. This love, says St John of the Cross, kills in order to give life:

> In killing You changed death to life
> (*Living Flame*, Stanza 2)

But in what way does it change us?

The Christian tradition, beginning with Paul and John, tells us that we die to ourselves in order to live to Christ. "Truly, truly, I say to you, unless a grain of wheat falls into the earth and dies, it remains alone; but if it dies, it bears much fruit. He who loves his life loses it, and he who hates his life in this world will keep it for eternal life" (John 12:24, 25). And so we lose our own centre to fall into that deeper centre which is the Word of God living in us. When this happens we can say with Paul: "It is no longer I who live but Christ who lives in me . . ." (Galatians 2:20). Christian mysticism is a transformation into Christ.

Obviously Buddhists would not accept this Christian interpretation of mystical experience. Yet for them too, I believe, there is a death and a resurrection. Let us remember that that mythical man who searches for the ox finally loses himself completely. No man and no ox remain. Just the big circle of nothingness.

But the big circle is not the end. The man comes to life again. Transformed and enlightened, the compassionate old sage returns to the market-place to save all sentient beings. Now his love is a new love and he is a new man – a new creation. Something has died and something new has been born.

11

Oriental Nothingness

I

The words "nothingness" and "emptiness" are constantly on the lips of Oriental mystics. In some sects of Buddhism it is even said that whoever grasps "nothing" or *mu* has reached the heart of the matter and is already enlightened. The distinguished Japanese philosopher Yoshinori Takeuchi goes so far as to say that nothingness or non-being is the very foundation of Oriental philosophy and religion whereas Western thought is based upon being. Here are his words:

> Whenever discussion arises, concerning the problem of encounter between being and non-being, Western philosophers and theologians, with hardly an exception, will be found to align themselves on the side of being. This is no wonder. The idea of "being" is the Archimedean point of Western thought. Now only philosophy and theology but the whole tradition of Western civilization have turned around this pivot. The central notion from which Oriental religious intuition and belief as well as philosophical thought have been developed is the idea of "nothingness". To avoid serious confusion, however, it must be noted that East and West understand non-being and nothingness in entirely different ways. (Waldenfels)

Now it is sometimes said that few Orientals and no Occidentals understand Oriental nothingness. Probably, however, this is an exaggeration. There are some Occidentals who have spent years or decades in assiduous Buddhist training and discipline and who undoubtedly have achieved insight into the mystery of *mu*. But I myself do not claim to be one of them. Consequently, I can do little more than introduce my reader to some of the basic problems of *mu* and then move on to nothingness in the Western mystical tradition which is more properly my field. I hope that some day we will receive an explanation of Oriental nothingness from the pen of an enlightened Buddhist, who will at the same time direct his inner eye to the corresponding problem in the West.

II

The *Upanishads* speak of many different layers of consciousness, the deepest of which is compared to a deep and dreamless sleep in which the mind is swept clean of all images and thoughts and subject-object relationships. This, an intense form of that pure or undifferentiated consciousness about which I spoke earlier in this book, has always been associated with the Sanskrit word *sunyata* which is generally translated as "emptiness" or "voidness" or "nothingness". Yet *sunyata* never means the death of all things or absolute negation: it has a positive connotation.

In the Buddhist wisdom literature composed in India between 100 BC and AD 600 the word *sunyata* continues to be of cardinal importance. Later it is brought to China and translated into Chinese by two vibrant characters which today are splendidly inscribed over the gates of Buddhist temples throughout Japan. The first character, pronounced *mu* in Japanese and *wu* in Chinese and translated into English as *nothing* is:

(By kind permission of Kakichi Kadowaki)

If you ask a Zen master to draw a character which expresses his deepest insight, it is more than likely that he will take up his brush and draw *mu*. This will be his parting gift as you leave the temple.

The second character is pronounced *ku* and is usually translated as *emptiness:*

(By kind permission of Kakichi Kadowaki)

This same character is also used for the sky: the great emptiness of the vault of heaven which resembles *sunyata*.

Now while these two characters and the ideas for which they stand sound disturbingly negative to Western ears, any authentic Buddhist will insist that they contain a very positive dimension.[1] That is why Takeuchi can say that the Eastern understanding of these words is quite different from that of the West and that "the absolute must be considered first as Absolute Nothingness" (Waldenfels).

On a more popular level, when Queen Elizabeth of Britain was visiting Japan, she was brought to a Zen temple over which the great character of *mu* was inscribed. "What does that

[1] A standard Japanese Buddhist dictionary renders *ku* as *sunyata*: "*Sunyata* does not deny the concept of existence as such. . . . it must not be confused with nihilism or a denial of the existence of phenomena in any form" (*Japanese-Buddhist Dictionary*, Daito Shuppansha, Tokyo, 1965).

mean?" she asked the Buddhist monk who guided her. "That means God", he answered. No doubt he felt that such an answer while not completely accurate or satisfactory was least open to misunderstanding.

*

But let me first refer to two aspects of *mu* which are less difficult to grasp.

The first I call cultural nothingness because it has penetrated Sino-Japanese culture in a remarkably way and is known to any educated person who lives in East Asia. It is found in the concept of no-mind (*mu-shin*) or non-self (*mu-ga*) which is central to the practice of the tea-ceremony, the flower arrangement and calligraphy as well as to the martial arts like fencing, judo and karate. It is closely associated with the Taoist non-action (*wu-wei*) about which I spoke in the last chapter, and is the mental state of one who submerges his ego or little self in order that the forces of life may begin to work within. The mind is emptied of reasoning and thinking, of all sense of subject and object, in order that the life-force which is centred in the belly may rise up – and it does rise up, giving extraordinary power to the person who has mastered this art of non-self or no-mind.

Yet non-self can be religious as well as cultural. At a temple near Tokyo famous for its great statue of the Bodhisattva Kannon, one can read the inscription: "The person of non-self (*mu-ga no hito*) can see with the inner eye." While the self remains, enlightenment will not come. It is when the illusory self dies that the real self is born and the inner eye awakens and comes to see.

A second aspect of *mu* which is central to Buddhist practice is the *ascetical mu*. That is to say the non-attachment, the abandonment of clinging and craving and inordinate desire. Repeating the word *mu* one drops all that superfluous baggage about which I have spoken, thus attaining to inner liberty and poverty of spirit. This again has Taoist influence and is based on the notion that when one abandons clinging, the Tao will act within.

As I have said, the cultural and ascetical aspects of *mu* are not difficult to understand. Much more mysterious and problematic is the ontological or metaphysical *mu* on which the others are built. For *mu* is regarded as an absolute and as perfect wisdom.

III

In the thirty-eight books which compose the *Prajnaparamita*, literature pride of place is given to the *Heart Sutra* of the perfection of wisdom, which claims to formulate the heart or essence or core of perfect wisdom and to put into words (impossible task) the experience of nirvana and of *sunyata*. In Chinese this sutra consists of only two hundred and sixty-two words which can be printed on a single page; and it is recited constantly in Zen temples. With something like awe I have attended the early morning liturgy at *Eiheiji*, the central temple of the Soto sect, watching a hundred monks, clad in Buddhist robes, march rhythmically to and fro to the sound of the gong while reciting the *Heart Sutra*. Although no translation will bring out the melody of those Chinese sounds, I would like to quote some of the sentences in English. The Sutra begins:

> When the Bodhisattva Avalokitesvara was in deep meditation of *prajnaparamita* (transcendental wisdom) he saw that all the five skandhas are empty; thus he overcame all suffering and ills.

Here the important word is "saw". The Bodhisattva, without the aid of discursive reasoning, got a direct intuition into the total emptiness of all things including the five skandhas.[2] And precisely through this enlightenment he was liberated from suffering and ill. This again is a notion that is deeply rooted in Buddhism: that through transcendental wisdom we are saved and liberated.

The sutra goes on to speak of emptiness, of *sunyata*. It does so in radically negative terms:

---

[2] According to Buddhist philosophy man consists of five heaps or layers known as *skandhas*. They are: body, feelings, perceptions, impulses and emotions, acts of consciousness. These five heaps are everything in man and the ego is illusory.

All that has its own characteristic or form . . . is empty of the form: no arising, no ceasing; no contamination, no lack of contamination; no increase, no decrease. Therefore, in emptiness is no physical component, no sensation, no representation, no will, no consciousness; no eye, no ear, no nose, no tongue, no body, no mind; no shape, no colour, no sound, no smell, no taste, no touch, no concept; no visible world . . . no consciously perceivable world; no ultimate ignorance, no extinction of ultimate ignorance, no ageing and dying; no suffering, no cause of suffering, no extinction of suffering, no practice which leads to the extinction of suffering; no knowing, no attainment, no non-attainment.

This array of negatives is a hymn in praise of *sunyata* or *ku* or nirvana. The same idea can be expressed pictorially by the great circle of nothingness or zero which is so characteristic of Zen art. It is the picture which we see when the ox has disappeared, the man has disappeared and only the voice cries out: "Not a thing is! Nothing!":

八   人牛俱忘

One way to approach nothingness is through the *koan* practice in Zen.[3] Sitting in the lotus with back straight and eyes slightly open, one simply repeats the word *mu* with the breathing. One repeats it again and again and again for hours, for days, for weeks, until eventually one comes to *realize mu* and to identify with it. This is a great enlightenment. Moreover, it is ongoing: one can get more and more insight into *mu:* there is no end to its treasures. The Master will ask questions to probe the depth of one's realization: "What is *mu?* Show me *mu.* What size is *mu?* What shape? What colour?" There is no fixed answer to these questions but an experienced master knows with unerring intuition whether or not the response comes from an enlightened consciousness. He can sense at once whether the student has become one with *mu* or is still separated from it.

In Zen, *mu* is called "the barrier without gates". One must strive with might and main to break through this great barrier which leads from the phenomenal world into the world of enlightenment. But one does not understand *mu* with the rational intellect. Here is a famous description of the approach:

> Now, tell me, what is the barrier of the Zen Masters? Just this *mu* – it is the barrier of Zen. It is thus called "the gateless barrier of Zen". Those who have passed the barrier will not only see Joshu clearly, but will go hand in hand with all the Masters of the past, see them face to face. You will see with the same eye that they see with and hear with the same ear. Wouldn't it be wonderful? Don't you want to pass the barrier? Then concentrate yourself into this *mu*, with your 360 bones and 84,000 pores, making your whole body one great inquiry. Day and night work intently at it. Do not attempt nihilistic or dualistic interpretations. It is like having bolted a red-hot iron ball. You try to vomit it but cannot. Cast away your illusory discriminating knowledge and consciousness accumulated up to now, and keep on working harder. After a while, when your efforts come

---

[3] *Koan* One way of practising Zen in the Rinzai sect is to keep before the mind's eye a riddle or enigmatic problem or *koan* which cannot be solved by discursive reasoning.

to fruition, all the oppositions (such as in and out) will naturally be identified. You will then be like a dumb person who has had a wonderful dream: he only knows it personally, within himself. Suddenly you break through the barrier: you will astonish heaven and shake the earth.

(Shibayama, p. 19)

In this way one becomes *mu*.

"What is *mu*?" asks the Master. "I am *mu*", answers the disciple. "Show me *mu*", says the Master. "You are looking at *mu*", retorts the disciple instantaneously. "What colour is *mu*?", asks the Master. "My colour," answers the disciple. "What shape is *mu*?", asks the Master. "My shape," answers the disciple. "*Mu* walked in through that door. *Mu* is talking to you." But this is only the beginning. There is no end to *mu*.

IV

Confronted with the mystery of Oriental nothingness, Western philosophers have frequently used words like nihilistic, life-denying, pessimistic. Some have not hesitated to call Buddhism atheistic. I believe (and I have already quoted Buddhists to support me) that this is a misunderstanding: we must not blind ourselves to the extremely positive elements which lie behind the negative language.

First of all we must remember that Buddhism is above all a religion of salvation. It claims to save man and woman from the illusions and snares and suffering of human existence. The four noble truths which are the basis of all forms of Buddhism declare that existence is suffering, but then hasten to add that *there is a way out:* man's situation is not hopeless: there is light beyond the darkness. Is not this a positive dimension?

Moreover, the way out is through enlightenment or a series of enlightenments culminating in the supreme experience of nirvana. Far from being negative, enlightenment is an experience of joy, liberation and release from anxiety. The *Heart Sutra* which I have quoted speaks of the fearlessness and joy of the person who has realized and attained to the perfection of wisdom. It is paralleled in all the mystical traditions where there comes a time when one is liberated from fear, and says with Julian of Norwich, "All will be well, and all will be well, and all manner of things will be well." All may not look well. It may look all wrong. But deep down in my heart I have a security and a certainty that everything is all right.

Again, let us remember that while the oxherding pictures originally ended with the great circle of *mu*, two pictures were subsequently added which are positive and deeply significant.

The first is called "the return of the source". It tells the myth of the eternal return. If you go on a journey you return to your starting point – like Chesterton's adventurous man who set sail from Plymouth on a journey of discovery and found England, or like the traveller in outer space who turns full circle and comes back to earth, or like all of us who return to the womb: to the womb of the earth. In the same way, the man who went in search of the ox, when the turmoil and conflict and ecstasy is over, returns to himself: he becomes his true self. Just himself, very ordinary, nothing special. Once again, trees are trees, rivers are rivers, valleys are valleys.

But in the last picture he goes one step further and returns to the market-place with great compassion to save all sentient beings. In other words he returns to action.

Now I believe that this compassion which fills his heart is connected with the *mu* and emptiness. For there is an old Buddhist saying that emptiness equals compassion (*ku soku jihi*). This is an emptiness which is akin to what the old Christian writers called humility. When I am humbly and totally empty I can receive others into my heart; when self is forgotten I have room for all men and women and for God.

*

There are good reasons, then, for concluding that while all expressions about the ultimate reality in Buddhism are negative that reality itself is positive and that Buddhism is by no means atheistic. There are indeed some Buddhist texts which point to such an interpretation. In the *Pali Canon* of Hinayana Buddhism we read: "Monks, there is a not-born, a not-become, a not-made, a not-compounded. Monks, if that unborn, not-become, not-made, not-compounded were not, there would be apparent no escape from this here that is born, become, made, compounded. But since, monks, there is an unborn . . . therefore the escape from this here is born" (*Udana*, 80, 81. See Woodward, p. 98). In other words, the very fact that there is salvation or deliverance points to the existence of an ultimate reality. We can only speak about it, however, in negative terms.

Yet when all is said and done, even the most enlightened among the enlightened does not grasp Oriental nothingness fully: anyone who claims to have plumbed the depths of *mu*, far from being wise, is a fool. For nothingness is truly a mystery, a mystery in the strictest sense of the word. And this in itself is deeply significant. Because, as I have repeatedly said, all the great religions point to a mystery which hovers over human life yet lies beyond a cloud of unknowing. It is precisely this sense of mystery and of the ineffable that we all have in common. If no one understands nothingness, neither does anyone truly understand God. No one understands Yahweh nor the Tao nor Brahman nor Atman. We are all reduced to silence in the face of mystery. We are all aware that we do not know.

12

Christian Nothingness

I

The apophatic mystics of the West, like their brethren in the East, are lavish in their use of words like nothingness, emptiness, darkness, obscurity and the cloud. Indeed, so dark and negative is their manner of speech that not a few fervent Christians have raised voices of protest. In an excellent book written in the early part of this century and entitled *Western Mysticism*, Dom Cuthbert Butler treats of contemplation in three great mystics of the West: Augustine, Gregory and Bernard of Clairvaux. In extolling enthusiastically the affirmative and deeply Christian dimension of these great giants of the mystical life, Cuthbert Butler shows himself a little uneasy about the nothingness and darkness and secrecy and unknowing of the Dionysian tradition. "The mystics", he writes, "heap up terms of negation – darkness, void, nothingness – in endeavouring to describe the Absolute which they have apprehended. It may be, of course, that their apprehension had such a fullness and richness of content that in human language it could only be described negatively. But one must at least point out that their method is the very opposite of the characteristically Christian one of affirmation; that where they say 'darkness' St John says 'light', and that St John says 'fullness' where they say 'void', and St Paul stresses not ignorance but enhanced knowledge, as the result of religious experience" (Butler, p. 179).

These words are representative of a number of deeply Christian contemplatives who react vigorously against the "neoplatonic contamination" which has infected the springs of Christian mysticism. They will agree that the Rhineland mystics had profound religious experience, but they are wary about the language in which this religious experience is expressed. They will agree that St John of the Cross was a great mystic, a great poet and a great saint – but they are less than happy with his negative theology. Most of all they are wary of an emptiness or nothingness that would negate the value and beauty of God's creation. Some distinguished Christian writers have labelled St John of the Cross Buddhist; and while this might sound complimentary to our modern ecumenical ears it was far from flattering in its original context.

This reaction against the negativity of the Dionysian mystics is even more pronounced today since we live in a culture which has the greatest esteem for human values, human feeling, human sexuality. Ours is a culture which delights in the saying of Irenaeus that the glory of God is man and woman fully alive. It is a culture which believes with Teilhard in the spiritual power of matter. It is a culture which looks with dismay on nothingness and emptiness.

And yet, in spite of all this, we still must ask if there is an authentic Christian *mu* or nothingness. Apart from other considerations, we owe this to the dialogue with our Buddhist brothers and sisters in the East.

II

At a Zen-Christian dialogue which I once attended in Kyoto one of the participants, a Japanese Christian who practices Zen with a small community in the Japanese Alps, was asked to explain his Zen. He rose to his feet and said quite simply: "The first thing is sincerity . . . My Zen is expressed in the words of Jesus on the Cross: 'My God, my God, why hast thou forsaken me?' " A Buddhist participant who was sitting behind me whispered under his breath: "Beautiful, beautiful!"

"Eli, Eli, lama sabacthani?" (Matthew 27:46). When Jesus uttered these words he had nothing, absolutely nothing. Previously he had said that his disciples would all be scattered and that they would leave him alone – "yet I am not alone, for the Father is with me" (John 16:32). But now even the Father has forsaken him, and Jesus is left in the void of nothingness and in the dark night of the soul.

These words are, of course, the opening lines of the Twenty-Second Psalm, and some scripture scholars hold that Jesus on the Cross recited the whole psalm or, at least, that the sentiments of the whole psalm were in his mind as he was dying. This is profoundly significant. For Psalm 22 is messianic – it is a cry of trust in the God who has protected our fathers and has drawn me from the womb of my mother. It ends with a cry of joy and of hope and of triumph:

> All the ends of the earth shall remember
>   and turn to the Lord;
> and all the families of the nations
>   shall worship before him
>
> (Psalm 22:27)

This is the cry of resurrection. The realization that in the total loss is the total gain. In the nothingness is the everything. In the death is the victory. "Truly, truly, I say to you, unless a grain of wheat falls into the earth and dies, it remains alone; but if it dies, it bears much fruit" (John 12:24).

*

Another example of nothingness is found in the Epistle to the Philippians where Paul speaks of the *kenosis* or self-emptying of Jesus – "who though he was in the form of God, did not count equality with God a thing to be grasped, but emptied himself, taking the form of a servant, being born in the likeness of men" (Philippians 2:6,7). Jesus emptied himself; and it is interesting to note that the Japanese Bible translates this as "Jesus became *mu*" (*mu to sareta*): Jesus became nothing. But he became even more than nothing because "being found in human form he humbled himself and became obedient unto death, even death on a cross" (Philippians 2:8). But there can be an even greater humiliation than this, and in another remarkable text Paul says that Jesus became sin: "For our sake he made him to be sin who knew no sin, so that in him we might become the righteousness of God" (2 Corinthians 5:21). Such was the humiliation, the emptiness, the nothingness of the Son of God. It is beyond words to describe.

But his emptiness is a way to fullness: his nothingness is a way to everything; his humiliation is a way to glory:

> Therefore God has highly exalted him
> and bestowed on him the name which is
> above every name, that at the name of
> Jesus every knee should bow, in heaven
> and on earth and under the earth, and
> every tongue confess that Jesus Christ
> is Lord, to the glory of God the Father
> (Philippians 2:9–11)

Here is the resurrection, hailed by every tongue with that formula which in the New Testament is the profession of faith: "Jesus Christ is Lord."

All this may seem a thousand miles away from Oriental nothingness. Yet I have heard of a Zen Master who, on reading this passage from Philippians, nodded his head and said: "St Paul really understood *mu*!"

*

Early in this book I spoke of the mystical experience of Jesus and I said that it was primarily Trinitarian. Now let me add another very obvious aspect of this experience: death and resurrection. The supreme mystical experience of Jesus entailed a total annihilation as a prelude to an endless glorification. And, moreover, this suffering and emptiness and death *was necessary*. "Was it not necessary that Christ should suffer these things and enter into his glory?" (Luke 24:26).

Now I have also said that the Christian mystical experience is that of "another Christ" – as Jesus became nothing in order to be glorified, so the Christian mystical life is a becoming nothing in order to be glorified by resurrection. But this pattern is not only Christian. It is found before the time of Jesus in Abraham who loses everything, absolutely everything, in order to become the father of a great nation. The story is told in Genesis and I have referred to it already in this book. Abraham is about to slay his beloved son, thus crushing all hopes that the promise will be fulfilled, but his hand is stopped by the angel of the Lord:

> By myself I have sworn, says the Lord,
> because you have done this, and have
> not withheld your son, your only son, I
> will indeed bless you, and I will multiply
> your descendents as the stars of heaven
> and as the sand which is on the seashore.
> And your descendants shall possess the gate of
> their enemies, and by our descendants shall
> all the nations of the earth bless themselves . . .
>   (Genesis 22:15–18)

Here Abraham dies; he becomes nothing in order to rise joyfully to the fulfilment of the promise.

I believe that this pattern of death and resurrection, of nothing and everything, of emptiness and fullness – this basic pattern is found in the big enlightenments or mystical experiences of all the great religions. In Buddhism it is said that there must come a "great death" prior to the awakening. Moreover, it is interesting to observe that when Zen masters speak to Christians they frequently use the example of the death and resurrection of Jesus, telling us that like Jesus we must die in order to be reborn. This is because they know from experience that death and resurrection are the warp and woof of human life and they see that Jesus is the archetypal man.

From all this I draw the conclusion that the Cross is the Christian *mu* and the Christian *koan*. Just as *mu* cannot be penetrated by reasoning and thinking, so also the cross is impervious to the rational intellect. But he who understands is flooded with unutterable joy and true wisdom – "we preach Christ crucified, a stumbling block to Jews and folly to Gentiles, but to those who are called, both Jews and Greeks, Christ the power of God and the wisdom of God" (1 Corinthians 1:23,24). These are not mere words. Paul glorified in the cross of Our Lord

Jesus Christ by which he was crucified to the world and the world to him; and many Christian mystics through the centuries have had the same foolish enlightenment. Their lives have changed radically when they came to understand, and then to love, the cross. This is something one cannot explain: it is folly and it is a stumbling block.

III

I believe, then, that the *kenosis* or self-emptying of Jesus is the basis and the inspiration for any Christian emptiness or nothingness or loss of self. And, moreover, I believe that the authentic Christian mystics of the Dionysian tradition thought so also. Those who call St John of the Cross Buddhist may overlook the profound significance of a few of the sentences with which he begins his practical advice for progress in the mystical path:

> First, have a habitual desire to imitate Christ in all your deeds by bringing your life into conformity with His. You must then study His life in order to know how to imitate Him and behave in all events as He would.
>
> Second . . . Do this out of love for Jesus Christ. In His life He had no other gratification, nor desired any other, than the fulfilment of His Father's will, which He called His meat and food (John 4:34) (*Ascent*, 1:13.3 and 4).

Similar passages could be quoted from the author of *The Cloud*, Meister Eckhart, and the other Christian Dionysian mystics. These men were impregnated with the spirit of the Gospel.

Yet, having said this, it is also true that other aspects of their spirituality are culturally conditioned. Just as theology changes according to culture and historical conditions (and what a change we witness today!), so also spirituality must change and be incarnated into each age. Consequently I am not at all certain that the overall approach of the mystics of darkness will appeal to modern men and women. I prefer to see it as one spirituality which was valid for people of a certain time and is valid for people of a certain temperament today. But I understand and respect the feelings of those who say that Eckhart and St John of the Cross are not their cup of tea.

Let me, however, select some aspect of the Western mystical nothingness which are worth discussing and may be of interest to Buddhists in our day.

*

St John of the Cross stresses the nothingness of the whole created universe. At the beginning of the *Ascent* he writes:

> All the creatures of heaven and earth *are nothing* when compared to God, as Jeremiah points out . . . "I looked at the earth, and it was empty and nothing; and at the heavens and I saw they had no light" (Jeremiah 4:23). *By saying that he saw an empty earth, he meant that all its creatures were nothing and the earth too was nothing.*

Here is a radical statement of the nothingness of the world, and it is followed by an even more radical declaration that "all the beauty of creatures compared with the infinite Beauty of God is supreme ugliness" (*Ascent*, 4:4,3)

Now in all cultures we find people who have a deep insight into the transiency and nothingness and vanity of all things. I am thinking of Qoheleth or of these modern Existentialists who speak of man as being-towards-death, and so on. But the nothingness of St John of the Cross is not like this. It is the realization of one who has had a glimpse of infinite beauty and who says that *by comparison* the rest of the world is supreme ugliness. Such a profoundly enlightened person must be forgiven for his poetic hyperbole. All the mystics are tempted to talk in this way. They talk of the light of the sun and the light of the candle, of the all and the nothing; and did not Thomas say that his writings were like straw?

Furthermore, the Thomistic theology which St John of the Cross studied under the Dominicans at Salamanca had integrated the Dionysian theology of negation and in consequence contained a startling paradox: on the one hand all created things are like God and reflect his glory, but on the other hand they are not like God and do not reflect his glory. For only God exists in the complete sense of the word. Things other than God are being and non-being. Seen from one aspect they are: seen from another aspect they are not.

Now is it possible to get an insight into the non-being or nothingness of all things? I think it is. But such an insight is closely associated with a realization of the allness of God. I believe that something like this exists in Hinduism where we are told that the world is only real and intelligible when seen as rooted in Brahman. Separated from him it is *maya* or illusion or nothingness, and the person who sees it cut off from its source lives in *avidya* or ignorance.

IV

I have spoken of the nothingness or non-being of the created universe. But is it possible to speak of the nothingness of God?

St John of the Cross will affirm that God is everything. He is light; he is fullness; he is all; he is the source of being and beauty. In this he would seem to be the very opposite of the absolute nothingness about which Oriental mysticism speaks. But (and here again we come against great paradox) while God is light in himself, he is *darkness to us;* while he is all in himself, he is *nothing to us;* while he is fullness in himself, he is *emptiness to us*. St John of the Cross does not say that God is darkness and emptiness and nothingness; but he does say that the human experience of God is darkness and emptiness and nothingness. For God is like night to the soul.

Nor is this mere theory. In the mystical life one enters into the void, into a cloud of unknowing which seems like nothingness. Indeed, a time may come when the darkness is so extreme that one feels abandoned by God – left high and dry with God absent. But if one waits in emptiness one comes to realize that the void is God: it is not a preparatory stage but the experience of God himself. And in the moment or period of enlightenment though one may say that God who was absent has returned, more correctly one will exclaim: "God was present all the time and I did not recognize him. I thought it was darkness but it was light. I thought it was nothing but it was all. It is not that the darkness has gone away but that I have come to love the darkness." As the light blinds the bat or as excessive light of the sun blinds the human eye, so the excessive light of God plunges the human person into thick darkness.

And God is approached in darkness and emptiness and nothingness simply because he is the mystery of mysteries, far above anything that the human eye can see or the human mind imagine, far above anything that can be conveyed in words: "No one has ever seen God" (John 1:18)

That God is mystery, unknowable, ineffable, unlike anything made by human hands or seen by human eyes – this is stressed all through the Old Testament. The Jewish historian Josephus tells the story of how the Roman Pompey, after capturing Jerusalem in 63 BC, strode into the holy of holies with some of his followers and found there *nothing, absolutely nothing*. This was the Hebrew way of representing the ineffable nature of Yahweh.[1] As for the apophatic mystics, beginning with Gregory of Nyssa, they constantly appeal to the example of Moses (to what extent the exegetes would support them I do not know) who ascended the mountain to meet God in the cloud of unknowing. For, as is said in Chronicles, "The Lord has said that he would dwell in thick darkness" (2 Chronicles 6:1). And the experience of Moses is one of nothingness and darkness even though his heart is filled with burning love. This is the darkness of faith, of naked faith which lives in the mind when all props are gone.

Some years ago while I was chatting with a Zen Master in Kyoto about *mu* and nothingness I cited the words of St John

---

[1] Pompey captured Jerusalem in 63 BC after a siege of three months. Josephus tells us that together with some of his followers he entered the sanctuary but that in accordance with his piety and virtuous character he touched nothing. In the innermost recess known as the holy of holies there was nothing whatever: *ouden holos* (Bellum Jud. 5, 5, 5). The Roman historian Tacitus also relates that Pompey saw into the holy of holies. It should be noted that this was the second, post-exilic temple. In the first temple, the temple of Solomon, the ark was placed in the holy of holies.

of the Cross which I have quoted earlier in the book, that in the mystical life there is nothing to guide me except the love which burns in my heart. I then observed that St John of the Cross was less radical than Zen because he says, "nothing except . . ." whereas Zen says, "nothing". The master smiled and said, "No. I don't think so. This is one example of the inadequacy of words. Because *'the love which burns in my heart' is also nothing.*" I immediately saw his point and was amazed at his perceptiveness. The love which burns in my heart is nothing because it is faith, pure faith, naked faith which is dark like night and is experienced as nothingness. Yet it is precisely the night and the nothingness which guide; and so St John of the Cross can sing:

> O guiding night
> O night more lovely than the dawn
> > (*Ascent*, Stanza 5)

It is in darkness and nothingness and emptiness that one experiences God. The darkness and the emptiness and the nothingness are guiding and leading me on. But let me add a word: the darkness and the nothingness are not necessarily dismal and bleak and unpleasant and painful, as the words themselves might indicate and as some writers have suggested. There are, of course, painful periods; but the nothingness is filled with joy and the night is more lovely than the dawn.

St John of the Cross, who was an artist as well as a mystic, has left us a sketch of the mystical path which leads to the summit of the mountain. At the very centre of the picture is *nothing* (the Spanish *nada*) and the saint writes:

> nothing, nothing, nothing,
> nothing, nothing, nothing,
> And even on the mountain nothing

Renunciation of all clinging and craving! I have mentioned it already: no gold, no silver, no copper in your belt, no bag for your journey, no two tunics, no sandals, no staff. A similar message is found in *The Cloud of Unknowing* where the author tells us to bury everything, absolutely everything, beneath the cloud of forgetting. All this is somewhat similar to the ascetical *mu* of Oriental mysticism. Only remember that this nothingness is not the renunciation of all things, but the renunciation of clinging to all things – and it is done in order that I may love these same things truly, as they are in themselves, without projections. Once liberated from self-centred craving one gets everything back and can cry with St John of the Cross:

> Now that I least desire them
> I have them all without desire

I have them all! Nothing is renounced. It is the mystic who really loves life and loves people and loves the cosmos and finds joy in all that is beautiful in the universe. He loves all but is the slave to nothing.

The all-important thing to remember (and here I hope I will be forgiven for repeating myself) is that this journey is the answer to a call and is made under the sweet influence of grace and the gentle guidance of the Spirit. Not one step is made except by the power of the same Spirit. This is the path of one who has seen the footprints of the ox and the treasure hidden in the field and sells everything joyfully to follow the ox or to buy the field. It is the renunciation of one who has heard the voice of the beloved: "Hark! my beloved is knocking" (Song of Songs 5:2). This is very important, because without the call of grace the whole doctrine of *nothing* becomes harsh, grating, inhuman and dismal.

Furthermore it must be remembered, as I have already said, that this loss of all things is eventually something that happens rather than something that I do. Remember the non-action, the *wu-wei*. I don't need to make violent efforts because the power of love which burns within is gradually and gently detaching me from all things, from all people, so that I may be attached to these same things and these same people in a true and nobler way.

And yet the voice of St John of the Cross does grate upon the ears of sensitive souls:

> To reach satisfaction in all
> desire its possession in nothing
> To come to possess all
> desire the possession of nothing,
> To arrive at being all
> desire to be nothing.
>
> To come to the knowledge of all
> desire the knowledge of nothing
> (*Ascent*, 1:13,11)

And in this *todo y nada* the Spanish mystic is not original. The same theme is sung centuries before in *The Book of Privy Counselling* and in Julian of Norwich where we hear of the "alling and noughting" (Johnston (2), p. 164).

I myself can never understand this in a purely philosophical or ascetical context. To me it only makes sense in view of the *kenosis* of Jesus about which I have spoken. In such a context it is nonsense which makes sense or, as Paul says, foolishness which is wisdom: "For the foolishness of God is wiser than men . . ." (1 Corinthians 1:25). That is why I believe that those who call St John of the Cross Buddhist and overlook the Christocentric dimensions of his work miss the whole point. Without Christ his doctrine would scarcely be human.

*

I have spoken of the journey and the way. But words are always inadequate; and of course there is no way. Abraham "went out, not knowing where he was to go" (Hebrews 11:8). Abraham had no maps. At the beginning there are guidelines and rules which are always helpful and valuable, but at the summit St John of the Cross can write:

> Here there is no longer any way
> Because for the just man there is no law
> He is a law unto himself

The just man is following his deepest spiritual instincts which tell him of the promptings of the Holy Spirit. He is beyond the law.

In Zen one often hears of a state which is "beyond good and evil"; and this kind of talk has been offensive to pious ears which have interpreted it as a *carte blanche* for licentiousness. But it is not so. It simply means that the enlightened person is beyond *the law* of good and evil because guided by the inner light. He or she is following the counsel of Jesus not to be anxious about what we should say because the Spirit will tell us: "It is not you who speak, but the Spirit of your Father speaking through you" (Matthew 10:20).

13

Journey Towards Union

I

I have described the mystical journey in negative terms; but I hope it has become abundantly clear that the journey itself is not negative or life-denying. It is a love-filled journey towards union with the All, a journey which can be described in all kinds of symbols and metaphors and figures of speech. Thomas Aquinas explains it theologically in terms of the Genesis myth. Man and woman created in the state of original justice lived happily in Paradise in harmony within themselves, harmony with one another and harmony with God. But by sin they were cruelly divided, split, scattered. Beguiled by the serpent, exiled from Eden, ashamed of their nakedness, they fell into that sadly divided state to which we their children are now reduced. But mysticism or contemplation is a return to harmonious union: it is a process of reconciliation, of inner unification, of magnificent justification. It is as the author of *The Cloud* (he was greatly influenced by Thomas) strikingly states, a one-ing exercise. That is to say, it makes us one with ourselves, one with the human race, one with the All which is God.

And the unity to which mysticism leads is much richer than the original justice which was lost. For "the free gift is not like the trespass" (Romans 5:13). The new union, found through the grace of Christ and his gift of faith, is ultimately that union for which Jesus prayed at the Last Supper when he asked the Father "that they may all be one; even as thou, Father, art in me, and I in thee, that they also may be one in us, so that the world may believe that thou hast sent me" (John 17:21).

As can be readily seen, this explanation situates mysticism at the very centre of the Christian life. The mystical life becomes the call to mysticism. For everyone is called to this union and reconciliation within the self, with the human race and with God. This is the message of Paul in Ephesians.

When it came to describing the psychological process by which this union was effected, the scholastics made use of the philosophy of Plato and Aristotle as it had been assimilated into the Christian tradition. Here the human soul is described as having faculties called exterior senses, interior senses, memory, understanding and will – while the centre or ground of the soul is the great mystery which we call God. Since these faculties have been dissipated and distorted, they must be purified in order that they may once more be focused on God who is their centre. This purification, achieved through darkness and dryness and emptiness about which I have spoken, leads to a great harmony. For the purified person has faith in the intellect, hope in the memory and love in the will, while the purified senses give light and warmth to the Beloved who dwells within. Indeed, this whole process is nothing less than a divinization of the person who now becomes another Christ, a child by adoption. The in-dwelling Spirit joins himself to the human spirit and cries out: "Abba, Father!"

In this book I accept this doctrine but I have preferred to use a different psychology which I consider more relevant for the men and women of our day. This psychology speaks in terms of state or layers of consciousness rather than faculties of the soul. In the mystical life one passes from one layer to the next in an inner or downward journey to the core of the personality where dwells the great mystery called God – God who cannot be known directly, cannot be seen (for no one has ever seen God) and who dwells in thick darkness. This is the never-ending journey which is recognizable in the mysticism of all the great religions. It is a journey towards union because the consciousness gradually expands and integrates data from the so-called unconsciousness while the whole personality is absorbed into the great mystery of God.

II

I have already described the journey as that of the man in search of the ox; but at the risk of some repetition I would like to describe it again with a different set of symbols.

And first of all let me recall that if we are inwardly divided this is partly because of the split between the conscious and the unconscious mind. I say unconscious but, as I have already observed, strictly speaking there is nothing unconscious in the psyche. What exists are higher and lower voices which sing in a great polyphony. But this polyphony is sometimes closer to a cacophony in that the higher voices lead in one direction and the lower in another; the higher voices plan and desire one thing and the lower voices lag behind – my conscious mind may want health while my unconscious mind wants sickness, my conscious mind may want life and my unconscious mind may desire death, my conscious mind may want to forgive but my unconscious refuses to co-operate. And at the very core of my being is the deepest voice of all which is that of the Spirit. Quite often I cannot hear this voice or I ignore it or I cannot distinguish it from the other voices. And the result again is cacophony and discord.

Mystical healing of this inner division begins with the call of love at the core of my being, at the centre of my soul. This is the voice of the Spirit calling to union through an obscure sense of presence or a deep interior silence or a longing for solitude or a simple desire for God. Hearing this voice I begin the inner journey, which is joyful because it is filled with love, but painful because, like Abraham, I must pass from the familiar to the unfamiliar, from a state of consciousness which enjoys one set of beautiful things to a state of consciousness which values another. I do not know where I am going; the territory is unfamiliar; I am entering into areas of the psyche that are ordinarily dormant and unconscious; I am listening to the deeper voices; my inner eye, which formerly was asleep, is beginning to awaken. Consequently, profound changes take place; I begin to see things in a new way; I may seem like a different person both to myself and to others. "At . . . times," writes St John of the Cross, "a man wonders if he is being charmed, and he goes about with wonderment over what he sees and hears. Everything seems so very strange even though he is the same as always. The reason is that he is being made a stranger to his usual knowledge and experience of things . . ." (*Dark Night*, 2:9.5). In all this process I am growing and growing; my consciousness is being expanded and deepened; I am becoming more myself; the most profound areas of my psyche are being actuated and brought to life; I am finding an inner unity resembling the original justice of the Garden of Eden.

Yet conflicts necessarily arise because, as Shakespeare adroitly remarks, the course of true love never did run smooth. I cling to what is familiar and dread the journey to what is unfamiliar, like the man who wants both to follow the ox and enjoy the pleasures of remaining in the forest. Moreover, as new layers of the so-called unconscious are opened I come to see that not everything in my psyche is beautiful – ugly things are released, things which shock and trouble, things I would prefer not to see. How am I to cope with them?

In the holy places of many Asian countries one can see a set or series of pictures depicting the life of the Buddha. In one of these pictures Shakamuni, the enlightened one, sits splendidly in the lotus bathed in celestial light, his features radiating majestic calm and peace and composure, while all around him are yawning beasts and crawling snakes and seductive women. And the serene enlightened one pays absolutely no attention to these diabolical distractions. He does not fear the beasts; he is not seduced by the women. He tranquilly continues his inner journey to the depths of his being, to the great goal of mystery called nirvana.

And this is what we must do. Pay no attention to those beasts – they cannot harm you if you do no meddle with them. Let the lewd women smile alluringly – they cannot seduce you if you ignore them. Laugh at the snakes – they are illusory.

Yet great storms do arise and they can shake us to the roots of our being. One can be almost overwhelmed by gusts of anger or by nameless anxiety and fear, or by tumultuous sexuality, or be fierce rebellion against God and human beings. If a person has any neurotic tendencies (and most people have some) this is the time when they will appear, sometimes in a greatly intensified form. If parts of the psyche have been unfulfilled, this is the time when they will clamour for fulfilment. This may be the time when, precisely because of the inner turmoil, one loses friends or fails in one's work or does something so utterly stupid that one looks like an idiot in the eyes of all. And this may continue for a long time. It is not for me to decide when it will end – this is not in my power. But the *kairos* or time of deliverance will come.

The old authors spoke of the storm at sea when Jesus came to his disciples walking on the waters: "They were frightened but he said to them, 'It is I; do not be afraid' " (John 6:20). This is a good illustration because the worst thing in this journey is fear or discouragement or despair. Do not be afraid. Do not be anxious. He will come walking on the the waters and the storm will immediately cease and give place to a great calm.

Happy the person who in this situation finds a sympathetic friend who will encourage and console and help him to understand the situation and see what is happening. Happy the person who can come to accept this situation and to cry out with Paul: "For the sake of Christ, then, I am content with weaknesses, insults, hardships, persecutions, and calamities; for when I am weak then I am strong" (2 Corinthians 12:10).

*

For the significant thing in this journey is the view of oneself – of one's own psyche with its weaknesses and its capacity for evil. Such an experience may be valuable in that it leads to compassion for others but it can also be very distressing. Those yawning beasts and slimy snakes and seductive women and grimacing devils – they are part of me. They are what Jung calls my shadow, the unacceptable parts of my personality with which I am now brought face to face. And what if secrets of the psyche are unlocked, secrets of my early childhood which I have refused to face – and now I get an untrammelled vision of self in fulfilment of those words of Jesus: "Nothing is covered

up that will not be revealed or hidden that will not be known"
(Luke 12:2).

A moment ago I said that like the Buddha I must pay no
attention to these monsters of the psyche. And now I repeat
this. But let me add that in paying no attention I am coming to
accept them and to accept myself as I am. And this self-acceptance is the first great key to integration of the personality. Once
accepted many of these monsters will melt or disappear into the
night – they were paper tigers anyhow. Yet this self-acceptance
is only possible in view of the growing experimental conviction
that I am loved by Another, profoundly loved. Yes, the first
thing is not that I love but that I am loved, not that I give love
but that I accept love.

Through the acceptance of self and of love I grow from
childhood to adulthood. "When I was a child, I spoke like a
child, I thought like a child, I reasoned like a child; when I
became a man, I gave up childish ways" (1 Corinthians 13:11).
So in this healing process neuroses and hang-ups of all kinds
melt away. One simply grows out of them, comes to look back
on them from a higher vantage point – the problem may still
be there but I see it in a new light and its crippling effects
have vanished. I am moving towards that integration of the
personality which Jung calls individuation.

III

I said that mysticism leads not only to union within oneself but
also to union with all men. This is indeed so. But once again
we are up against paradox: for union only comes through isolation and conflict. In the early stages mystical experience often
separates people from the crowd. They are out of step because
they have heard a different drummer. Often they are for some
time misfits in society, though they may have a few friends who
understand them and share their aspirations. But the isolation
is there, a painful consequence of the decision to follow the ox
or to buy the field in which lies the treasure.

And yet, even while this separation is taking place, union with others is being enacted at another level. One reason for this is that all prayer, but especially contemplative prayer, leads to forgiveness and to the collapse of those unconscious barriers which cut us off from others. By barriers I mean things like suppressed anger, buried resentment, lack of forgiveness – all those neuroses which have existed in our unconscious since childhood or have even been inherited through the collective unconscious. Quite often these barriers are a neurotic relationship with one's parents.

Here let me digress for a moment to say that some modern psychologists have highlighted the supreme importance in human life of interior fidelity to the fourth commandment of the Decalogue – to love and honour one's parents. For relationship with parents (even when these parents are already dead) seems to be the key to success in other adult relationships. Nor can it be taken for granted that everyone honours his parents with an adult love. Quite often suppressed anger and resentment and fear and childish fixations linger on. And it is precisely here, in the deep, deep unconscious, that barriers fall down in the mystical journey. Love penetrates to the caverns of the unconscious, allowing the suppressed anger and fear and clinging to surface. Exposed to the light they melt away and a deep, adult, ongoing love for one's parents becomes the basis for universal love. Indeed, there can be an experience of enlightenment in which all barriers which separate me from others collapse, and I discover that I am one with the human race, that no one is excluded from my compassion and love, that no rancour exists in my heart. This experience of union with the human race can be found. I believe, in the mysticism of all the great religions.

In Buddhism it is beautifully incarnated in the Bodhisattva Kannon whose statue stands magnificently throughout Asia. The name Kannon, literally Kan-ze-on, means "beholder of the cries of the world" and this god or goddess (Kannon is originally a man but acquires the features of a woman and is often spoken of in feminine terms) with a gentle smile of compassion looks benevolently on all mankind. Kannon is one of the most beloved of Buddhist saints. But to return to my point.

Authentic mystical experience necessarily brings with it a

great love for all mankind. It can lead to remarkably deep friendship and intimacy in those who share the same experience; it also leads to a great compassion for the poor, the sick, the oppressed, the down-trodden, the imprisoned, the underprivileged. Buddhist compassion is an emptying of self in order to take to one's bosom the suffering people of the world; and Christian compassion is a discovery of Christ in the suffering people of the world. For he himself said: "For I was hungry and you gave me food, I was thirsty and you gave me drink . . . as you did it to one of the least of my brethren you did it to me" (Matthew 25:35,40).

This union or solidarity with the poor and the oppressed is of the very essence of Christian mysticism. Even if the contemplative decides to spend her days in a solitary cave in the Himalayas or a tumbledown hut in the desert she is still united with the suffering world for which she intercedes and for which she offers her life. But not all mystics are on the mountain or in the desert. We find Christian mystics struggling for the liberation of the poor or picking up the dying in the streets of the big cities. This they do because they find Christ in the afflicted, and become more and more closely united with him.

But again conflict! Love of the oppressed may bring one into conflict with the rich and powerful and with the establishment. So it was with Jesus, so it will be with his followers.

It will be remembered that in the oxherding pictures the wise old man returns to the market-place to save all sentient beings. This is a picture of beautiful compassion. But I have sometimes felt that had the pictures been composed in the Christian West they would have ended with yet another picture which would hold the caption: *The Wise Old Man is Assassinated*. For the inner eye of this enlightened and compassionate sage would immediately see the terrible social injustice and the oppression of the poor. He would raise his voice in protest and even in holy anger, calling for liberation. And he would suffer the cruel fate of all the prophets, from the just Abel to Martin Luther King.

And so union with Christ will mean union with the poor and the underprivileged, and it will lead to conflict until such time as we reach the Omega point of convergence when Christ hands all to the Father and God is all in all. Until that time those who are united with Christ will be at odds with a large percentage of the human race. "They are not of the world, even as I am not of the world" (John 17:14). And yet in a paradoxical way they will be united with the very people whom they criticize and against whom they fight. For they will love their adversaries and be united with the Christ in them, the Christ whose visage is often obscured and distorted but who lives in all men and women.

IV

I have spoken of inner union and the process of becoming another Christ. I have also spoken of union with the human race, particularly with the poor, through Christ. But all this is built on the deepest union of all: union with the Father through Christ.

To speak about this let me first return to the inner union about which I spoke at the beginning of this chapter, when I said that the deepest thing within us is the great mystery of mysteries which we call God – God who is the very ground and source of our being.

I said that the significant thing in this inner journey is a self-acceptance which is enacted at various levels. At one level there is myself with all my neuroses and complexes and capacity for evil and with my murky past – myself with my anxieties about health and reputation, myself with my irrational fear of rejection. When this self is accepted as loved (marvel of marvels!), at first through anguish and then with a sense of humour, there is another level of self: the existential level. Now I see myself as limited being, as being-towards-death, as potentially separated being. This is a whole new experience, a whole new level of existential anguish; and it can be terrible. Divorced from the totality, divorced from God I am *nothing*. All other human fears and anxieties are built on this realization of my own contingency – on the realization that I could be separated: "My God, my

God, why hast thou forsaken me?" (Matthew 27:46). This is the night of faith. I see myself as limited being, as separated being, all alone. Of course I believe and hope that I am united with God and with the totality; but this faith is dark and I feel totally and existentially alone. "Oh my God, I cry by day, but thou dost not answer; and by night, but find no rest" (Psalm 22:2).

Now most people feel flashes of this existential anguish and loneliness at some time in their lives; but they escape from it to play tennis or watch television. But in the mystical life one is brought face to face with this fact of contingency. To see our own limitation and the possibility of separation from the totality which is God – this is to get a glimpse into hell. And it is truly terrible.

Mystics have sometimes spoken of the vision of hell; and we imagine big fires and little devils with pitchforks. This may be the artist's way of depicting it; but the reality is beyond words and images. The reality is a picture of contingent being isolated and separated from the whole. To see this possibility is an inevitable state in the mystical life; it is an experience which is found in all the great religions. In Buddhism the most terrible thing imaginable is to build up one's ego and to be separated from the totality. This is the Buddhist hell. The doctrine of hell, like so much religious teaching, arises from the mystical experience of mankind.

But the vision of hell is not the end. For again he comes walking on the waters. "It is I; do not be afraid" (John 6:20). And we realize not the separation from the totality but the identity with the totality. "It is no longer I who live, but Christ who lives in me" (Galatians 2:20). This is Christ who dwells in the Father and who can say: "I and the Father are one" (John 10:30). Through Christ and as another Christ I am one with the Father. Just as the vision of my separateness from the totality is hell, so the vision of my union with God is heaven.

*

We know little about God our Father. He is like night to the soul and he is surrounded by thick darkness. But one thing is clear; namely, that the higher stages of the mystical life are very ordinary. There is no ecstasy, no rapture, no flash of light, no bells, no incense. I am now my true self. It is sometimes said by Christian writers that the peak-point of mysticism is found in a vision of the Trinity. This is very true. But do not think of this vision of the Trinity as an extraordinary, earth-shaking vision of three in one. Not at all. It is a very simple and quite realization that God is my Father and I, another Christ, am truly his son or his daughter, and that the Holy Spirit dwells in me. This is the Christian self-realization. The Spirit who has transformed me, joins himself to my spirit and cries out: "Abba, Father!"

14

Journey of Love

I

Throughout this book I have stressed the fact that mysticism is a journey of love. It is the answer to a call of love; and every stage is enlightened and guided by a living flame, a blind stirring, a love which has no reservations or restrictions. This is the love which, Paul says, is superior to any charismatic gift and has no limitations whatsoever. It "bears all things, believes all things, hopes all things, endures all things ... love never ends" (1 Corinthians 13:7,8). And for Paul this is an incarnational love which is patient and kind, not jealous or boastful, not arrogant or rude.

This love burns at a very deep level of consciousness and is so different from what is ordinarily called love that perhaps we need a new word to describe it. The early Christians seem to have felt this need, and so they spoke of *agape*, a word which is little used in classical Greek. As for Buddhist mystics, they are reluctant to use the word love at all – since they feel that it scarcely fits the experience of nothingness which is fundamental to their lives. Yet I myself believe that *agape* exists in Buddhism and in Buddhist hearts. It is a question of getting clear what we mean by love.

II

The Christian mystics, then, speak constantly about love. But many (though not all) make use of the Song of Songs in a way which disturbs the exegetes and gives something of a Freudian shock to people like Dean Inge – who called the influence of the canticle "deplorable". And yet the man-woman motif keeps turning up in the Hebrew-Christian drama; and in our own day Bernard Lonergan (whom I have quoted abundantly), when he speaks of authentic religious experience, returns to the theme of the bride and the bridegroom, speaking of "other-worldly falling in love" and of the union of marriage. In this manner of speech he is part of a long tradition which goes back to the prophet Hosea in the eighth century BC and perhaps even further.

For Hosea, Yahweh is the bridegroom who loves his people passionately and even foolishly in spite of their infidelity and harlotry. In his own private life the prophet has experienced all the pain and anger of rejection by the woman he loves and whom he has chosen as his bride. But he will still love her passionately and take her back to his bosom. And in the same way Yahweh tenderly loves his people and will call them back:

> I will heal their faithlessness
> I will love them freely
> > (Hosea 14:4)

Some scripture scholars tell us that this Hosean description of the love of Yahweh was a scandal to those who first heard it; and they also tell us that while Yahweh "loves" his people, the people do not "love" Yahweh in precisely the same way. But in Deuteronomy (which was influenced by Hosea) Yahweh asks for a radical and unrestricted love when he speaks unequivocally to the people: "Hear, O Israel: The Lord our God is one Lord; and you shall love the Lord your God with all your heart, and with all your soul, and with all your might" (Deuteronomy 6:4).

The bride-bridegroom theme is taken up by Jeremiah who writes about Israel's first love in the wilderness in contrast with her marital infidelity in the land of Canaan. And again in Isaiah: "As the bridegroom rejoices over the bride, so shall your God rejoice over you" (Isaiah 62:5). In the New Testament, too, Jesus stands forth at Cana as the true bridegroom who changes the water into wine. And elsewhere he answers the Pharisees with the enigmatic words: "Can the wedding guests mourn as long as the bridegroom is with them? The days will come, when the bridegroom is taken from them, and then they will fast" (Matthew 9:15). Jesus is the bridegroom, and the people, the church, the community, are his bride.

Underlying all this is the notion of a very powerful and unrestricted love of God for his people and the very total love which he asks in return. In the Bible this is framed in terms of God and the community; but from the early centuries of the Christian era we hear of the love affair between God and the individual devout soul. This way of speaking is found in Origen, whose commentaries on the Song of Songs, translated by Jerome and Rufinus, were widely read in the West. It is also found in Augustine and Gregory and Cyprian; but the person most responsible for the wide diffusion of the bride-bridegroom theme is Bernard of Clairvaux whose *Sermons on the Canticle* exerted incalculable influence on subsequent Christian spirituality. Consequently, we find this way of speaking in Bernard's younger contemporary Richard of St Victor, and later in Jan Ruysbroeck, St Teresa of Avila, St John of the Cross and a great number of mystics.

As I have already said, this mystical use of the Song of Songs has been a source of embarrassment to many devout Christians. But let us remember that these love songs, like many literary masterpieces, can be read at different levels of consciousness; and let us also remember the wise observation of T. S. Eliot that there is more in the poetry than the poet himself realizes. For it is an undeniable fact that authentic mystics have read and reread the canticle with overflowing joy, have resonated with its vibrant sentences, have somehow identified with the passionate love described therein. They have felt deeply the wound of love and have exclaimed:

> You have ravished my heart, my sister, my bride,
> You have ravished my heart with a glance of your eyes
> (Song of Songs 4:9)

They have felt an immense longing which consumes their whole being and makes them cry out:

> Upon my bed by night
> I sought him whom my soul loves;
> I sought him, but found him not;
> I called him, but he gave no answer.
> I will rise now and go about the city,
> in the streets and in the squares;
> I will seek him whom my soul loves.
>
> (Song of Songs 3:1,2)

Such words have risen spontaneously to the lips of mystics after they have experienced a momentary enlightenment which, like a wound of love, has filled them paradoxically with ecstatic joy and with deep suffering. Where is he whom I love? They have been fascinated with a beauty which has touched them momentarily with such power that they have been forced to exclaim: "Turn away your eyes from me for they disturb me" (Song of Songs 6:5).

Yes, the fact is that mystical experience, at one stage in its development, is a very passionate existential love which possesses the whole person, creating the most enormous thirst and longing for the infinite. Once touched by this love, people will travel the length and breadth of the earth, endure incredible suffering with joy, give up everything with a smile. This is the love which filled the heart of the psalmist when he cried: "I stretch out my hands to thee, my soul thirsts for thee like a parched land" (Psalm 143). It is the love which inundated the heart of Paul when he exclaimed: "My desire is to depart and be with Christ . . ." (Philippians 1:23).

Earlier in this book I said that all anguish is based on an existential anguish which is nothing other than the fear of contingent being separated from the totality. I said that this existential anguish in its pure form can be a vision of hell. And now let me add that just as there is an existential anguish at the root of all anguish, so there is an existential longing at the root of all longing. This is the love of contingent being for the totality, the love of the part for the whole, the love of the creature for the creator. Just as man is incomplete without the feminine – "It is not good that man should be alone" (Genesis 2:18) – so contingent being is incomplete at the existential level without the totality. As man longs for woman and woman for man, so the human heart is restless until it rests in the totality.

Such is existential love. What is not often realized is that this love is an all-consuming and passionate fire which can envelop the personality and tear people asunder. It is particularly consuming and passionate in the heart of one who has experienced even to a small degree God's passionate love. If God has shown his face even for a moment, if he has unlocked the smallest of his secrets, if he has wounded my heart, then it is easy to make my own the words of the Song of Songs:

> Many waters cannot quench love,
>   neither can floods drown it.
> If a man offered for love
>   all the wealth of his house,
>   it would be utterly scorned
> (Song of Songs 8:7)

I am speaking here in a Christian context; but I do not doubt that this same existential love exists in Buddhist mystics and in the mystics of all the great religions. Let us remember that in Buddhism the greatest evil is the desire for separate existence, and the longing for existential completeness is the greatest good. It is this existential longing that I speak about here.

*

Assuredly existential love need not be expressed in terms of the erotic; and many mystics do not appeal to the Song of Songs at all. But nevertheless it *is* frequently and persistently expressed in erotic man-woman language; and the question is asked: Why? What is the relationship between the erotic and the mystical?

Let me be frank and confess that I could never attempt to answer this question adequately and can do no more than add a few words of tentative explanation.

And first let me say that the existential love of which I speak is not purely spiritual. It has its roots in matter; it has its roots in the body; it does not reject physical or emotional or erotic love but simply goes beyond them, further and further beyond.

Now it is also true that in the passionate, romantic love with which the mystics resonate, this existential and universal dimension is already present. Hence the extravagant and hyperbolic expressions of lovers – protestations that their love is the greatest the world has known, that it will not die, that it is unrestricted. Such love differs from mystical love, however, in that it is not detached from its expressions; it is not detached from clinging and self-centredness; it is filled with projection; it is not open to the infinite. It may be, so to speak, mystical in embryo but it has to grow; and this can only happen through a process of detachment – through the emptiness, the nothingness, the void, the *mu*. All this nothingness does not kill love. By no means. It simply detaches it from its expressions and from its restrictions (for love is deeper and more mysterious than any of its expressions) so that it may be purified. In other words, the existential dimension which already exists in erotic love must grow, expand, develop until it is universal and unrestricted, open to man and God.

And so there is a process of growth from the erotic to the mystical. Jung traces this growth through symbols which are: Eve (biological love); Helen of Troy (romantic love); the Virgin Mary (devotional love); and Sapientia or Wisdom (mystical love). The idea of Jung is that, ideally speaking, human love should grow and develop through these stages – though he admits that in our day very few people reach the fourth and mystical stage.

Jung here speaks of masculine love for the feminine; but perhaps we could trace the growth in a way which would apply equally to men and to women. This would speak first of an *individual* need, love by which we love someone of the opposite sex in order to forget our loneliness. Next comes growth to *personal* love, by which two people really share their being in a deep communion. Here there is more profound fulfilment, always joined to the danger that the two people may isolate themselves from society in a common solitude. Out of this they must break into a *cosmic* or *eternal* love, in which the barriers of space and time are overcome and they are united with the cosmos, with Christ in one another and in all people, and with the Father.

Such mystical love is incarnational in that man loves individual women and woman loves individual men. But extraordinary powers of loving have now been awakened so that they see the eternal incarnate in the temporal, the infinite incarnate in the finite: they see and love God in man. This means that in the face of the other they see Christ who is masculine as the *logos* and feminine as *sapientia*.

When love reaches this stage, however, it must go beyond the existential longing about which I spoke earlier. For it should be remembered that the existential longing of the contingent for the absolute is still based on need and is a form of spiritual passion. That is why Buddhists would be slow to accept it as the final stage in growth: it contains too much of the craving from which they wish to be liberated. Therefore we must go on and on – and there is yet another stage in which one is liberated from all craving, however spiritual, in order to love in complete liberty.

III

When it comes to describing the highest stage of love, the symbolism of the Fourth Gospel which speaks of father and son, and of friendship, is extremely valuable.

Before speaking about the Fourth Gospel, however, let me recall that while the bride-bridegroom theme is found in the New Testament, it could scarcely be called central; and Jesus never uses it to describe his own mystical experience and his own union with God. No. Jesus always speaks of himself as Son; and his mystical experience is that of a son who loves his father and is loved by him. Furthermore, when Jesus teaches us to pray (and teaches us to pray mystically) he tells us to call God our Father. In other words, the central symbolism of the New Testament is not that of the bride and the bridegroom but of the father and the child.

Furthermore this is described by St John in terms of indwelling. In human life we know that mutual indwelling of friends is a fact of experience no less real than the love of the bride and the bridegroom. It sometimes happens that love so unites friends that despite miles of separation they are close to one another and dwell in one another. And when speaking of his relationship with his Father, Jesus keeps telling us that he dwells in the Father and the Father in him: "Do you not believe that I am in the Father and the Father in me?" (John 14:10). Here is the mysticism of Jesus, a mysticism which extends to his friendships. For just as he dwells in the Father so his friends dwell in him. "As the Father has loved me, so have I loved you; abide in my love" (John 15:9). Or again we have those striking, eschatological words: "In that day you will know that I am in my Father, and you in me, and I in you" (John 14:20).

And so in the Fourth Gospel we get a remarkable picture of mystical union joined to the highest personalism. We dwelt in Jesus; Jesus dwells in the Father; we all dwell in one another. We are completely one with God and others and the universe; and yet we become our truest selves, reaching the apex of human personalism and authenticity. And in this kind of indwelling there is a great absence of the clinging and craving and need which Buddhists regard as an imperfection in human loving.

Now I said earlier in this book, and I repeat it now, that the model of Christian mysticism is Jesus himself. As he is son by nature, we are sons or daughters by adoption. As he dwells in the Father, we dwell in the Father; as he dwells in us, we dwell in one another.

Concretely, the peak-point of mysticism in interpersonal relations is reached when we open the door of our hearts to a friend who is knocking in the name of the archetypal friend: "Behold I stand at the door and knock; if anyone hears my voice and opens the door, I will come in to him and eat with him, and he with me" (Revelation 3:20). Yes, I hear the knocking on the door; but what freedom I have! I need not open; there is no compulsion; and if I refuse, even the best of friends must remain outside. But if I do open, there ensues an intimate indwelling and a loving banquet in which friends dine together without craving or clinging or dependence and without that exclusivity which is almost necessarily present in the bride-bridegroom relationship. For such mystical friendship is not confined to one friend. It can embrace several people and leads to an indwelling in the Christ who identifies with the sick and the oppressed.

IV

Whatever symbolism is used, mystical love is never sterile but is intensely creative. We know from modern reflection on inter-personal relations that just as the physical union of man and woman creates the child, so the union of loving hearts can create great works of art and literature. This is an aspect of creativity which greatly claims the interest of modern people.

And mystical indwelling leads to creativity. Jesus says that his words and his actions are those of the Father who dwells in him: "The words that I say to you I do not speak on my own authority; but the Father who dwells in me does his works" (John 14:10). And he speaks of the creativity of the disciples with the symbol of bearing fruit, fruit which will remain. The indwelling of Jesus in his disciples and of the disciples in Jesus is like the branch in the vine and the vine in the branch – this is a union which is always fruitful. In the same context Jesus speaks of the woman giving birth to her child. "When a woman is in travail she has sorrow, because her hour has come; but when she is delivered of the child, she no longer remembers the anguish, for joy that a child is born into the world. So you have sorrow now . . ." (John 16:22).

The disciples to whom Jesus spoke would later bear their child. They would go out into that Mediterranean world with great joy and great love. Intensely creative people, they would build up something that would remain, a spiritual kingdom that will last to the end of time. This kingdom was born of their union with the Father through Jesus in the Spirit.

And so their work continues through the indwelling of God in man. Such a union is *necessarily* creative: "He who abides in me, and I in him, he it is that bears much fruit . . ."(John 15:5).

The precise nature of this creativity in a given instance cannot be spelled out. For some will create the kingdom through love for the sick and dying, others through intellectual research, others through a passionate search for social justice, others through the silence of intercessory prayer and contemplation. There are varieties of gifts but the same Spirit of love inspires them all.

15

Enlightenment and Conversion

I

I have already indicated that the great fact on which Buddhism is built is the enlightenment of Shakamuni beneath the Bodhi tree at Bodh Gaya in the sixth century BC. This was an event which shook the world. And it is an event which has been repeated in the lives of Buddhists everywhere, even when they have belonged to different sects and to different cultures. Enlightenment is nothing other than the awakening of the third eye, the inner eye, the eye of the heart. This eye, represented in Indian culture by the round spot on the forehead, is single and sees the world of unity, as opposed to the two eyes of the flesh which see an illusory world of duality. When the inner eye is opened one enters the void or *sunyata* which is the realm of true wisdom, known as *prajna*. Here one is released from suffering and from the oppressive *karma* which has accumulated in this life and in past lives. In this way one is saved.

In some sects, such as Zen, enlightenment is achieved by personal effort (called *jiriki*); while in other sects, such as the Pure Land, one relies on the grace of another (*tariki*). But in either case enlightenment is an ongoing process. In some sects there are a series of sudden illuminations culminating in the supreme experience of Nirvana; in other sects illumination is a gradual process. Dogen, founder of the Soto sect of Zen, held that the very sitting is in itself an enlightenment. In this prolonged sitting in the lotus posture, one's consciousness is gradually changed and the inner eye comes to see.

What matters is the change of consciousness; and a good

master can detect very rapidly the presence or absence of enlightenment in the consciousness of the one to whom he speaks. He may judge from the breathing or from the posture. Or he may ask questions and judge from the spontaneity (or lack of spontaneity) of the answer. I believe it is not too difficult to recognize the deeply enlightened consciousness: for the Buddhist who speaks from the depth of his own enlightenment has a humility, a compassion and an inner security which command respect and are quite different from the erudition of one who talks about books.

Be that as it may, it is this enlightenment which attracts many people in the West; and sincere Christians ask to what extent they can participate in this Buddhist treasure which has been handed down from master to disciple through many centuries. This is a question which I have already discussed; and I need not repeat myself here.

II

The Gospel also speaks of enlightenment, and Jesus refers to the eye of the heart when he says: "The eye is the lamp of the body. So if your eye is sound, your whole body will be full of light; but if your eye is not sound, your whole body will be full of darkness. If the light in you is darkness, how great the darkness" (Matthew 6:22, 23). Here we are told in no uncertain terms that what matters in life is illumination or enlightenment; and the same theme runs through the Fourth Gospel where the blind man comes to see that Jesus is the light of the world. We are that blind man and our life should be a sudden or gradual awakening. But the terrible thing is that as we can awaken so we can become blind. "For judgement I came into that world, that those who do not see may see, and that those who see may become blind" (John 9:39). And so our life is a struggle against darkness. We possess the inner eye but we must awaken from sleep. "Having eyes do you not see . . . ?" (Mark 8:7).

But what do we see when our inner eye awakens? Here again the Fourth Gospel is clear:

We have seen his glory
(John 1:14)

The glory of the Risen Jesus cannot be seen with the eyes of the flesh but only with the eye of love. That is why Jesus rebuked Thomas who could not be satisfied until he saw Jesus with the eyes of the flesh and Jesus says equivalently: "Thomas, because you see with your physical eyes you are willing to worship me. But blessed are those who do not see with their physical eyes but see with their inner eye." The awakening of this inner eye is a wonderful experience through which one comes to see "the fullness of him who fills all in all" (Ephesians 1:23). One sees his glory in the cosmos; one sees his beauty on the faces and in the eyes of the friends one loves; one sees his suffering in the afflicted and oppressed.

Now the awakening to the reality of his glory is an authentic Christian experience which has occurred frequently in Christian lives since Paul met Jesus on the road to Damascus. People have awakened to the stupendous fact that Jesus is the centre of their lives – that he truly is. Such an experience sometimes comes gradually, as one repeats the Jesus prayer and comes to realize that *Jesus is Lord*. Or it comes like a sudden shock at an unexpected moment when one experiences the glory of the Lord; "If you confess with your lips that *Jesus is Lord* and believe in your hearts that God raised him from the dead, you will be saved" (Romans 10:9).

But the inner eye also sees the Father, for Jesus has said that he who sees him sees the Father also; and Paul assures us that every tongue will confess that "Jesus is Lord *to the glory of God the Father*" (Philippians 2:11). In other words, when my inner eye is awakened and Jesus is the centre of my life I spontaneously look up to heaven and cry out: "Abba, Father!" This is the cry of the Spirit of Jesus within me. It is the Trinitarian experience about which I have spoken throughout this book. It is the Christian enlightenment.

III

I have spoken of enlightenment, but the Bible speaks also about conversion or *metanoia* or change of heart. This is a great revolution in human life which is described graphically by Ezekiel:

> A new heart I will give you and a new spirit. I will put within you; and I will take out of your flesh the heart of stone and give you a heart of flesh. And I will put my spirit within you, and cause you to walk in my statues and be careful to observe my ordinances.
>
> (Ezekiel 36:26,27)

Here we have the radical change of mind and heart and body which is to find fulfilment in the gospel cry: "Change your hearts, for the kingdom of heaven is at hand" (Matthew 3:12). This is a theme which recurs throughout the symphony of Christian history. It is something very real in the Acts of the Apostles where people change their hearts and change their lives; it has been something very real wherever the Gospel has been preached. In Protestant theology it has always had a place of honour. Less so in Catholic theology until recently, when Bernard Lonergan builds his *method* on this inner experience. As I have already said, Lonergan distinguishes religious, moral and intellectual conversion, thus pointing to a tremendous revolution in the personality. For by religious conversion one falls in love without restriction; by moral conversion one's values change; by intellectual conversion one sees into a world of being.

The process is well illustrated in the experience of Paul. He fell in love with Christ in an unrestricted way so that for Paul to live was Christ and to die was gain. His values changed in such a way that what he previously considered important is now like refuse compared with the great grace of knowing Christ Jesus his Lord. His outlook on life changed in such a way that he now sees a world no longer bounded by the law but without any horizons. His vision is now universal.

*

In the contemplative life as conceived by Buddhists and Christians alike, there are ordinarily periods of joy and consolation together with periods of darkness and boredom. There are also flashes of insight or illumination when one comes to understand some words of scripture or revelation. But there may also be times of upheaval and inner revolution, times of momentous change when conversion is likely to occur. In other words, there are natural turning-points, crossroads or periods of crisis when the human psyche demands a conversion in its process of growth.

In this connection, Jung speaks of four crucial stages on the way to individual or psychic fulfilment; and he calls them four births. The first is when the child leaves the womb of its mother and steps into life. The second is at puberty when the adolescent, liberating self from parental authority and from psychic fusion with father and mother, enters adult life as an independently responsible person. The third is when the spiritualized person emerges from the conflicts of middle age and discovers the true self. The final stage is when the person departs from the world and is born into the huge unexplored land beyond death, the land from which he or she came.

Jung, however, believed that the majority of people do not pass successfully through these crises and are never fully born – principally because they fear the death which necessarily precedes birth. They shrink from the suffering and the pain; and so they are only born once and never reach integration.

Now I believe that the mystical life ordinarily develops through these Jungian stages of death and rebirth, because in mysticism, as I have frequently stated, one does not transcend the human condition but becomes authentically human under the guidance of faith and love. Let me, then, consider here the third birth, that of middle age, which is particularly relevant for contemporary men and women.

*

In many of his writings but particularly in his autobiography *Memories, Dreams, Reflections*, Jung speaks about the death and rebirth which, ideally speaking, should take place through the crisis of middle age. Within us there are two personalities. Number one is the personality we show to the world, the person who in our youth and adolescence we think we are, the personality which becomes a doctor or a businessman or a teacher – our self-image derives from this personality. But much deeper than this slumbers another personality, number two, and here is the true self. Scarcely visible in early life, it is so smothered up by external things that only one who loves and understands us deeply can get a glimpse of it. We are not yet ourselves. But as life enters its middle period this deeper personality awakens, begins to assert itself and to rise to the surface of consciousness. It is now that conflict begins.

Is number two friend or foe? This I do not know. I only know that number one is now captain of the ship and does not wish to lose control or to be dislodged. And yet certainly, if vaguely, I realize that number one must die if number two is to emerge into life. My old self must die if my new self is to be born. This can be an agonizing and fearful feeling; and it may precipitate a great crisis. This crisis is particularly acute if my vocation is at stake – if I fear that a wrong choice has been made and that fidelity to my deepest self may demand the adoption of a new path in life. Such a step may mean losing everything, like Saint Paul who left a privileged position in his Jewish community to enter a world which he did not know.

This is indeed a great parting of the ways. Small wonder if many or most people, shrinking from the sacrifice involved, never allow their true personality to be born, never become their true selves. But, on the other hand, those who face up to the real issues find that the new personality is born with overwhelming joy. "When a woman is in travail she has sorrow, because her hour has come; but when she is delivered of the child, she no longer remembers the anguish, for joy that a child is born into the world; (John 16:21).

At this point Jung half-humourously suggests that there should be schools for the middle-aged. And then he reflects that after all there are such schools: the great religions, if they do their work, are schools for the middle-aged. Here Jung has a real insight into the religious dimensions of this great crisis. I believe that in this psychological turmoil grace is working gently, if painfully, in the unconscious, inviting our number two personality, our true selves, to emerge from the womb into fullness of life. Quite often this whole process of middle age crisis is nothing less than a mystical experience of death and resurrection to a new life which is filled with true joy.

*

I believe that the psychological process leading to deep conversion has something in common with that which frequently precedes great activity. Here a stillness or even a listlessness descends upon a person, as though power were being withdrawn from the conscious mind into the unconscious where it simmers for some time, prior to a breakthrough into consciousness and the creation of great art or great scientific achievement or whatever. Conversion also is a creative process – for what is more creative than giving birth? – and it demands the marshalling of all the forces of the unconscious mind. But for the breakthrough to take place two conditions are ordinarily present.

The first is a period of solitude. This may be the solitude of a monastery or of a sick bed or of a prison cell. Or it may be hours and hours, days and days, of sitting in the silence of Zen. It is in this way that the upper layers of the mind are swept bare in preparation for the breakthrough of grace from the unconscious. In such a situation there is no escape from one's self, no escape from one's number two personality which is rising up to vanquish us and give us joy.

The second condition, as we have already seen, is some kind of shock. Remember that Paul was blinded and neither ate nor drank for three days. In other cases the shock may come from acute rejection which causes great pain. Think of the prophet Nathan pointing the finger at David: "You are the man" (2 Samuel 12:7). And David was shaken to the core. "And David said to Nathan: 'I have sinned against the Lord'" (2 Samuel 12:13). Shocked into self-realization! Or again when Peter protested against the suffering of his master, and Jesus turned on him: "Get behind me, Satan! For you are not on the side of God but of men" (Mark 8:33). For Peter it must have been a

profound shock to be treated in this way by the Master he
loved. But it had to be. His way of thinking was wrong; he did
not understand the Cross; and only the deep pain of apparent
rejection by Jesus could awaken him to the way of thinking that
is of God.

And so a great rejection, especially rejection by those we love,
can precipitate death and herald the joy of resurrection. Only
in this context can I understand the words of Jesus: "Blessed
are you when men revile you and persecute you and utter all
kinds of evil against you falsely on my account. Rejoice and be
glad, for your reward is great in heaven..." (Matthew
5:11,12). Taken as a command to rejoice in rejection these
words might sound inhuman; but seen in the light of *metanoia*,
seen in the light of death and resurrection, they are the quintess-
ence of wisdom and enlightenment. Rejoice and be glad because
the pain of rejection is the herald of unutterable joy.

The art, the cruel yet compassionate art, of shocking a person
into enlightenment is part of authentic spiritual direction in all
religions and is well known to the skilled master in the Orient.
Not that he shocks for the sake of shocking – that would be
disaster – but he sternly confronts the disciple with the vision,
the true vision, of his self in its inadequacy and weakness. "You
are the man!" "You are not on the side of God but of men!"
And the painful view of the truth, the painful view of death and
of hell, tears away the veil of illusion and leads to the joyful
vision of a total truth which heralds resurrection.

To shock into enlightenment is, as I have said, a great art.
Only the person of powerful insight, rigorous detachment and
profound compassion can kill and change death to life.

IV

I have said that fidelity to one's deepest self, to one's number
two personality, may demand the choice of a new path. This is
often the most distressing aspect of this crisis and conversion.
For who wants to be uprooted in middle years? Yet such was
the case with St Paul. Such was the case with John Henry

Newman: "Lead, kindly light!" And this is an anguishing choice which confronts not a few religious people in our troubled times. When my true personality rises to the surface, will it demand that I change my state in life?

In the *Spiritual Exercises* (where St Ignatius intends primarily to lead the exercitant to conversion and choice of a state in life) this problem is faced squarely. And Ignatius insists from the beginning that there are certain immutable decisions or irrevocable choices in human life which cannot even be reconsidered. Most people would agree with this. A decision which involves the happiness of other people cannot lightly be revoked – unless I do so out of fidelity to truth which must always be obeyed. But still, in our complex age it is by no means easy to say which decisions are irrevocable and which are not.

Here I cannot enter into the complex ethical controversies which have arisen on this point. What I want to say is that there is a solution which arises from the depth not of an ethical, but of a religious, conversion. That is to say, a solution that is connected with my falling in love without restriction and is nothing less than a religious enlightenment. Let me explain what I mean.

The solution I speak of depends upon prayer, upon prolonged prayer like that of Jesus in the wilderness. And I believe that if one devotes oneself to this prolonged prayer in silent non-attachment, the answer will come not from ethical reasoning but from the Spirit who dwells in the depth of the so-called unconscious. The enlightenment which thus arises will not be an ethical one: it will not tell us that this path is morally correct and the other wrong. Rather will it be a vision of the truth which makes us free. For a Buddhist it may be a moment of profound enlightenment after which he sees with great clarity what he should do. For a Christian it may be a great upsurge of love which makes him cry out: "Jesus is Lord." And then, as a second step, love will tell him what to do. Or it may be something much less dramatic. Just a quiet realization repeated again over weeks and months, always accompanied by joy and consolation, giving birth to a conviction that the Spirit has spoken.

As can be seen, I am here distinguishing between the ethical and the religious conversion. I am trying to say that the religious happening will often come first and that the ethical decision will flow from it. But this is always the work of grace.

V

I have spoken about conversion but one may ask about its contrary. What about breakdown? What abut counter-conversion?

One aspect of breakdown, I believe, is simply the refusal to grow, the refusal to allow the true personality to emerge, the refusal to be born. This means that I get stuck at a lower level of psychic development and never allow myself to be fully born. I do not use my talents: much of my potential remains untapped. To some extent this is the fate of all of us; we shrink from the suffering entailed in conversion; we run away from the hound of heaven. And so we are never fully born; we never realize our full potential.

This is sad. But there can be something more terrible; namely, a breakthrough to evil, a conversion in reverse. For just as grace works in the unconscious gradually leading to enlightenment and a change of heart for good, so in the same way evil can gradually build up to a breakthrough into consciousness and a change of heart for evil. And this, too, could be accompanied by great joy – a conversion to evil, and enlightenment from Satan.

St Ignatius indicates this in the *Spiritual Exercises* when he says that those who go from evil to evil are drawn on by Satan *with consolation*. This is because diabolical influence is, so to speak, in harmony with their inner dispositions and so it comes as a sweet messenger of joy: "When the disposition is similar to that of the (evil) spirits, they enter silently, as one coming into his own house when the doors are open" (Ignatius (I), p. 149). When the dedication of such people to evil is total, the counter-conversion is complete. Now they experience security and peace in the accomplishment of evil. This is a terrible consideration. One is reminded of the First Epistle of John which, speaking about prayer for sinners, goes on to say that some sin is so deadly that we need not bother praying for it: "There is sin which is mortal; I do not say that one is to pray for that" (1 John 5:16). At this stage of dedication to evil only great grace can effect conversion. But grace is always present.

*

Finally let me say a word about group conversion. This surely seems to be the great need of our day, a time of upheaval and revolution; and the Second Vatican Council made a call for communal conversion.

Such conversion took place when the Spirit descended upon the apostles at Pentecost. But I believe that such Pentecosts are rare. More often the salvation of the group is achieved through the conversion of the few. "For the sake of ten I will not destroy it" (Genesis 19:32). There are people who, following Jesus in Gethsemane, take upon themselves the suffering of the world. We need such people today. What the future holds we do not know.

PART IV

MYSTICAL ACTION

16

Towards Action

I

I have already indicated that mystical action flows from *wu-wei* or non-action. It is not based on reasoning and thinking and conscious effort but rather on letting things happen, letting the Tao act, letting God work in me and in the world. In a Christian context, mystical action reaches its climax when I surrender to the Spirit so totally that I can make my own words of Paul: "It is no longer I who live but Christ who lives in me" (Galatians 2:20). When these words live in me the Spirit of Jesus governs my life, my action is no longer my own, and what appears to be conscious effort is the activity of a deeper power which dwells within. All I have to do is to accept. Was not one of the world's greatest decisions made by one who said: "Behold, I am the handmaid of the Lord; let it be done to me according to you will" (Luke 1:38)? Here conscious effort fell into the stream of non-action.

But submission to the Spirit is an art which is only learnt through years of trial and error, success and failure. Only gradually does one come to possess a delicate sensitivity to the inner motions of grace so as to be moved by the Spirit in one's life. And the art or gift by which we come to recognize the inner voice of the Spirit is called discernment.

Discernment is of the essence of mysticism in action. The medievals were greatly interested in it, and they kept asking a number of simple but intriguing questions: How am I to know when to eat and when to fast, when to sleep and when to watch, when to go into solitude and when to go into action? How am

I to discern the voice of the Spirit so as to follow that gentle guidance? And of course they could ask even more weighty questions like those I discussed in the last chapter – questions about vocation and state of life.

Such weighty and even agonizing questions are confronting sincere people in our day – people who work in the world of science or of business or of politics. Such people may be called on to make decisions which will affect the lives of millions of men and women. Often these decisions cannot be made through unquestioning obedience to ethical laws but only through a process of discernment and listening to the Spirit. But how am I to discern the voice of the Spirit in my life?

II

A great master of discernment was Ignatius of Loyola. His experiments (if I may call them that) began when he was a young soldier, wounded in the leg at the siege of Pamplona and compelled to lie on a sick bed in a lonely Spanish castle. Out of sheer boredom and because there was nothing else available, he began to read the lives of saints and then (and here is the interesting thing) *he began to listen to himself*. He began to listen to his own feelings which were sometimes joyful and sometimes sad. He himself describes in the third person what happened:

> When he was thinking of the things of the world *he was filled with delight* but when afterwards he dismissed them from weariness *he was dry and dissatisfied*. And when he thought of going barefoot to Jerusalem and of eating nothing but herbs and performing the other rigours he saw that the saints had performed, he was consoled, not only when he entertained these thoughts, but even after dismissing them he remained cheerful and satisfied. But he paid no attention to this, nor did he stop to weigh the difference until *one day his eyes were opened a little* and he began to wonder at the difference and to reflect on it, learning from

experience that *one kind of thought left him sad and the other cheerful*. Thus, step by step, he came to recognize the difference between the two spirits that moved him, the one being from the evil spirit, the other from God.

(Ignatius (2), p. 10)

Here Ignatius listens to himself, listens to his own feelings of consolation and desolation, and on the basis of this he eventually makes the greatest decision of his life; namely, to give up "the things of the world" and to travel barefoot to Jerusalem. This, in turn, is a symbol of a deeper decision to dedicate himself totally to Christ.

Now the practice of listening to one's own feelings is advocated by a number of modern psychologists. Jung, particularly in his later years, spoke about listening to his *anima* or feminine principle and, needless to say, he was constantly listening to what the unconscious was saying through dreams. More recently Carl Rogers advocates attention to, and acceptance of, one's feeling. "I find myself more effective", he writes, "when I listen acceptantly to myself, and can be myself. I feel that over the years I have learnt to become more adequate in listening to myself; so that I know, somewhat more adequately than I used to, what I am feeling at any given moment – to be able to realize that I *am* angry, or that I *do* feel rejection towards this person; or that I feel very full of warmth and affection for this individual; or that I am bored and uninterested in what is going on; or that I am eager to understand this individual or that I am anxious and fearful in my relationship to this person. All of these diverse attitudes are feelings which I think I can listen to in myself. One way of putting this is that I feel I have become more adequate in letting myself be what I am."[1]

[1] (Rogers, p.17) In the same book, Rogers writes of the good life: "The individual is becoming more able to listen to himself, to experience what is going on within himself. He is more open to his feelings of fear and discouragement and pain. He is also more open to his feelings of courage, and tenderness, and awe. He is free to live his feelings subjectively, as they exist in him, and also free to be aware of these feelings. He is more able fully to live the experiences of his organism rather than shutting them out of awareness"(p. 188).

For Carl Rogers, listening to one's feelings is a way to fullness of life and to the actuation of one's potentialities. But it is more than this. The great psychologist maintains that the process of listening to one's self leads to right action or (to use his terminology) to the good life. It is precisely in obeying one's deepest self, one's total self, that one's actions become truly human. This is because man's basic nature is positive and trustworthy. In this regard I would like once more to quote some of his words:

> One of the most revolutionary concepts to grow out of our clinical experience is the growing recognition that the innermost core of man's nature, the deepest layer of his personality, the base of his "animal nature" is positive in nature – is basically socialized, forward moving, rational and realistic . . . . This point of view is so foreign to our present culture that I do not expect it to be accepted . . . . Religion, especially Protestant Christian tradition, has permeated our culture with the concept that man is basically sinful, and only by something approaching a miracle can his sinful nature be negated.
>
> (Rogers, p. 91)

Quite frankly, the above astonished me. To me what Carl Rogers has discovered is not revolutionary at all. I had always taken it for granted that man's basic nature is good since he was created in the image of God. Moreover I was educated in a Thomist philosophy which taught something similar to what Rogers is saying; namely, that the norm of morality is human nature and that by obeying the fundamental dictates of human nature one's activity is right. Original sin, of course, is there. But it is a wound which weakens, without corrupting, human nature. I believe that all the great religions hold ultimately that man's basic nature is good since at the core of his being is Brahman or Atman or the Buddha nature or the Holy Spirit.

*

Coming, however, to religious discernment, one might reasonably ask how it differs from the listening to one's feelings advocated by psychologists like Carl Rogers.

And to this I would answer that in religion new elements enter in.

The first new element is faith. Religious faith had taught Ignatius and those like him that the Spirit who dwells in the depth of our being guides and directs and comforts and teaches, as is written in the Fourth Gospel. It further taught him the reality of sin. While it is true that human nature is fundamentally good, we cannot take it for granted that the lives of all men and women are orientated towards good; there is the possibility of choosing sin and evil. Again, faith taught Ignatius that there are forces of evil outside us and distinct from us. These he calls evil spirits.

Consequently, while Ignatius is aware of his feelings and interior movements in a way that reminds one of Jung and Rogers, he differs from them in his great preoccupation with *the origin* of these feelings and with *their goal*. And so he asks further questions: Are these inner movements from the spirit of love who dwells within and guides me towards love? Or are they from the evil spirit? Or are they from my little ego? Will the following of this inner stirring lead me to a life of unrestricted love or will it isolate me in loveless solitude? Are these feelings leading to *metanoia* or to breakdown?

To answer these questions, says Ignatius, I must first investigate my basic dispositions. If my thrust is towards evil (which God forbid!) then these so-called positive feelings of joy and consolation may be confirming me in my evil path. If, on the other hand, I am basically orientated towards good (and I have no doubt that all of my readers are) then feelings of joy and consolation are a sign of the action of the Spirit. In short, my basic disposition is of crucial importance.

But even when my basic dispositions are good, I still must scrutinize my thoughts, asking myself in what direction they are leading me, since self-deception is always possible. "We must carefully observe the whole course of our thoughts. If the beginning and middle and end of the course of thoughts are wholly good and directed to what is entirely right, it is a sign that they are from the good angel. But the course of thoughts suggested to us may terminate in something evil, or distracting, or less good than the soul had formerly proposed to do. Again, it may end in what weakens the soul, or disquiets it; or by destroying the peace, tranquility and quiet which it had before, it may cause disturbance to the soul. These things are a clear sign that the thoughts are proceeding from the evil spirit, the enemy of our progress and eternal salvation" (Ignatius (1), p. 148).

Yet another element which psychology does not ordinarily take into account is the presence of mystical experience. As I have already indicated, this is an experiential and undeniable psychic fact which has been described as a living flame of love, a blind stirring of love, an obscure sense of presence, a murmuring stream, a small fire, the voice of the Spirit and so on. And in the mystical life, listening to one's feelings means above all hearkening to this deepest of all feelings. The important thing is to be faithful to this and to act in harmony with its promptings. When I do so, I feel joy and peace and security, even in the midst of conflict and suffering. When I act against it I immediately feel upset and inner turmoil.

The medievals urge us to be constantly attentive to this inner flame. "Hold yourself at the sovereign point of the spirit!" is the good advice of the author of *The Cloud*. That is to say, remain at the level of awareness where the flame of love is living. Do not be carried away by superficial feelings of any kind – be they feelings of joy or sadness, of elation or depression. If you remain poised at this deep point of recollection and at the ground of your being, Satan will not be able to disturb you (for he cannot enter these innermost mansions) and you will be open to the directives of the Spirit. Indeed, a time will come, says St John of the Cross, when the inner flame will tell you what to do in your daily life. Speaking of advanced contemplatives the Spanish mystic writes: "For God's Spirit makes them know what must be known and ignore what must be ignored, remember what ought to be remembered . . . and forget what ought to be forgotten, and make them love what they ought to love, and keeps them from loving what is not God" (*Ascent*, 3:2,9). And he adds an example: "At a particular time a person will have to attend to a necessary business matter. He will not remember through any form, but without knowing how, the time and suitable way of attending to it will be impressed on his soul without fail" (*Ascent*, 3:2,11).

And yet such a stage of mystical union is not common. Ordinarily we must search for the voice of the Spirit, sometimes with anguish. Quite often we are in illusion or bogged down by indecision. At other times we are completely in the dark. Consequently, to aid us in the process of discernment the Christian tradition worked out a whole science which is still alive today.

III

The science of discernment has its roots in the New Testament. The early Christians were aware of the movements and stirrings which arise in the human heart and in the human community; and they asked about the spirits from which these movements originated. "Beloved," writes St John, "do not believe every spirit, but test the spirits to see whether they are of God; for many false prophets have gone into the world" (1 John 4:1). In other words, do not follow your feelings and whims indiscriminately, however pious and holy they may appear – you might easily deceive yourself. So test the spirits. And John goes on to give a clear-cut norm:

> By this you know the Spirit of God: every spirit which confesses that Jesus Christ has come in the flesh is of God: and every spirit which does not confess Jesus is not of God.
> (I John 4:2,3)

From this it is clear that "Jesus" is the first norm: Jesus who has come in the flesh. The same idea is found in Paul. "Therefore I want you to understand that no one speaking by the Spirit of God ever says 'Jesus be cursed' and no one can say 'Jesus is Lord' except by the Holy Spirit" (I Corinthians 12:3).

"Jesus is Lord" was, as we have seen, one expression of faith and of *metanoia*. And this Jesus was not only the risen Jesus who is lord of the cosmos but also the Jesus who has come in the flesh and is present in his brethren, the Jesus who taught that blessed are the poor and meek and the merciful and the peace-lovers and the persecuted. Consequently, we can say that the New Testament norm is very practical. It means that thoughts and deep feelings of compassion for the poor, the sick, the underprivileged and the rejected; joyful desires of poverty and even of persecution with Jesus persecuted – in short whatever is in conformity with the Gospel of Jesus Christ – is from the spirit of God; whereas thoughts and feelings which lead to rejection of Jesus, to hatred of his brethren, to dissension and violence, to lust for money and power – these are not from the Spirit of God. Elsewhere in the New Testament Paul is to spell this out when he speaks of the works of the flesh and the works of the Spirit: "Now the works of the flesh are plain; immorality, impurity, licentiousness, idolatry, sorcery, enmity, strife, jealousy, anger, selfishness, dissension, party-spirit, envy, drunkenness, carousing and the like . . . But the fruit of the Spirit is love, joy, peace, patience, kindness, goodness, faithfulness, gentleness, self-control" (Galatians 5:19–23).

As can at once be seen, the norm of morality in the New Testament is not fidelity to the law but fidelity to the Spirit – that is fidelity to the law of love which includes every other law since "love is the fulfilling of the law" (Romans 13:10).

*

The science of discernment was developed by the Church Fathers; and later, in the Middle Ages, we find the author of *The Cloud* composing a charming treatise on discernment of stirrings. And to this same tradition belongs Ignatius.

The young soldier about whom I have spoken, later elaborated a whole mysticism of action based on a sensitivity to the presence of God and the working of the Spirit. Two further points in his mysticism are worth noting.

The first is his stress on what he calls *indifference*. This simply means holding oneself poised at the sovereign point of the spirit, ready to follow the voice of the beloved in whatever direction it may call. But to maintain such a position one must be liberated from inordinate affections, and one must possess an inner liberty which is not unlike the non-attachment demanded by the Buddhist mysticism.

The second is that Ignatius always recommended a rational check. That is to say, he asks us to bring our conclusions before the bar of reason, insisting that any feelings which run contrary to reason cannot be from God.

*

The disciples of Ignatius further elaborated his doctrine: and we find the Jesuit Louis Lallement, who is representative of a school of Jesuit mysticism in seventeenth-century France, advocating this same inner awareness as a way of life.

> Let us watch with care the different movements of our soul. By such attention we shall gradually perceive what is of God and what is not. That which proceeds from God in a soul subjected to grace is generally peaceable and calm. That which comes from the devil is violent, and brings with it trouble and anxiety.
>
> (McDougall, p. 109)

And so we have a way of life in which one is always open to the inner vibrations and in touch with one's deepest feelings. It pre-supposes what modern people call "emotional honesty". That is to say, I recognize the movements that are within me and even give them a name, admitting that I am angry or lustful or fearful, or that I am joyful or optimistic or courageous.

Ignatius spoke frequently of *examination of conscience* and he recommended that people examine their conscience again and again and again during the day. This, alas, was taken in an ethical sense, as though we ought constantly to accuse ourselves of sins and defects of all kinds. But more recently a whole new interpretation of this process has been made, an interpretation which is surely more faithful to Ignatius. For now we hear not of *examination of conscience* but of *examination of consciousness*. Obviously this is healthier. And it leads to a constant awareness of the action of the Spirit in one's life.

I have said that discernment is nothing less than a way of life and the very basis of mysticism in action. It is something that goes on all the time. One is constantly open to the breath of the Spirit, to the action of God in one's life and in the world; one is always poised in readiness to hear the voice of the beloved and to follow where it leads. This is one's daily bread and one's food: "My food is to do the will of him who sent me, and to accomplish his work" (John 4:34). But there will, of course, be special times – times when great decisions arise. And then, as Jesus prayed for forty days in the wilderness before beginning his ministry, as he prayed all night before choosing his disciples, as he prayed in Gethsemane before his passion, it will be necessary to pray, to reflect, to consult with others, to search out the divine will.

IV

From what has been said it will be clear that for discernment we need an objective view of ourselves and our feelings. As long as we are entangled in our own anger or vanity or lust or fear of craving we cannot be poised and ready to follow the call of the Spirit of love. How, then, can we attain this objectivity and inner freedom?

The principal way is by prayer and reflection on the meaning of life, thus deepening our inner experience and entering into a new level of awareness where craving and attachment no longer tyrannize our lives. But it is also useful to write a journal or to sketch or to paint or to engage in any creative art. For this has the effect of objectifying our thoughts and feelings and of liberating us from their domination. All this is good. But when all is said and done, I believe there is no substitute for opening one's soul to another – to one who accepts, who loves, who listens, who does not judge, who reflects back to me what is in my mind and heart, who helps me to recognize the voice of the Spirit in my life.

This is spiritual guidance. It differs from counselling in that it is a *religious experience* enacted between two people. That is to say, it is the experience of two people who are in love without reservation or restriction and who meet at the level of psychic life where the Spirit of God dwells. Such a religious experience exists in an authentic relationship between master and disciple. It exists in its painful, yet loving, form when the master shocks his disciple into self-realization. But ordinarily he does not do this. He accepts; he listens; he loves; he shares. Sometimes he says nothing; and then there is a bond of silence which unites more deeply than words and communicates immense wisdom. The master gives and receives the Holy Spirit – because this is a two-way path, a mutual giving and receiving.

Such a relationship can become extremely deep and can develop into a mystical friendship. For the time may come when the master finds that he is no longer a master. He must make his own the words of one who said: "No longer do I call you servants . . . but I have called you friends, for all that I have heard from my Father I have made known to you" (John 15:15). In this way, the relationship becomes one of equality, of mutual indwelling and of common indwelling with God.

*

The art of discernment is still developing; and I believe it will be of cardinal importance in the decades which lie ahead. This is because, as I have said, complex and difficult decisions are arising in the lives of good people and a legalistic ethic is unable to cope with them. In the evolution of discernment I see two important factors.

The first is dialogue between spirituality and modern psychology. As we all know, an outstanding characteristic of modern culture is its discovery of, and appreciation for, human feeling. By feeling I do not just mean emotion but the deeper and more subtle inner movements of the psyche, which have been analysed and clarified as never before. Moreover, the movement which stems from Carl Rogers and others to love oneself, to accept one's feelings, to trust one's feeling, to love one's body – all this will teach many and valuable lessons to spirituality and to religions.

The second factor is Christian dialogue with Buddhism. For the art of listening to one's body and one's feelings and even to one's thoughts and one's innermost spiritual activities is highly developed in Buddhist mediation and is called *mindfulness*. About this I will speak later in this book. Here only let me say that one becomes aware of one's breathing, of one's body, of one's feelings, of one's thoughts. In this total awareness, one experiences an inner liberation in such a way that one is not dominated or controlled by inner craving of any kind. Yet all the time one accepts these feelings and listens to them with great objectivity. Moreover, in this kind of meditation one learns to listen not only to the feelings but also to the body. And there is enormous wisdom in the body. It can tell us when to eat and when to fast, when to sleep and when to watch. But we must learn how to listen!

By watching the body and the breathing and the posture a skilled Oriental master can learn a lot, almost everything, about the spiritual attainment of his disciple. That is why he often needs no words. And we, too, can learn to listen to the Spirit through our own bodies and that of others. Here is an important field for discernment in the years which lie ahead.

17

Intercession

I

If the modern world is interested in meditation it is also greatly fascinated by the prayer of petition. This is partly because our contemporaries, efficient, practical and materialistic, have suddenly awakened to the fact that intercessory prayer gets results. Things happen. The sick are healed, the sun begins to shine, projects that looked hopeless start to prosper. Surely this is worth investigating! And so we find parapsychologists conducting experiments on plants and fields of wheat. People pay for growth in some fields while other fields are left unprayed for – and the results are carefully tabulated. On the basis of this and other evidence, theories have been elaborated about spiritual vibrations, subtle energy and the rest. Is there, after all, in the universe a form of energy as yet unknown to science?

How far these speculations are valid I do not know. It is not impossible that subtle, spiritual vibrations are at work and that science will some day tap an energy which is now unknown to us. But even if it does, I believe that even deeper than this and at the root of all is the great mysterious power of God which no scientific instrument will ever touch. This is the power which we call grace; and it is associated with faith and love.

But quite apart from all this, the great religions attach the utmost importance to the prayer of intercession. In one sect of Buddhism which has recently become extremely popular in Japan, believers chant again and again the mantra: "Honour to the lotus sutra"; and it is claimed that the vibrations thus aroused tap the life-force which governs the activity of the whole universe.[1] This means that by reciting these words with faith and perseverance one can achieve remarkable results. Devout believers kneel before their sacred scroll chanting the mantra thousands and thousands of times for the success of their projects, for the prosperity of their business, for the triumph of their political party, and for world peace.

This kind of belief is closely associated with the Oriental notion of *karma*. Just as the pebble thrown into the pond causes ripples that extend to the bank, so every thought and action has its ripples throughout the whole universe. In consequence, no prayer or aspiration is wasted but is always resounding through aeons of existences. But likewise (and this is more sobering) no evil deed or thought is without its sad consequences. Believers in *karma* are confirmed in their conviction by the modern scientific notion of a close-knit universe in which the tiniest movement of one particle exercises influence on the whole.

In this form of Buddhism words are used. But words are not necessary. The silent sitting in meditation itself communicates wisdom and goodness to all, and we find a Buddhist saying: "The sun radiates its splendour on all alike: in like manner the *tathagata* radiates the truth of noble wisdom without recourse to words on all alike." Surely this is a beautiful picture of the enlightened one communicating wisdom and goodness to the whole world.

Yet another altruistic prayer, practised in the East and now adopted by some Christians, centres around the breathing. One sits cross-legged and breathes goodwill to the whole universe. With the exhalation of each breath I send out vibrations of love and compassion to all men and women and to all living creatures. This is beautiful. But it should be noted that it presupposes a certain degree of interior purification. We are warned to take care lest we breathe out our anger and frustration and hatred and envy. The moral is: get rid of all that first and then breathe out love and compassion.

Granted, however, that some degree of inner purification is

---

[1] The formula *Nama-Myoho-renge-kyo* is used by many branches of the Nichiren sect.

effected, we can intercede for friends by breathing the Spirit to them – imagining that they are present and that we are imposing hands on them, communicating the Spirit as did Jesus when he breathed on his disciples saying: "Receive the Holy Spirit. If you forgive the sins of any, they are forgiven . . ." (John 20:23). I know Christians who pray in this way, communicating the Spirit to their friends, always returning to Christ who is the source from whom the Spirit flows. Indeed, through breathing with faith the Spirit can be communicated to the minds and hearts and bodies of others.

II

In the Hebrew-Christian tradition the prayer of intercession has pride of place. Never think that one, so to speak, grows beyond the prayer of petition to enter into the cloud of mystical prayer – as though intercession were for beginners and mysticism for proficients. Not at all. For at the head of the Hebrew tradition stands Moses the mediator, praying for his people with out-stretched arms. The great prophet is the type and forerunner of Jesus, the mediator between God and man. As Moses prayed for Aaron, so Jesus prays for Peter: "Simon, Simon . . . I have prayed for you that your faith may not fail" (Luke 22:32). Remarkable words! Where and when did Jesus pray for Peter? Perhaps Peter's name arose in his mind during those long nights when, alone on the mountain, he prayed to his Father for the world. Again, in that long, priestly prayer in the seventeenth chapter of the Fourth Gospel, Jesus intercedes for his disciples and for us who are their disciples – before praying for himself in Gethsemane and offering his life to the Father on the Cross: "Father, into thy hands I commit my spirit" (Luke 23:46).

And we are told to ask and to keep asking – for ourselves and for others. "Ask, and it will be given you; seek, and you will find; knock, and it will be opened to you" (Matthew 7:7). But it is important that the asking spring not from our little ego but from the Spirit who dwells within us. That is why Jesus tells us to ask *in his name*. Not in our name but in his name.

"Hitherto you have asked nothing in my name; ask and you will receive, that your joy may be full" (John 16:24). It sometimes takes discernment to find out in whose name we ask. It may be that we are asking in our own name; and then the prayer lacks conviction and quickly peters out. But at other times the prayer arises constantly and perseveringly with the unshakeable conviction that it will be heard – and this is the prayer which comes from the indwelling Spirit. St Teresa of Avila speaks of occasions in which the inspiration to pray for another rose spontaneously and unexpectedly in her heart. It was as though she was not deciding who she would intercede for: that decision was made by another. This is prayer in his name. This is prayer with faith.

And so throughout the centuries the Christian community has raised its voice to God our Father asking for daily bread, for forgiveness of sin, and to be delivered from evil. And the prayer is always heard. Just as Eastern religions speak of a life-force which runs through all things and unites all beings in the universe, so Christians speak of a living breath of love, a Spirit who dwells in the whole world and in the hearts of men and women everywhere. It is because we are all united in the Spirit that prayer in Tokyo has repercussions in New York, and intercession in Delhi affects Berlin. We are one in the spirit, always affecting one another.

If I were asked to speak of a mystic who uses intercessory prayer, I would immediately quote Paul. The opening verses of his letters are filled with references to his prayer for those whom he loves. "God is my witness," he writes to the Romans, "that without ceasing I mention you always in my prayers" (Romans 1:9). It is as though on those journeys by land and sea the prayer of intercession was constantly and lovingly in his heart and even on his lips. This is a prayer which rises not from Paul's little ego but from Christ who lives in him. And as Paul prays for others, so he humbly asks the Colossians to pray for him. After all, is it not a great art to receive the prayer of others? Just as we must learn to receive love, so we must learn to open our hearts gratefully to the loving prayers that others offer for us.

*

There are, of course, various levels of intercessory prayer. There is the almost casual prayer of one who intercedes for others because he has promised to do so. This is all right. But there is another form of intercession in which one becomes deeply involved with another person or with other persons. This is a prayer which may be accompanied by fasting and watching and suffering like that of Moses: "Then I lay prostrate before the Lord as before, forty days and forty nights; I neither ate bread nor drank water . . . and I prayed for Aaron also at the same time" (Deuteronomy 9:18–20).

Such a prayer demands a going out from oneself, a forgetfulness of self (and forgetfulness of self is always an indispensable condition for enlightenment) and a total empathy with another person in whose place one stands. But (and here is the difficult thing) I cannot become attached to the person for whom I intercede. I must allow myself to be drawn up into God, leaving the person for whom I pray in order to find him or her again in God.

The process is beautifully described by a Russian *staretz* who describes his prayer for the workers who have been entrusted to him. He prays at first in a very concrete way for particular persons for whom he feels compassion:

> Lord, remember Nicholas, he is so young, he has left his newborn child to find work because they are so poor he has no other means of supporting it. Think of him and protect him from evil thoughts. Think of her and be her defender.

> (Bloom, p. 14)

Here is a prayer of empathy, a prayer in which the *staretz* suffers with the people whom he loves. But as he perseveres he finds that he is drawn up into the cloud of unknowing. Just as the man in search of the ox finds that the ox disappears, so the holy *staretz* finds that Nicholas and his wife and child disappear. And not only for them. Everything is forgotten and the *staretz* is alone, immersed in the silence of God:

> Thus I pray but as I feel the presence of God more and

more strongly I reach a point where I can no longer take notice of anything on earth. The earth vanishes and God alone remains. Then I forget Nicholas, his wife, his child, his village, his poverty and am carried away in God.

(Bloom, p. 14)

This loss of self corresponds to the big circle of nothingness where one forgets everything and is totally lost in the absolute. Wonderful prayer of intercession! *The Cloud of Unknowing* insists that by remaining in silent mystical prayer I am in fact helping the whole human race and the souls of the dead. I do not think explicitly of anybody, but I am helping everybody.

But this total forgetfulness is not the last step. Just as the wise old man returns to the market-place, so the *staretz* must return to Nicholas, his wife and his child. And so he writes:

Then deep in God I find the divine love which contains Nicholas, his wife, his child, their poverty, their needs – this divine love is a torrent which carries me back to earth and to praying for them. And the same thing happens again. God's presence becomes stronger, earth recedes. I am carried again into the depths where I find the world God so greatly loves.

(Bloom, p. 15)

And so in the last stage he sees through the eyes of God. Now it is God who loves through him; and this is unrestricted love which is unattached and liberated from craving.

III

It may happen that someone has a calling or vocation to intercessory prayer for another person or for other persons or for the world; and this prayer will consume her whole being and draw her up into the cloud of unknowing in the silent love I have described. Here she will be in the emptiness, the nothingness and the void, in a state of detachment from all thinking or reasoning or feeling; but her very being, her existential being, is an offering to God like the offering of Jesus on the Cross.

The Book of Privy Counselling speaks of such prayer, and the author seems to regard it as the apex of the mystical life. He describes how, naked of self and clothed with Christ, one offers oneself to the Father with the words:

> That which I am and the way that I am with all my gifts of nature and grace you have given me, O Lord, and you are all this. I offer it to you principally to praise you and to help my fellow Christians and myself.
>
> (Johnston (1), ch. 3)

This is a remarkable prayer. It is existential: a total offering of one's being. "You are all this" – in other words, God is my being and I am (as the author says elsewhere) worshipping God with himself. This is Trinitarian in that one offers oneself in Christ to the Father. Moreover, the offering is made for a three-fold intention: to praise God, to help my fellow Christians, to help myself. How interesting that the prayer of intercession should reach its climax in praise – "principally to praise you"!

*

The notion of sacrificing oneself in intercession is deeply embedded in human nature. It entered increasingly into the heart of Gandhi as his death drew near. All his life Gandhi had been aware of the power of suffering and non-violence and the Cross; but at the end he saw clearly that the most powerful force in the world was the offering of one's life in martyrdom. He became increasingly fascinated by the thought of Christ and his sacrifice. While in Rome we are told that he wept before the crucifix in the Sistine Chapel; and later, the only picture on the bare walls of his little room was that of Christ. Whereas the activist Gandhi had loved the prayer of Newman: "Lead, kindly light", the later Gandhi turned to the Christian hymn: "When I survey the wondrous Cross". Killed by the bullet of a fellow Hindu while walking to a prayer meeting, he died with the name of God on his lips: "Ram, Ram!"

For all his faults (and he had plenty) Gandhi is for me a Christ-like figure. He is one of those great religious personalities who becomes more and more universal, who takes upon himself the suffering of the human race, who offers himself to God for the salvation of the world. In this one sees the potential greatness of human nature.

IV

All that I have said leads to a vitally important conclusion; namely, that the greatest force in the world is not the conscious efforts of men and women who make plans, construct buildings, travel continents and change the face of the earth. All this is good and I would be the last person to oppose human progress. But there is another power at work in the universe and it is a power that can be tapped by men and women of faith. As I have said, Oriental religions speak of the life-force and of *karma*; Christians have always spoken of grace and faith and love. It is precisely here that there lies the power to move mountains and to shake the earth. This was the point of Jesus when he spoke of the widow who dropped her mite into the donation box. "Truly, I say to you, this poor widow has put more than all those who are contributing to the treasury. For they contributed out of their abundance; but she out of her poverty has put in everything she had, her whole living" (Mark 12:43,44). Her mite contributed little; but her loving sacrifice – this shook the universe, and the universe is still shaking under its impact.

This can be applied to social action. It is the cup of water given in the name of Jesus that counts. This principle was admitted by such a great activist as Gandhi. Tagore had given him the name of Mahatma, the great-souled; and Gandhi could reply: "My Mahatmanship is worthless. It is due to my outward activities, due to my politics which is the least part of me and is therefore evanescent. What is of abiding worth is my insistence on truth, non-violence and Brahmacharya, which is the real part of me. That permanent part of me, however small, is not to be despised. It is my all" (Duncan, p. 166).

This is the Gandhi who insisted that his non-violence was a creed, not political expedience. Belief always creates something, even when we do not see tangible results. Some people have said that Gandhi failed – that he left India in a political and economic chaos from which it never recovered. Others have said that he was magnificently successful and changed the course of history. But in either case we must measure the achievement of Gandhi by his own standards – "My Mahatmanship is worthless." His faith and love, like that of the widow, gave birth to spiritual vibrations which will always remain.

The same can be said of Mother Teresa of Calcutta. Judged in terms of economics, she and her sisters have done little to alleviate the poverty of the Indian sub-continent. But their love and compassion generate a spiritual power which remains. Let me again quote her words:

> We can do very little for the people, but at least they know that we love them and that we care for them and that we are at their disposal. So let us try, all of us, to come closer to that unity of spreading Christ's love wherever we go, love and compassion; have deep compassion for the people.

This again is the power which shakes the universe.

*

Now while I emphasize the power of compassion and love and enlightenment, it is by no means my intention to downgrade human efficiency, plans for economic progress, political acumen and conscious effort. Far from it. The great challenge of our day is to unite these two forces. In other words, the great challenge of our day is mysticism in action. Our age demands not only men and women who will retire to caves in the Himalayas and huts in the desert to intercede for mankind but also men and women who will enjoy mystical experience in the hurly-burly of politics and economics and social action. The activity of such people will bear fruit because it is rooted in the Tao, rooted in non-action, rooted in God. In them human action falls into the stream of non-action and progress is made.

18

Mysticism in Action

I

Critics of mysticism frequently point to the immense social problems of our day – the hunger, the air pollution, the social injustice, the racial discrimination, the political corruption, the danger of nuclear war, the exploitation of the poor by the rich, the torture of political prisoners. And then they ask about mysticism. How will this help solve contemporary problems? Is it not a luxury to retire to the desert while large sections of humanity face utter destruction? Surely the first duty of modern people is to stretch out a helping hand to fellow man and women, to alleviate their suffering, to bring peace and happiness to the world.

These statements and these questions are all very reasonable. Of course we must marshal our forces to help suffering humanity and to build a better world. The only problem is: how? Activists sometimes overlook the undeniable fact that unenlightened, unregenerate, unconverted men and women can do nothing to solve the vast problems with which we are confronted. Not only will they do nothing but they may do immense damage. They may line their own pockets with the money which should go to the poor (and, alas, we have seen this happen very often); or they may be carried away by passionate anger and violently create more problems than they solve; or they may simply lack the depth and vision to see the roots of the problems. The weakness of human nature is something we cannot with impunity overlook. Buddhism teaches that prior to enlightenment we are in illusion – we are lost in the woods and don't even see the footprints of the ox. And then Christianity teaches about original sin. In either case, to work for humanity one must be enlightened. What the modern world needs is enlightened men and women.

Once enlightened we no longer rely on our little ego but on a power which is greater than ourselves. "Apart from me," says Jesus, "you can do nothing" (John 15:5). And Paul, carried away to boast that he has laboured more than all the others, is forced to correct himself: "It was not I, but the grace of God which is with me" (1 Corinthians 15:10). Yes, Paul. You never said a truer word. It was not your strength; it was a greater power within you to which you surrendered. Your strength was in weakness. Your action was rooted in non-action.

And so if we are in any way to solve the problems of our day we must rely on the power of another, not on our own power. And this is non-action which, I have tried to say, is the most powerful action of all. It manifests itself in the human heart as a blind stirring of love, as a living flame of love. Sometimes, it is true, this inner fire drives people into solitude where they intercede for mankind and unleash a power which shakes the universe. But the same inner fire drives others into the midst of action with a passionate love for justice and a willingness to die for their convictions. Indeed, this flame of love may suddenly become dynamic in the heart of a solitary – who suddenly discovers that he is called to action and that he cannot refuse the invitation. Such was the shepherd-prophet Amos who protests: "I am no prophet, nor a prophet's son; but I am a herdsman, and a dresser of sycamore trees, and the Lord took me from following the flock, and the Lord said to me, 'Go, prophesy to my people Israel' " (Amos 7:14,15). Poor Amos! Like Jeremiah and Jonah he did not want to be involved in tumultuous action; but the inner flame, the inner voice, drove him on and, under its influence, he thundered against the rich:

> Hear this, you who trample upon the needy
> and bring the poor of the land to an end
> (Amos 8:4)

Here is the action which is the overflow of mysticism. It is filled with compassion for the poor and needy and underprivileged.

II

I have said that the mystical flame sometimes drives hermits or solitaries into action. But I can immediately hear the objection: "But the mystic who has spent long periods in solitude knows nothing about the world. How, then, can he solve its problems? Let him subscribe to *Time* or *Newsweek*. Let him read *The Times*. Or, better still, let him take a guided tour around Calcutta and be 'exposed to the poor'. Then we'll listen to him."

Well, well. I wonder. Let us never underestimate the wisdom of the desert. For the fact is that the person who has spent long periods in authentic prayer and meditation knows about the suffering of the world because he has experienced it all within himself. How often has a repentant sinner, filled with remorse for his iniquities and failures, gone to the solitary monk to confess his crimes – and, lo and behold, he has found someone who understands the whole story. For the monk has experienced it all within himself – in another way. He has met the devil and seen his own awful weakness and potentiality for evil. It does not shock him to hear about murder and rape and violence – and he is filled with compassion for the weakness of a human race to which he himself belongs. Moreover, like Kannon, who with that exquisite smile of compassion hears the cries of the poor, mystics also have in their own way heard the cries of the underprivileged, the downtrodden, the victims of violence and deceit and exploitation – just as Jesus knew it all in Gethsemane. Of course it will do them no harm to read *Time* and *Newsweek* also. And if they do, they will find there things which the authors of the articles did not realize.

*

In the midst of solitude, then, a person may receive a prophetic vocation like that of Amos. And he may struggle against it. But his struggle will be in vain; and he will be pursued by the inexorable words: "To all to whom I send you you shall go, and whatever I command you you shall speak. Be not afraid of them, for I am with you to deliver you, says the Lord" (Jeremiah 1:7). And so he goes into action and his action is fruitful because the Lord is with him, and because he sees problems at their root and in their totality. His enlightened eye penetrates through the lines of *Time* and *Newsweek* to the basic cause of all our problems, which is that mysterious reality that Christians call sin and Buddhists call blindness and ignorance.

I have spoken of the solitary who is called to action. But the mystic in action need not have been solitary. She may (and this is the Ignatian ideal) be a person who has spent her years in a cycle of contemplation-action-contemplation-action; and in this way she has attained to enlightenment. The important thing is not whether or not she has spent years in solitude. What matters is that she should be enlightened – that her eye of love penetrate beyond the superficial appearances to the root cause of our problems and to the ultimate solution which lies beyond the cloud of unknowing.

*

But what, you may ask, will he or she do? And to this I can only answer, as in my previous chapter, that he or she will follow the guidance of the inner light. Nor is this an easy task, because following the light is different from following an idea or an ideology. It demands liberation from ideology so that one can listen to the voice of the beloved which will, at times, run counter to all ideologies. But one must discern that voice; and we find that the true mystic in action is always praying for light, always searching for the way. The initial call points out the general direction, but it does not enlighten every step of the path. Quite often there will be anguish and fear and uncertainty and conflict like that of Jeremiah: "Woe is me, my mother, that you bore me, a man of strife and contention to the whole land!" (Jeremiah 15:10).

This inner light leads in the most surprising ways. Prophetical people are quite unpredictable. Often they are socially unacceptable, strident, exaggerated, apparently unorthodox. Like Jeremiah they are often ridiculed and put in the stocks. Usually they are put to death, either literally or metaphorically. But the distinctive thing is the quality of their love which "bears all things, believes all things, hopes all things, endures all things" (1 Corinthians 13:7).

Consequently there is no blueprint to tell us what the mystic in action will do. He might do anything. But, on the other hand, he will have his charisma which he must faithfully follow. And this is true of all of us. We are not called to serve in the same way. "Are all apostles? Are all prophets? Are all teachers? Do all work miracles? Do all possess gifts of healing? Do all speak with tongues? Do all interpret?" (1 Corinthians 12:29). We cannot ask that every prophet walk in peace marches or teach the blind or visit the sick or denounce the politically corrupt. Each must follow a distinctive charisma.

And we must have our ears to the ground to listen for the true prophets, to recognize them, to follow their guidance and not to kill them. This is the great challenge of our day. Around us are prophets and false prophets. By their fruits we shall know them; by their fruits only can we distinguish the authentic from the pretenders. And Paul has spoken of those fruits of the Spirit which are "love, joy, peace, patience, kindness, goodness, faithfulness, gentleness, self-control" (Galatians 5:22). If these are present we should listen to the prophet, even when his words run counter to what we hold sacred and believe.

III

St Paul says that the important thing is love. After extolling the various charismatic gifts he goes on to say that what is, or should be, common to them all is love. Without love the gifts are useless. And so he begins his canticle: "If I speak in the tongues of men and of angels, but have not love, I am a noisy gong or a clanging cymbal" (1 Corinthians 13:1).

Gandhi recognized this; but in his peculiar circumstances he preferred to speak of non-violence or *ahimsa*. This included compassion for the poor, love of the aggressor, love of justice.

It renounced all hatred and use of force; but it believed in force of another kind: *satyagraha* means the force of truth.

To build one's activity on love and non-violence demands the greatest inner purification. One must constantly rid one's heart of inordinate desires and fears and anxieties; but above all one must cleanse oneself from anger.

*

In our day anger seems to be the chief enemy of love and non-violence. By anger I mean the inner violence which lies not only in the conscious but also in the unconscious mind of individuals and of whole nations. This is an inner violence which has sometimes been nurtured by decades of oppression and injustice; sometimes it has been further nurtured by domestic strife in the home; always it is the source of great insecurity, inner fear and awful weakness. This is the anger which may erupt into sexual crimes or irrational murder and terrorism.

Now if I come to recognize the anger which is in me (and this is already great progress in the journey towards human maturity), and if I ask a psychologist what I am to do with my anger, the odds are that he will tell me, among other things, to get it out of my system. "Get it out somehow! Imagine that your enemy is seated beside you and just roar at him – tell him what you feel! Or thump a pillow or a punch-ball or a sack of hay! But get it out!"

Now this may sound a thousand miles away from mystical experience. But in fact it is not. Because in the mystical path anger comes out – it rises to the surface of consciousness. Remember that I spoke of the Buddha sitting serenely in meditation while the beasts roar and the dogs bark. These are manifestations of my hidden anger. As I have already said, I must not make violent efforts to chase them away, neither must I enter into dialogue with them. I simply pay no attention to them – and in doing this I accept them. And then they vanish. In some cases, of course, it may also be necessary to speak about them to a friend or counsellor. But in any case I get them out of my system.

But when this is done, something still remains. And this is

just anger. In other words, my anger has not been annihilated but has been purified. Now it is the anger of one who has seen, and still sees, real injustice in his own life and in that of others and refuses to countenance such evil. It is an anger which could be more properly called *love of justice* and is accompanied by a willingness to die in the cause of justice. In itself this is nothing other than a mystical experience. It is the living flame of love orientated towards action.

Such was the righteous indignation of the prophets. Such was the anger of one who made a whip and drove the money-changers out of the temple: "Take these things away; you shall not make my Father's house a house of trade" (John 2:16). Gandhi, too, was moved by this just anger: he spoke frequently of marshalling all one's spiritual forces against the oppressor, and he fought injustice by fasting, by suffering, by accepting imprisonment and by non-violence.

IV

From all that has been said and from a perusal of the Fourth Gospel it will be clear that mystical action is chiefly a matter of bearing fruit. It is not a question of frenetic activity, of getting a lot done, of achieving immediate results. Rather is it a question of unrestricted love which goes on and on and on.

Such love always bears fruit. Such love always leads to a union which creates something new. But the new creation may be quite different from what the mystic and her followers expected. Her life, like that of Jesus, may end in apparent failure. But when it does, people in another part of the world and perhaps in another era will reap the fruit. For "here the saying holds true, 'One sows and another reaps'. I sent you to reap that for which you did not labour; others have laboured and you have entered into their labour" (John 4:37,38).

19

Training for Mysticism (1)

I

Throughout this book I have stressed the fact that mysticism is the gift of God and the work of grace. And yet it is also true that the great religious traditions have used human means to educate people and introduce them to mysticism. How these two factors, divine grace and human effort, are theologically reconciled need not concern us here. Enough to say that monastic life, whether Christian or Buddhist, has always attempted through training and discipline to educate the contemplative faculties which exist in all men and women and which are of particular importance for those who would devote themselves to meditation and prayer. Such contemplative faculties concern that realm which we call "the heart" but they are also deeply embedded in the body; and in Asia there has always been particular skill in educating and forming a contemplative body. These faculties, however, have become blunted in modern life by the tremendous bombardment to which our senses have been exposed. Consequently, modern people are looking for a new spirituality and a new asceticism which will enable them to benefit from the good points of scientific progress while at the same time developing and training those mystical faculties which lead to enlightenment. This is quite a challenge.

In the Sino-Japanese tradition spiritual training is called *gyo* and is represented by the character which means going and walking and which originally pictured a road or a crossroads (see page 339). This character translates the Sanskrit *carya* and is defined in a standard Buddhist dictionary as: "Religious acts, deeds or exercises aimed at taking one closer to the final goal of enlightenment.''[1] In other words, as the very core of Buddhism is the awakening or enlightenment so *gyo* includes anything that carries one along the way to this goal.

Buddhist monasticism contains a very elaborate and meticulous *gyo* which gives instructions on how to walk, how to sit, how to dress how to eat, how to fast, how to sleep, how to breathe, how to bathe, how to train the body and make it flexible, how to develop vital energy, how to be authentically detached, how to act in time of sickness. It also gives instructions on certain ascetical practices such as running around the mountain (I speak here of Mount Hiei) for days or weeks, sitting for long periods in the lotus posture, reciting the sutras, copying the sutras, bowing and touching the ground with one's forehead, prostrations, striking the gong while reciting the name of Amida – and so on, and so on.

Naturally enough, this *gyo* has had its difficulties and its critics. As happened in similar circumstances in the West, it often deteriorated into an external legalism which simply put burdens on people without bringing them to the coveted goal of enlightenment. And so we find the saintly Japanese monk Shinran (1173–1263) rebelling against the asceticism of the Tendai and Zen sects, and proclaiming the pre-eminence of faith and of grace. Shinran himself had spent much time practising *gyo* on Mount Hiei near Kyoto and had profited little from it all. And so he proclaimed faith in Amida as the one means of salvation. Everything is a gift, he declared; everything is grace: one drop of the mercy of Amida is of more value than all the *gyo* in the wide world. He was the first Japanese Buddhist monk openly to abandon celibacy and to take a wife – for celibacy was part of the *gyo* which he rejected. He has frequently been compared to Luther, all the more so since he preached a doctrine which appealed not only to monks but to ordinary working persons who had neither the time nor the capacity for the prolonged austerities of Tendai and Zen. Simply call on the name

[1] *Japanese-English Buddhist Dictionary* (Daito Shuppansha: Tokyo 1965, p. 93).

(By kind permission of Kakichi Kadowaki)

of Amida with faith – this was his message. Recite the name of Amida (and this was called the *nembutsu*) and you will be reborn in the Pure Land which lies to the West.

Shinran preached the doctrine of reliance on another (*tariki*) as opposed to the self-reliance (*jiriki*) of Zen. While Zen proclaimed the difficult *gyo (nan-gyo)*, Shinran and his followers proclaimed the easy *gyo (i-gyo)* as the way to salvation. Yet in practice his path is not so easy. The very renunciation of asceticism is a *gyo* in itself. It demands a total detachment.

II

In the Christian tradition, too, there has been training and education for enlightenment and conversion. St Ignatius speaks of "spiritual exercises" (and this might be the best translation of the word *gyo*) and he describes these exercises: "For just as taking a walk, journeying on foot, and running are bodily exercises, so we call spiritual exercises every way of preparing and disposing the soul to rid itself of all inordinate attachments, and, after their removal, of seeking and finding the will of God in the disposition of our life for the salvation of our soul" (Ignatius (1), p. 1). Here is an interesting parallel to Buddhism: detachment leading to enlightenment or conversion and salvation. For Ignatius this conversation entails the discovery of God's will.

Ignatius, of course, is appealing to an ancient tradition in which asceticism is associated with the Hellenistic games just as Buddhist *gyo* is associated with the martial arts like judo, karate, fencing and wrestling. St Paul refers to the sports of his day:

> Do you not know that in a race all the runners compete, but only one receives the prize? So run that you may obtain it. Every athlete exercises self-control in all things. They do it to receive a perishable wreath, but we an imperishable.
>
> (1 Corinthians 9:24,25)

The thought of the games is often in Paul's mind – Paul who is running towards the goal without looking back, Paul who has fought the good fight, who has finished the course, who has kept the faith.

As the art of asceticism developed, the old authors began to speak of interior and exterior asceticism. The orthodox teaching was that the exterior, which included fasting, watching, observance of silence and discipline of all kinds, was only of value in so far as it led to the interior which meant love of neighbour, compassion for the suffering, humility and simplicity of life.

And yet in Christianity, as in Buddhism, wise people were always acutely aware of the dangers of asceticism and of minute fidelity to law. For one thing they realized that the exterior could be over-emphasized to the detriment of the interior, thus leading to pride, self-centredness and the building up of the very egoism it was meant to destroy. Indeed, the prophets of the Old Testament had kept insisting that Yahweh wants our hearts rather than our sacrifices: rend your hearts and not your garments. This is particularly stressed in Isaiah:

Is not this the fast that I choose . . . Is it not to share your bread with the hungry, and bring the homeless poor into your house; and when you see the naked, to cover him, and not to hide yourself from your own flesh?

(Isaiah 58:6,7)

This is also a central theme in the Gospel: the observance of the sabbath, the washing of hands, fasting and all kinds of external observance are subordinate to justice and truth and charity. And is not this a theme that must always be replayed? Because the dangers of legalism are perennial.

And so in East and West we find the same tension. On the one hand, some training or education is necessary; on the other hand, all depends on grace. On the one hand, we must strive; on the other hand, our striving is itself a gift. On the one hand, asceticism is necessary; on the other hand, it is spiritually dangerous. In practice the problem has been solved by a principle which states that we should strive with our human abilities as though all depended on ourselves, and yet we must wait for the gift as though all depended on God.

III

In our own day the Western wave of interest in meditation and mysticism brings with it a great interest in asceticism. Modern practical people want to know *how to do it*. They want to be shown the way. And so their eyes turn towards the *gyo* of the East – towards the foothills of the Himalayas and the temples of Kyoto. Who will give me a methodology, a spirituality, a system? Where will I find a master?

And while these questions are asked, thinking people are also acutely aware of the grave defects and failures of the asceticism of the past. Apart from the dangers which I have already mentioned and which are stressed in the Gospel, there is the additional voice of protest from many people who have gone through the training and found it ineffective – even counter-productive. They faithfully observed all the rules of a religious or monastic system; but the whole thing did not touch their innermost being, did not penetrate beyond the surface. It all remained external;. and they did not even reach the threshold of contemplation. This is a complaint which one hears from Christians and Buddhists alike. Why was the law never internalized? What was wrong?

Again, an objection raised in the West is that the traditional asceticism has paid little attention to the training of human feeling and affectivity. Modern people are peculiarly sensitive to this, since they live in a culture which has rediscovered the beauty of matter, of feeling, of sexuality. Read Teilhard de Chardin on *The Evolution of Chastity* and you find a powerful statement of the inadequacy of the old approach which frequently warped and crushed that human feeling which should blossom and bloom through the message of the Gospel.

Now it seems to me that we will not find a new asceticism or spirituality simply by delving into the past of either Buddhism or Christianity. This is an area in which, recalling that religions are evolving, we must turn to dialogue between the great religions and their common dialogue with modern psychology and culture. Furthermore, this is an area in which we will not get instantaneous results, for neither psychology nor religion can claim an adequate understanding of human feeling and human sexuality. We have a long way to go; and a great challenge lies before us. Let me, then, mention a few points which are no more than guide-lines; and then in the next chapter I will select some aspects of Buddhist *gyo* which may be of interest to modern people.

IV

First of all let me say that if the old asceticism failed in many ways this was principally due to lack of love. The trouble with the Pharisees was not that they kept all the rules (their observance was praiseworthy) but that they did not love enough.

And that is why their rules remained external. Similarly, in any ascetical training the only thing which will internalize the outer observance of the law is love – that human and religious love which is unrestricted, which goes on and on and on. That is why I have spoken about the interior law of charity and of love which is above all laws and rules and observances. That is why I have spoken of the living flame of love, the blind stirring of love, the small fire and the murmuring stream.

And it should be remembered that this love must be directed to ourselves. Love of self is important. Though this is proclaimed in Deuteronomy and reiterated even more strongly in the Gospel, it has been a weak point of traditional asceticism. It is so easy to fall into a holy self-hatred, as it was sometimes called; it is so easy to fall into a morbid delight in doing the difficult thing. And it has taken modern psychology to remind us that we must love ourselves, accept ourselves, listen to ourselves, trust our deepest feelings and instincts. Only in this context can austerity be holy and enriching.

Again, there is love of God, love of the Gospel, love of the community. Buddhist texts, as I have frequently said, do not make much of love and do not talk about love. But this does not mean that love and commitment are absent. It is interesting to recall that Buddhist temples everywhere resound with an archetypal invocation which is the very essence of their religious practice:

> I take refuge in the Buddha
> I take refuge in the *dharma* (the law)
> I take refuge in the *sangha* (the community)

Here is total commitment to what is called the triple jewel. Is this not an expression of love? And is it not interesting to see the very personal nature of the first invocation, the dedication of oneself to Shakamuni, the enlightened one?

I said that the triple invocation is archetypal. And, of course, the corresponding Christian commitment could be expressed in the words:

> I take refuge in Jesus
> I take refuge in the Gospel
> I take refuge in the Church

Here is a great love, an unrestricted love for the whole universe and for its source. When *gyo* is practised in this setting and when it leads to such commitment it cannot but be human, it cannot but be internalized.

Put in other words, faith is the very core and essence from which all asceticism flows and to which it returns. Buddhist faith develops into total commitment to the Buddha, to the *dharma*, to the *sangha*. Christian faith develops into total commitment to Jesus, to the Gospel, to the Church. Both, I believe, move on to faith in the great mystery which lies beyond the Buddha, the *dharma*, the *sangha* – to the great mystery which lies beyond Jesus, the Gospel, the Church. This is the great mystery which Christians call God our Father and the Father of Our Lord Jesus Christ.

*

I have spoken of the *sangha* and the Church. This recalls the vitally important fact that we cannot practise asceticism and meditation alone; we cannot arrive at mysticism alone. Just as Paul had to go to Ananias to receive the imposition of hands after his initial encounter with Jesus on the road to Damascus, so we also need other people. We need people whom we love and by whom we are loved; we need a climate of trust and of union. Only in such a community can mysticism develop – "if we love one another, God abides in us and his love is perfected in us" (I John 4:12).

Obviously this does not mean that we must live under the same roof with the whole community. It simply means that we must be united with them even when distance or the need for solitude separate us physically. Ordinarily Christians are united with a small group and through it with the whole Church and the human race; Buddhists are united with their *dharma* brothers and sisters, then with the whole *sangha* and then with the universe.

As for the precise nature of the smaller community which leads to mysticism, I would not restrict myself to one format. There are innumerable possibilities.

The traditional type of community in Christianity and Buddhism alike tends towards monasticism. It centres around a master who guides his disciples to enlightenment, to conversion, to mysticism. Such a master reads the Scriptures and comments on them – not in the scholarly fashion of the exegete but in the enlightened manner of one whose inner eye of love sees in the Scriptures treasures which are hidden from the wise and prudent. Again, he explains the *dharma* or the Gospel. He interviews his disciples one by one, enjoying with them the religious experience about which I have spoken in this book. Sometimes this religious experience will be expressed in words but at other times words will be unnecessary – the two can remain in silent and communal contemplation. In this way the teacher mediates the God experience; he brings the disciple to enlightenment. Indeed, enlightenment (sudden or gradual) may take place precisely during this interview.

Yet this meeting has a profoundly human dimension also. A story is told that when Ignatius (who was one of the great directors of Western Christianity) saw that one of his disciples was glum and downcast he danced a Spanish tango to cheer him up. When one reflects on the game leg of Ignatius, the legacy of Pamplona, one can imagine that the disciple quickly snapped out of his desolation.

Master and disciples form one kind of community. But it is only one. There are, as I have said, other possibilities. The founders of the religious orders had different ideas about the nature of community – some advocating stability, others advocating constant travel on the road. Again, in our day and before our eyes new forms of community are emerging. There are charismatic communities in which each member has his or her special gift. "To each is given the manifestation of the Spirit for the common good" (I Corinthians 1:7). In such a community, as Paul says, some will teach, others will speak in prophecy, others will interpret, others will heal. What matters is that they love and trust one another, and in this way cultivate a soil in which authentic mysticism can grow and develop.

I would not, then, limit community to one particular format. This is an area in which modern people are searching; and it is scarcely possible to imagine the form which communities will take in the decades which lie ahead.

20

Training for Mysticism (2)

I

I have indicated that Buddhist *gyo* or asceticism is extremely meticulous and extends to every area of human activity. Consequently I cannot treat it here in detail but must content myself with outlining a few general principles which may be useful for my reader in his or her quest for enlightenment.

But first let me recall that the Buddhist asceticism found in Japan owes a great debt to Taoism and the whole stream of Sino-Japanese culture – and it is about this that I will principally speak. To understand it one must to some extent grasp its peculiar approach to the human body, an approach which is quite different from the Hellenistic body-and-soul way of thinking that became traditional in the West. The East Asian approach is found pre-eminently in Oriental medicine – in acupuncture, moxibustion, and the many forms of massage. It is also in evidence in the martial arts like karate, judo, aikido and sumo; and even in the fine arts like the tea ceremony and the flower arrangement.

In all these activities the centre of gravity is not the head but the belly or *hara*. (It is interesting to note, in parenthesis, that in the *yin-yang* scheme of things the belly is *yin*. That is to say, it is feminine; and in this sense contemplation, as envisaged by Chinese philosophy, is a feminine activity.) And particular attention is paid to the area which lies a couple of inches below the naval. This is called the *tanden* or *kikai*, the latter word meaning literally "the sea of energy".

When I use the word energy I am thinking of the Japanese *ki* (pronounced like the English *key*), the Chinese *chi* and the Sanskrit *prana*. All these words point to a certain cosmic energy or vital force which courses through the whole universe, linking all things together, and courses also through the human body when it is healthy. One who possesses a wealth of *ki* can perform extraordinary feats; and yet it differs from muscular energy in that it nourishes spiritual activities like meditation and, according to some, reaches its peak at the moment of death when physical strength is ebbing away.

And yet *ki* heals. One can learn to direct it to the affected part of the body, thus healing oneself. Or by imposing hands on another one can allow the *ki* to flow through one's body into the body of another, thus imparting healing and strength. Indeed, the Japanese word for healing is *teate* literally meaning "imposition of hands", and in the ancient Oriental world people healed others by laying their hands on them.[1]

Closely associated with this *ki* is another concept which has already appeared in my book; namely, *muga* meaning non-self or *mushin* no-mind. This is the art of losing self, emptying one's mind, entering into a state of relaxed awareness. This emptiness is, it should be noted, a state of profound concentration in which the mind is liberated not only from reasoning and thinking but also from hatred and passion and fear, so that a great calm descends upon the person. Losing oneself in this way, one can "become the object", whether that object be a flower or a bow or a flowing stream.

Only in this state of no-mind will the *ki* flow through one's body, and only in this state of no-mind can one impart healing to another. For the *ki* is blocked by tension or anxiety or hatred or rancour of any kind.

A good Oriental master is aware of his own *ki* and he can, so to speak, catch the *ki* of his disciple. He can learn very much

---

[1] Scientific studies have been made on this *ki* or vital energy; but modern physics is not yet prepared to assert that it exists. It is possible that we have here a phenomenon which does not fall under the aegis of science and does not obey the laws of physics as we know them. Some people claim that an understanding of *ki* would throw light on parapyschological phenomena like telepathy, clairvoyance and thought projection.

by observing the eyes, the throat, the breathing. Sometimes he has a gaze which is embarrassingly piercing and penetrating. All this is part of his process of discernment.

But remember that this *gyo* is, so to speak, neutral. Obviously it is very good to lose one's self in order to be filled with the Holy Spirit. It is also good to lose self so that the inner creative and artistic powers may surface. It is also healthy when one is trained to lose self in sports like judo. But the non-self state can also be dangerous. In some forms of ecstatic religion one empties the mind in order to allow a spirit to take over or in order to enter into a frenzy. For this reason an authentic master teaches his disciple to enter into emptiness with great discipline and purity of intention. For *muga* and *mushin* and *ki* are not things to be treated lightly. They are very serious.

*

But now, keeping in mind these fundamental concepts, and also keeping in mind what I said in the last chapter about the supreme importance of faith and love, let me consider three aspects of Buddhist ascetical training: *control of the mind, control of the breathing, control of the body*. These three approaches converge at the desired goal of heightened awareness and even, under certain circumstances, at enlightenment.

II

First, then, is control of the mind. Eastern thought stresses what we all know from experience: that the human mind is restless, untamed, undisciplined like the wind. We constantly think of the future either with expectation or with apprehension; or we think of the past with nostalgia or with guilt. Seldom do we live in the present moment; seldom do we live in the here-and-now. We are always escaping from what we are and from what is.

Now the East has developed certain techniques for controlling the mind and bringing it to a standstill. And central among these is the art of concentrating on a single object so that the mind enters a state of one-pointedness.[2]

Concretely, one can concentrate on a part of the body – the space between the eyebrows, the tip of the nose, the lower abdomen. Or one can concentrate on a single thought. Or, as in Zen, one can concentrate on a *koan* or riddle. Or one can repeat a single sound or sacred word. Or one can become aware of the breathing. In all these cases one is concentrating on a single thing and, in consequence becoming interiorly unified so as to enter the *mushin* or no-mind state about which I have spoken.

Or one can listen not to one sound but to every sound – a practice about which I spoke earlier in this book. Or one can watch every object that enters one's field of vision. And in this way one becomes totally aware of present reality.

Presence to each moment is a great ideal in Buddhist *gyo*; and there is an old saying that "a saint is one who walks when he walks, who talks when he talks, who does not dream while listening, who does not think while acting". And, as I have said, a similar attentiveness is found in the arts. A teacher of calligraphy once told me that he can immediately tell from the ideographs where the writer lost one-pointedness and became distracted. His lapse affected his brush and appears in the writing.

Never underestimate one-pointedness. It gives remarkable power. It is the key to controlling the psychic energy or *ki* about which I have spoken; it is the key to influencing (and, alas, sometimes to manipulating) other people. I know a young Japanese man who can smash a heap of tiles with his forehead; and this he attributes to one-pointedness through the breathing. I myself believe that the secret of many feats, like those of the Fiji fire walkers (whom I watched in Suva) or the yogis who pierce their cheeks with skewers, can be traced to this same one-pointedness. For in this state a latent dynamism of the human psyche is brought to the surface and people experience great

[2] *One-pointedness* seems to be the best translation of the Sanskrit *ekagrata* ("on a single point") and the Japanese *seishin toitsu* ("unification of spirit").

power. If Asia has been labelled "the mystic East" this is partly because Westerners have unconsciously adverted to the prevalence of one-pointedness in its life and culture.

Though one-pointedness is so central to all Asian culture, it is little known in the West outside the religious and mystical tradition. That is why transcendental meditation, which is a form of one-pointedness, has made such an impact. It has brought a new dimension into Western culture and has introduced many Westerners to a dynamism hitherto latent in their psyche. By taking a comfortable position and quietly repeating a mantra one comes to the deeper level of consciousness where one-pointedness resides. This gives relaxation, joy and renewed strength. It is interesting to note that transcendental meditation has made almost no impact in Japan or even in India, its country of origin. No doubt this is because these countries already possess one-pointedness in their culture. Transcendental meditation offers nothing new . . . .

*

One-pointedness looks very like mysticism. But do not be deceived! It is here that one must use discernment. For mysticism (and please forgive me for repeating it again) is centred on faith, whereas profound one-pointedness can be achieved without any faith whatever. It can be practised in a purely secular situation in order to develop human potential and ability to play ping-pong or golf. It can be used for good or evil, to heal or to destroy – a grim fact which is well known in Japan.

Zen masters distinguish clearly between those who sit in the lotus to develop human potential or to improve their karate and those who sit with faith, committing themselves totally and unconditionally to the Buddha, the *dharma* and the *sangha*. That is why an authentic master will quickly ask you what you want in your practice. And he will direct you accordingly.

A Christian example of one-pointedness is Mary Magdalen sitting at the feet of Jesus. "One thing is needful" (Luke 10:42). Or again, Jesus tells us to live in the present without anxiety about the future. And here again the dimension of faith is stressed: "Your heavenly Father knows that you need them all" (Matthew 6:32).

In general it can be said that mysticism is a form of one-pointedness; but not all one-pointedness is mysticism.

III

The second point was control of the breathing.

In all forms of Oriental meditation the breathing is of cardinal importance. Western medicine will agree that deep abdominal breathing is health-giving and invigorating; the Oriental thought adds to this belief that breath or air is the principal source of life-giving *prana* or *ki* or cosmic energy. In yoga there are many breathing exercises and techniques; but in Buddhist meditation one just breathes naturally without in any way interfering with the inhalation or exhalation and without retention of breath. If one keeps the back straight, the breathing automatically becomes abdominal; and the aim in Buddhist asceticism is simply *to become aware of the breath*. This is called mindfulness (I referred to it earlier in this book), and it can be achieved first by counting the breath and then becoming aware of the breath without using any words. One may be aware of the breath at the nostrils, or of the rise and fall of the abdomen until, eventually, one becomes aware of one's whole body. "The wise man breathes from his heels" says an old Chinese proverb; and this well explains the awareness of the breath or the *ki* which flows through the body in this kind of meditation. Here is an ancient Buddhist text which describes mindfulness through the breathing.

> A monk who has gone to a forest or the root of a tree or to an empty place, sits down cross-legged, holding his back erect, and arouses mindfulness in front of him. Mindful he breathes in, mindful he breathes out. Whether he is breathing in a long or a short breath, he comprehends that he is breathing in a long or a short breath. Similarly when he is breathing out. He trains himself, thinking: "I shall breathe in, I shall breathe out, clearly perceiving the whole body."
>
> (Conze, p. 56)

In this way the monk becomes aware of the vital energy and enters into one-pointedness.

The breath is of crucial importance because it gives access to the deeper levels of the psyche which are ordinarily unconscious. If we have a voluntary and involuntary nervous system, the former governing actions which can readily be controlled and the latter governing the inner functions like digestion which are normally outside of our control – if we look at the body in this way, then breathing stands between these two. Ordinarily it is involuntary; but it can easily be controlled and made rhythmical. And once one has learned to control the breathing, control of the remaining areas of the involuntary nervous system may follow. That is why the skilled yogi can control his digestion, his sleep and even his heartbeat. That is why he can penetrate to deep states of consciousness. "By making his respiration rhythmical and progressively slower," writes Mircea Eliade, "the yogin can penetrate – that is, he can experience, in perfect lucidity – certain states of consciousness that are inaccessible in a waking condition, particularly the states of consciousness that are peculiar to sleep" (Eliade, p. 56).

*

Another important aspect of the breath is the fact that it symbolizes life – "Then the Lord God formed man of dust from the ground, and breathed into his nostrils the breath of life" (Genesis 2:7). When I am breathing mindfully I become aware of the life within me; I become aware of my body; I become aware of the core of my being. I am reminded of the words of Jesus: "Is not life more than food, and the body more than clothing?" (Matthew 6:25). How true! It is life that counts: the breath and the body. Other things like food and clothing are secondary.

Moreover in all the great religious traditions breath symbolizes something cosmic. *Ki* and *prana* have a cosmic dimension; and that is why they are associated with telepathy and thought-projection and the rest. Again, in the Hebrew-Christian tradition breath or *spiratio* symbolizes the Holy Spirit who fills the whole universe, who envelops us with his presence, who dwells within us. It is a wonderful fact of experience that, in those who have faith, mindfulness of the breathing can lead to a relishing of the presence of the Spirit. Some people's meditation consists in just breathing silently and wordlessly in the Spirit.

IV

The third point is control of the body.

There is a form of Buddhist meditation in which one becomes totally aware of one's body – it is a variation of the mindfulness about which I have already spoken. One simply sits on a chair (though in ancient times the cross-legged position was always used) with back erect, eyes closed, hands on thighs; and one experiences or feels the sensations of the body. The touch of the clothes on one's shoulders, the back pressing against the chair, the hips, the hands, the thighs, the soles of the feet. One does not *think about* the body; one *experiences* the body – moving one's awareness from one part of the body to the other until a profound relaxation is attained to. Here again the *ki* or vital energy courses through one's whole being.

But what, you may say, has this to do with religion, this body awareness? And to this I would answer that one passes through the body to the spirit. The same is true also of *hatha yoga* which is not just a form of physical training but a way to union – union with oneself and union with God. Some authors speak of mysticism of posture; and while I do not accept this use of the word mysticism I sympathize with the underlying idea.

*

While there are many bodily postures in Oriental meditation, pride of place is given to the lotus. It is the perfect posture. With the left leg on the right thigh and the right foot on the left thigh, the back straight, the chin in, the strength in the abdomen – this posture brings one into silence and one-pointedness.

Sitting in the lotus is an art and an accomplishment. It is not mastered in one day but takes years of assiduous practice. One may, of course, learn the physical position in a short time. But sitting in the lotus means more than this: it means that the stream of consciousness and the stream of the unconscious are brought to a standstill. One is "just sitting", grasping the present moment in its totality, transcending time, liberated from anxiety and fear about future or past. This in itself is enlightenment.

When the bodily posture is correct one is enlightened. *The posture is the enlightenment.* That is why Suzuki Shunryu can write: "When you have this posture, you have the right state of mind, so there is no need to try to attain some special state" (Suzuki p. 22). Since mind and body are two sides of one coin, perfect bodily posture brings spiritual enlightenment.

V

Finally, let me recall that all the great mystical traditions speak of extraordinary powers which may, or may not, appear in the course of the mystical journey. Such powers, alas, have caught the imagination of modern people, many of whom identify mysticism with telepathy, clairvoyance, out-of-the-body experience, thought projection, psychic auras and the like. Yet it is a mistake to pay too much attention to these things. They are no more than side-effects or by-products. What matters is faith and love.

Yoga speaks of *siddhis* or miraculous powers. These include the ability to read hearts, to see the future, to see things that are happening at a distance. Others, which are less authenticated and the existence of which I question, are the ability to walk on water, to travel through the air, to pass through solid matter.

In yoga the appearance of psychic powers is significant in that it tells the master that his disciple is making progress. Yet no authentic master will encourage a disciple to seek such powers. Indeed, one must be wary of them because of the danger of vanity or what moderns might call "inflation". Moreover, there is the danger that, fascinated by the allure of power, one may be distracted from the principal goal which is salvation, total liberation, *moksa.*

Zen is even more radical in its rejection of extraordinary powers. The *mu . . . mu* about which I have spoken includes a rejection of any extraordinary power which may arise in the course of one's practice. All such things are treated as illusions like the *makyo* or "world of the devil" through which one must pass on the way to enlightenment.

As for St John of the Cross, his attitude is somewhat similar. The nothing or *nada* which runs through his work entails a renunciation of clinging to all things, including psychic powers and supernatural gifts. Yet he sometimes speaks positively about enhanced vision as when he observes that "the Holy Spirit illumines such souls . . . in many . . . present or future matters and about many events, even distant ones" (*Ascent*, 3:2, 12). Here he attributes this knowledge to the Holy Spirit; but elsewhere he speaks of a natural cause:

> We affirm that those who have reached perfection or are already close to it, *usually* do possess light and knowledge about events happening in their presence and absence. *This knowledge derives from their illumined and purified spirits*.
> (*Ascent*, 2:26, 13)

It is as though the body is spiritualized or sensitized in such a way that one's faculties penetrate beyond time and space and into the hearts of others. "It is worthy of note," he writes, "that those *whose spirit is purified* can naturally perceive – some more than others – the inclinations and talents of men and what lies in the heart of the interior spirit. They derive this knowledge through exterior indications (even though extremely slight) such as words, gestures and other signs" (*Ascent*, 2.24, 14)

Even though such knowledge may carry remarkable conviction, the Spanish mystic is always wary of it. It is not necessary; it may be a source of illusion. What matters is faith, naked faith, dark faith, the inner eye of love.

In a slightly different context St Paul speaks about charismatic gifts. He says that they are good in themselves but without love they are useless. "If I speak in the tongues of men and angels, but have not love, I am a noisy gong or a clanging cymbal . . . And if I have prophetic powers, and understand all mysteries and all knowledge, and if I have all faith, so as to remove mountains, but have not love, I am nothing" (I Corinthians 13:1,2). And the same can be said of psychic powers or enhanced vision. All these things are good in themselves but without love they are nothing.

*

And so I conclude where I began, recalling that mysticism is a question of love, a love which arises in the heart in answer to a call, a love which leads through the darkness of the cloud of unknowing to the great mystery which is light in itself but darkness to us. In East and West and in all the great religions, we find men and women who are in love without restriction and who look upon the world with eyes of love and compassion. Most of them are little known or talked about. Yet as long as such people walk the earth we can have unshakeable confidence in the future.

BOOKS AND ARTICLES QUOTED IN THE TEXT

Abbot, Walter M (editor): *The Documents of Vatican II* (Guild Press, New York, 1966).

Bloom, Anthony: *Courage to Pray* (Paulist Press, New York, 1973).

Butler, Edward Cuthbert; *Western Mysticism* (E. P. Dutton, New York, 1923).

Conze, Edward (editor); *Buddhist Texts* (Harper Torchbooks, New York, 1964).

Duncan, Ronald (editor): *Selected Writings of Mahatma Gandhi* (Fontana, London, 1971).

Eliade, Mircea (1): *The Two and the One* (Harper and Row, New York, 1965).

(2): *Yoga: Immortality and Freedom* (Princeton University Press, New York, 1969).

French, R. M. (translator): *The Way of a Pilgrim* (The Seabury Press, New York, 1970).

Griffiths, Bede (1): *Christ in India* (Charles Scribner, New York, 1966).

(2): *Return to the Centre* (Collins, London 1976).

Heiler, Friedrich: *Prayer* (Oxford University Press, New York, 1958).

Ignatius of Loyola, St (1): *The Spiritual Exercises of St Ignatius*, Louis J. Puhl (editor), (Loyola University Press, Chicago, 1951).

(2): *St Ignatius' Own Story*, William Young (translator) (Regenery, Chicago, 1956).

Inge, William Ralph: *Christian Mysticism* (Methuen and Co, London, 1899).

James, William: *The Varieties of Religious Experience* (Fount Paperbacks, London).

John of the Cross, St: *The Collected Works of St John of the Cross*, (translated by Kieran Kavanaugh, OCD, and Otilo Rodriguez, OCD (Institute of Carmelite Studies, Washington, DC).

Johnston, William (editor) (1): *The Cloud of Unknowing and The Book of Privy Counselling* (Doubleday, New York, 1973).

(2): *The Mysticism of "The Cloud of Unknowing"* (A. Clarke Books, London, 1978).

(3): *Silent Music* (Collins, London, 1974 and Harper and Row, New York, 1974).

(4): *The Still Point* (Fordham University Press, New York, 1970).

Kadloubovsky, E. and Palmer, G. (translators): *Writings from the Philokalia* (Faber and Faber, London 1967).

Lonergan, Bernard (1): *Method in Theology* (Darton, Longman and Todd, London, 1972).

(2): *A Second Collection* (Darton, Longman and Todd, London, 1974).

McDougall, A. (editor): *Spiritual Direction of Louis Lallement* (Newman, Westminster, 1946).

McKenzie, John L.: *Dictionary of the Bible* (Macmillan, New York, 1965).

Rogers, Carl: *On Becoming a Person* (Houghton Mifflin Co, Boston, 1961).

Shibayama, Zenkei: *Zen Comments on the Mumonkan* (Harper and Row, New York, 1974).

Suzuki, Shunryu: *Zen Mind, Beginner's Mind* (Weatherhill, New York, 1970).

Tanquerey, Adolphe: *The Spiritual Life: A Treatise on Ascetical and Mystical Theology* (Newman, Westminster, 1947).

Teresa, Mother: "The Poor in Our Midst" in *New Covenant* (Ann Arbor, Michigan, January, 1977).

Valera, J. Eduardo Perez: "Toward a Transcultural Philosophy" in *Monumenta Nipponica*, volume XXVII (Tokyo, 1972).

Waldenfels, Hans: "Absolute Nothingness" in *Monumenta Nipponica*, volume XXI (Tokyo, 1966).

Ware, Timothy (editor): *The Art of Prayer: An Orthodox Anthology*, compiled by Igumen Chariton of Valemo (Faber and Faber, London, 1966).

Woodward, F. L.:*The Minor Anthologies of the Pali Canons* (Oxford University Press, London, 1948).